W9-CCW-514

Other books by Gordon Williamson:

The Iron Cross: A History, 1813–1957
Knights of the Iron Cross: A History, 1939–1945

ACES
OF THE
REICH

Gordon Williamson
Foreword by Otto Carius

ARMS AND
ARMOUR

First published in Great Britain
in 1989 by Arms and Armour Press,
Artillery House, Artillery Row, London SW1P 1RT.

Distributed in the USA by Sterling Publishing Co. Inc.
387 Park Avenue South, New York, NY 10016–8810.

Distributed in Australia by Capricorn Link (Australia) Pty. Ltd,
P.O. Box 665, Lane Cove, New South Wales 2066, Australia.

British Library Cataloguing in Publication Data
Williamson, Gordon
Aces of the Reich.
1. World War 2. Air operations by Germany, Luftwaffe
I. Title
940.54'4943
ISBN 0-85368-986-5

Designed and edited by DAG Publications Ltd. Designed by
David Gibbons; edited by Michael Boxall; typeset by
Typesetters (Birmingham) Ltd, Warley; camerawork by
M&E Reproductions, North Fambridge, Essex;
printed and bound in Great Britain by
Richard Clay Ltd, Bungay, Suffolk

CONTENTS

Foreword by Otto Carius   7
Introduction   9
Acknowledgements   11

Insignia of the Aces   13
The Knight's Cross, 13; The Oakleaves, 15; The
Oakleaves and Swords, 16; The Diamonds, 17; The
Golden Oakleaves, Swords and Diamonds, 17; The
German Cross in Gold, 18; Other Awards, 19

The Land Aces   23

The Air Aces   91

The Sea Aces   147

Appendices   189
Highest Decorated Panzertruppen Personnel, 189; Top
Fighter Aces of the Luftwaffe, 190; Top Night-Fighter
Aces of the Luftwaffe, 195; Jet Fighter Aces of the
Luftwaffe, 195; The Luftwaffe's Most Highly Decorated
Pilots, 196; U-Boat Ritterkreuzträger, 197; Top Twenty
U-Boat Aces, 201; List of all E-Boat Ritterkreuzträger,
201; The Most Highly Decorated Aces of the U-Boats,
E-Boats and Auxiliary Cruisers, 202; Einzelkämpfer
(Single-Action) Ritterkreuzträger, 203; Auxiliary Cruiser
Ritterkreuzträger, 203; Military Unit Organization, 204;
The Iron Cross, First and Second Classes, 205

Bibliography   207
Glossary   211
Index   215

FOREWORD
BY OTTO CARIUS

We old soldiers must thank the author for recognizing the achievements of the German armed forces during World War Two. The book is, to us, extraordinary because it was written by a person who belongs to a nation which we had to fight. It is even more remarkable because in Germany the post-war political and military situation has prohibited all connections to the swastika and sometimes even prevented us from publishing our own account of the conflict. Our thanks are most sincere because this book is appearing in a changing social climate; where we are witnessing the erection of memorials to the unknown deserter; and while places of remembrance for our dead comrades are being desecrated.

All active participants in the war will confirm that the average German soldier fought with decent bravery in a disciplined manner. However, soldiers of all nations are connected by the common bond of obedience to their commanders, and this book must be looked upon not only as a biographical collection of individual cases but also one that represents the achievements of all.

Personal performance, accurate assessment of the situation, the right decisions, determined action and tactical success were the criteria for awards of distinction, but great military performance was demanded from everybody in the unit, and the soldier's extraordinary achievements began only when individuals thought they had already reached their psychological and physical limits. Of course, it is easy to obey at those times when the bond of comradeship as well as faith in the leadership is strong and when the essential of soldier's good luck plays its role.

I only experienced pleasure in wearing the Knight's Cross when at the Front. It made the accomplishment of one's own goals easier, even when faced with formidable obstacles. The award also influenced the rest of the unit in a positive manner. Even soldiers not belonging to my unit, who did not know me or had perhaps only heard of me by repute, were more forthcoming with their trust when they saw the award. On the other hand, of course, the Knight's Cross also placed the wearer under great strain because he could not afford to show his weaknesses. Above all, he had to demonstrate that the trust placed in him by others was justified.

The wish of all people, especially the soldier at the Front, is for the following generations to experience peace in which to build their future. If this is not achieved, then all the sacrifices have been in vain. To work towards the fulfilment of such an objective has to be the foremost aim of us all, especially those who lost dear friends and relatives in the war. We must not give up hope that one day commonsense will prevail and make it possible for all people on earth to live together in peace.

INTRODUCTION

The term 'ace' in modern usage, is generally taken to mean a champion or particularly skilled exponent of some sport. The military usage can be said to have gained widespread use and popularity during the First World War when air warfare was in its infancy, and the daring airmen in their flimsy aircraft caught the imagination of the world with their exploits.

Germany's armed forces produced the First World War's greatest aces of air and sea. Pilots of the calibre of Manfred von Richthofen (80 victories) and Werner Voss (47 victories) became legendary the world over. Lesser known but no less impressive were the feats of Germany's first U-boat aces such as Lothar Arnauld de la Periere who sank more than 200 enemy ships, and Otto Weddingen whose *U9* sank three British cruisers, *Aboukir*, *Hogue* and *Cressy*, in a single engagement.

During the Second World War, the Germans once again produced the world's greatest aces. Warfare has changed so much since then that it is extremely unlikely that the achievements of Erich Hartmann, Otto Kretschmer or Michael Wittmann will ever be matched, let alone surpassed. Many theories have been put forward in an endeavour to account for the successes of the Third Reich's aces, and many of them are convincing. These will be looked at more closely in the appropriate sections. One thing is clear, however; Germany's weapons designers came up with some of the best military hardware of the period. At various points in the war, Germany boasted the world's finest aircraft, Me 262, the world's most powerful tank, Königstiger, and the world's most advanced submarine, Type XX1.

Much doubt has been cast on some of the achievements claimed by some of Germany's aces, but post-war research has shown that in the main the claims made were very accurate and in several cases even higher scores might have been justified.

Many of the Luftwaffe's top aces are fairly well known outside of Germany. A few of the top U-boat commanders are also well known, but few readers – other than military history buffs – will be familiar with the exploits of the top Panzer commanders or the assault gun aces.

So many German aces reached high scores, that a whole series of books would be required to cover them all. This book will restrict itself to offering the reader a representative selection. No book on aces can possibly exclude men like Hartmann, Galland, Prien, Kretschmer or Wittmann, but in this work I have sought to balance the picture by depicting many of the lesser-know aces whose scores were comparatively small, but whose achievements were impressive by any standards. Many of these gallant soldiers, whose bravery, skill and selfless dedication to duty brought them their country's highest awards, lost their lives in the process.

It is to be hoped that now, fifty years after the outbreak of the Second World War, we can look at the achievements of our former enemies objectively, unobscured by the hate propaganda which warring nations inevitably hurl at one another, and which unfortunately tends to linger for years afterwards and inhibit the forging of new bonds of friendship.

EDINBURGH
January 1989

ACKNOWLEDGEMENTS

In compiling this work I have once again been fortunate enough to have been assisted by a considerable number of contributors. Successful aces have always been the subject of coverage in the popular Press of the day, and the aces of the Wehrmacht were no exception. Books, propaganda magazines, picture postcards, etc., are a valuable source of information; but in addition, the assistance of the many people who have contributed to this book has been invaluable, and the willingness with which so many of the surviving aces themselves have supplied photographic and documentary material has been most gratifying.

I should like to express my particular thanks to the following:

ARTUR BECKER-NEETZ. The OdR official with responsibility for liaison with collectors of photographs and information from the UK, USA and Canada, Herr Becker-Neetz has been of considerable assistance to this and previous works by helping me to make contact with numerous *Ritterkreuzträger* (wearers of the Knight's Cross).

HEINRICH SPRINGER. Although not himself featured in this book, my good friend Hein, a Knight's Cross winning veteran of the élite Leibstandarte SS 'Adolf Hitler', has been of inestimable help and encouragement, making introductions to many of his former Waffen-SS comrades.

ERNST BARKMANN. This top Panzer ace graciously received me in his home and spent an afternoon showing me his considerable photograph archives and reminiscing on his wartime experiences and former comrades.

Tiger tank aces Otto Carius, Max Wirsching and Albert Kerscher took the time to answer my numerous questions and supplied a number of excellent photographs. My good friend Jim Skeldon from Edinburgh undertook a considerable amount of tedious research work on my behalf, checking statistical data on the ships sunk by U-boat aces. Fellow-collectors and enthusiasts Chris Ailsby, Malcolm Bowers, David Littlejohn and Fred Stephens were as helpful as ever in allowing the use of photographs from their collections. Finally, special thanks are due to Josef Charita. Although I have only known M. Charita for a short time, he has been overwhelming in his generosity. Each request for help to locate photographs of a particular ace seemed to be answered with masses of material from which to choose. His help has been truly invaluable.

The following list of contributors includes many of the aces featured in this book. To them and to the *Ordensgemeinschaft der Ritterkreuzträger* (Association of Knight's Cross Bearers) I offer my grateful thanks. Chris Ailsby, Friedrich Arnold, Günther Bahr, Klaus Bargsten, Erwin Bachmann, Ernst Barkmann, Heinz Baurmann, Ernst Bauer, Georg Bose, Malcolm Bowers, Ernst Börngen, Artur Becker-Neetz, Sepp Brandner,

Hermann Büchting, Otto Carius, Josef Charita, Martin Drewes, Arnold Doring, Paul Egger, Georg Peter-Eder, Heinz Franke, Josef Flögel, Karl-Heinz Gustavsson, Hermann Graf, Reinhard Hardegen, Fritz Henke, Willi Hein, Willi Heinrich, Herbert Ihlefeld, Willy Jähde, Erhard Jähnert, Hans Joachim Jabs, Frederick Jope, Clemens Graf von Kageneck, Einrich Köhler, Norbert Kujacinski, Albert Kerscher, Paul-Albert Kausch, Wolfgang Koltermann, Werner Kraus, Otto Kretschmer, Siegfried Koitschka, Friedrich Kemnade, David Littlejohn, Jakob Lobmeyer, Karl-Heinz Marbach, Karl-Friedrich Merten, Waldemar Mehl, Johannes Mühlen-kamp, Karl Nicolussi-Leck, Rudolf von Ribbentrop, Hubert Rauh, Johann Sailer, Hans Sandrock, Remy Schrijnen, Emil Seibold, Paul Senghas, Gerd Suhren, Heinrich Schroeteler, Hans Siegel, Jim Skeldon, Heinrich Springer, Fred Stephens, Wilhelm Wegner, Max Wirsching, Helmut Witte and Otto Westphalen.

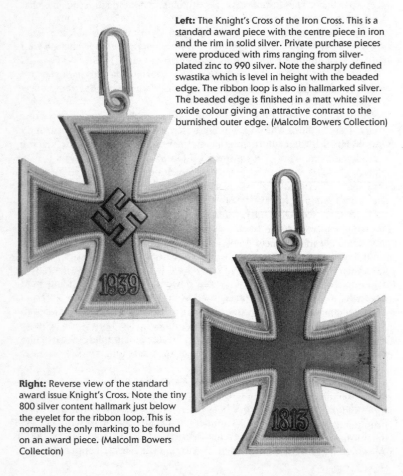

Left: The Knight's Cross of the Iron Cross. This is a standard award piece with the centre piece in iron and the rim in solid silver. Private purchase pieces were produced with rims ranging from silver-plated zinc to 990 silver. Note the sharply defined swastika which is level in height with the beaded edge. The ribbon loop is also in hallmarked silver. The beaded edge is finished in a matt white silver oxide colour giving an attractive contrast to the burnished outer edge. (Malcolm Bowers Collection)

Right: Reverse view of the standard award issue Knight's Cross. Note the tiny 800 silver content hallmark just below the eyelet for the ribbon loop. This is normally the only marking to be found on an award piece. (Malcolm Bowers Collection)

INSIGNIA OF THE ACES

Germany's top generals, often awarded the Knight's Cross or its higher grades in recognition of their part in the successful outcome of a crucial battle or even a campaign, could not compete with the young aces of the armed forces where public adulation was concerned. These young daredevils in their glamorous uniforms, competing in deadly combat with often superior enemy forces, captured the imagination of their nation. The propaganda machinery of the Third Reich was not slow to capitalize on their deeds. All major newspapers and such quality magazines as the famous *Signal* carried regular accounts of the successes of the aces of land, sea and air. Photo-postcards of these young heroes were avidly collected by Germany's youth, and such prominent war artists as Willrich produced many portrait studies of the better-known aces in heroic poses.

Details of the history and development of the Knight's Cross series of awards is more fully covered in the author's earlier works: *The Iron Cross – An Illustrated History 1813–1957* and *Knights of the Iron Cross*, both published by Blandford Press. Only a very basic look at the Knight's Cross and its higher grades will be given here, and the reader is referred to the above books if further information is required.

THE KNIGHT'S CROSS

The Knight's Cross of the Iron Cross was instituted on 1 September 1939. This was a completely new grade in the Iron Cross series of awards. Its introduction was necessitated because, since the end of the First World War, when the *Pour le Mérite* ceased to be awarded, there existed no suitable decoration between the Iron Cross First Class and the Grand Cross of the Iron Cross.

The Knight's Cross was worn at the neck from a 45mm-wide ribbon and consisted of a blackened iron centre held within a silver frame. The obverse centre featured a swastika above the date '1939' in the lower arm. The reverse was devoid of design with the exception of the date '1813' in the lower arm, i.e., the same design as the Iron Cross Second Class of 1939.

The vast majority of officially awarded pieces bore the silver content stamp '800' on the reverse upper edge just below the eyelet for the ribbon loop, and on the ribbon loop itself. Occasional specimens may be encountered with makers' code marks (i.e., 'L/12') alongside the silver content mark. Generally speaking these are privately obtained 'extra' pieces purchased at the bearer's own expense. Having said this it must also be

Above left: Seen in its original award case, this view shows the reverse of a Knight's Cross manufactured by C. E. Juncker of Berlin, one of only three firms permitted to manufacture the Knight's Cross for supply to the Ordenskanzlei. The manufacturer's code number L/12 can be seen next to the 800 silver content mark. (Peter Huckstepp)

Above right: An award set of Oakleaves to the Knight's Cross of the Iron Cross shown here in the original award case. The oakleaves have a matt silver finish with the outer edge and central rib burnished. The case is of identical pattern with that used for the Swords and Oakleaves. A full-length portion of neck ribbon is also included. (John Shaw)

noted that such marked examples were occasionally used as award pieces, and the same can be said regarding maker marked examples of the Oakleaves, and Swords and Oakleaves clasps.

The Knight's Cross was awarded with a small black case, the base of which was covered with black velvet and recessed to the shape of the Cross and compartmented to accept a length of ribbon. The lid interior was lined with white silk or satin. At the presentation the Knight's Cross was generally hung around the recipient's neck using the full length of ribbon. Afterwards, the recipient would 'tailor' the ribbon to a suitable length and whatever type of fixing device he chose. While several recipients purchased duplicates for wear in combat and kept the original award safe at home, this practice was not widespread and most winners had only the original award, which was worn in action throughout the recipient's subsequent combat career.

It may be of interest to the reader to consider the way in which an award of the Knight's Cross was recommended and approved. If we consider an 'ideal' case from the early part of the war when the full award system was carried out in the majority of cases, the procedure was as follows.

1. The soldier's unit commander would report the action for which the Knight's Cross was recommended giving a brief but detailed review of the action as well as a brief pen-picture of the nominee.

2. The report would be passed to the divisional commander, usually of junior General rank, who would add his own report on the action and its importance, and confirm his support of the recommendation.

3. The next stage would be to forward the report to the General commanding the Army Corps to which the Division was attached. He would add a short comment and signify his approval of the recommendation.

4. The report would then reach the General or Field Marshal commanding the Army Group, who would also signify his approval before sending the report on to Army High Command.

5. At this, the penultimate stage, the Commander of the Oberkommando des Heeres (OKW) would usually signify his approval by appending a single-word message such as *Befürwortet* (approved).

6. At this stage only one final approval was required, that of the Supreme Commander Armed Forces, Adolf Hitler. Again, a one-word comment, *Verliehen* (awarded), was all that was usually required.

Once Hitler had approved the award, the recipient would be notified via his unit by telegram. An entry would be made in his paybook, and a *Vorläufiges Besitzzeugnis* (Preliminary Certificate of Entitlement) was issued. At a later date the recipient, in the early stages of the war at least, was presented with a very elaborate hand-crafted and lettered parchment award document or *Urkunde*, contained in a red morocco leather bound folder, embossed with a gold eagle and swastika. This was also hand crafted. These documents were made with such meticulous care that it was impossible for the small team of artisans to keep up with demand and most Knight's Cross winners received only the Preliminary Certificate.

THE OAKLEAVES

The Oakleaves were instituted on 3 June 1940 to recognize further acts of gallantry or meritorious conduct after the award of the Knight's Cross. The award consisted of a cluster of three oakleaves with the central leaf overlapping two lower leaves. The award was die-struck in solid silver with a slightly concave reverse on to which was soldered a replacement ribbon loop.

The standard award pieces were marked with only the silver content code '800' or '900' on the left reverse. Occasional pieces are found with makers' codes on the right reverse. The piece was awarded in a small black case. The black velvet base was slotted to accept the ribbon loop, and held a replacement length of ribbon. Overall size was 20mm × 20mm.

THE OAKLEAVES AND SWORDS

This clasp, introduced to reward further acts of merit or gallantry after the award of the Oakleaves, was instituted on 21 June 1941. It consisted of a standard set of Oakleaves as described above, but with a small set of crossed swords measuring 24mm in length at the base. On the original official award pieces, the reverse of these swords were plain. This fact has been confirmed by the original manufacturers. Several pieces exist with double-sided swords, and these are generally found in conjunction with a maker's code number such as '21' on the right reverse. These are in fact private-purchase pieces which recipients could acquire at their own expense. This situation was confused by the fact that occasionally such elaborate specimens were actually used for award pieces, which perhaps explains the fact that for many years the elaborate pieces were thought to be the official awards, and those with the plain reverse were thought to be jewellers' copies or duplicate private-purchase pieces. The clasp was presented in a case similar to that for the Oakleaves. It should be noted that original examples of both the Oakleaves and the Oakleaves and Swords exist in silver-plated bronze or brass. Knight's Crosses also exist with silver-plated rims.

Below left: This standard award issue set of Swords and Oakleaves was produced by the original manufacturer, Steinhauer & Lück. The finish is identical with that of the Oakleaves, being matt silver with burnished highlights. Note that the ball ends to the crossguards of the swords touch the opposing blades. Some examples have this joint slit through. (Chris Ailsby) **Below right:** Reverse view of the standard award piece. Note that the original specifications called for the reverse of the swords to be left blank. Once again, only the silver content mark is found, on the left-hand side. Examples with double-sided Swords and having makers' marks, etc., once thought to be the official award pieces, are now known to be private enterprise de luxe items. (Chris Ailsby)

Right: An original set of Swords, Oakleaves and Diamonds. This is one of the award pieces manufactured by the firm of Klein in Hanau. Made of platinum, it is fitted with numerous individually claw set diamonds. The reverse of the Sword handle is marked with the manufacturer's code and the hallmark. (Josef Charita)

THE DIAMONDS

This, the penultimate grade in the Knight's Cross series, was instituted on 15 July 1941 and was awarded only 27 times. Unlike the one-piece Oakleaves, or the two-piece Oakleaves and Swords, the Diamonds clasp was of multi-piece construction. The standard piece, if such a thing can be said to exist where so many variants exist in an award which was granted so few times, was crafted in white gold or platinum and set with 53 diamonds in the oakleaves and the sword hilts. The total weight was about 18.7 grammes. On the reverse of the sword was impressed the manufacturer's mark 'K' for Klein, together with the hallmark stamp.

Each recipient was also given a duplicate piece in silver, which was normally set with sapphires or paste stones. Otherwise it was identical with the standard piece. Some early examples of the Diamonds are said to have been made from standard Oakleaves and Swords blanks.

THE GOLDEN OAKLEAVES, SWORDS AND DIAMONDS

This beautiful award, granted only once, to Stuka ace Hans Ulrich Rudel, was instituted on 29 December 1944. Manufactured by the same jewellers as the 'ordinary' Diamonds, Klein of Munich, it was of identical design with the normal piece, but was crafted in 750 grade gold, and set with a total of 58 diamonds. Both the original award, and the duplicate presented along with it, are still in the possession of the late Oberst Rudel's family.

THE GERMAN CROSS IN GOLD

Another important award was the German Cross in Gold. This decoration was introduced on 28 September 1941 in an attempt to bridge the considerable gap which existed between the Iron Cross First Class and the Knight's Cross of the Iron Cross.

It was required that the recipient of the German Cross in Gold already possessed the Iron Cross First Class, but it was not a requirement that a proposed Knight's Cross recipient possess the German Cross in Gold. The fact that many Knight's Cross winners held the German Cross before winning the Knight's Cross was coincidental; many other Knight's Cross winners did not receive the German Cross until long after being awarded the Knight's Cross. The German Cross in Gold was a decoration in its own right and should not be considered as a part of the Iron Cross series of awards.

The Cross of the title was in fact the swastika in the centre of the award. This decoration took the form of a sunburst star and not a cross. The German Cross consists of a large heavy matt silver-coloured sunburst star of 63mm diameter. Over this is set a slightly smaller black radiant star, so

Below left: The German Cross in Gold. A large and impressive award, the German Cross can be seen worn on the right breast pocket by many of the aces covered in this work. **Below right:** Cloth embroidered version of the German Cross in Gold. This specimen is embroidered on to black backing cloth for the Panzer uniform.

that only the edge of the outer star is seen. In the centre is a matt silver disc upon which is set a black enamelled swastika with a gilt laurel wreath surround. At the base of the laurel wreath is the date of institution '1941'. It was worn on the right breast pocket by a hinged pin attachment on the reverse of the silver outer star. Embroidered versions were also produced. Hand-stitched to a piece of cloth of the same colour as the wearer's uniform, the only metal part featured was the laurel wreath.

A total of approximately 17,000 of these decorations were awarded to members of the Heer and Waffen-SS, from a total award figure of some 30,000. Generally speaking, the German Cross in Gold was awarded in recognition of a number of achievements rather than for a single meritorious or gallant deed. Two examples of the Vorschlag or recommendation for the German Cross in Gold in the author's possession have 55 and 11 separate incidents respectively, cited in support of the recommendation for the award. Each action is briefly described in a short paragraph of 80 or 100 words and the document is signed by the Divisional commander.

As with the Knight's Cross, the German Cross was often awarded with a *Vorläufiges Besitzzeugnis* or preliminary certificate often to be followed later by a larger and more elaborate *Urkunde*. The preliminary certificate was printed on a small, A5-sized document with the recipient's details typed in and an authority signature and rubber stamp found at the bottom of the document.

The Urkunde was much larger, at about four times the size of the preliminary certificate. These were normally signed by the Commander-in-Chief of the branch of the armed forces to which the recipient belonged, i.e., Keitel for the Army, Raeder or Dönitz for the Navy and Göring for the Luftwaffe.

The high regard in which these decorations are held may be judged by the fact that a German Cross holders' association similar to that for holders of the Knight's Cross is being formed.

OTHER AWARDS

There were of course several other awards, decorations, campaign medals, qualification badges, etc., which would have been worn by the aces mentioned in this book. However, the few badges described here would have been worn only by soldiers who had seen considerable combat service and in many cases only by those who had already been decorated with the Oakleaves to the Knight's Cross. This is by no means a complete list of such badges, but only includes those directly relevant to the branches of service of the aces described in this book.

The Combined Pilot-Observers' Badge with Diamonds This award was instituted by Hermann Göring in 1935 and was a personal gift from the Commander-in-Chief of the Luftwaffe and not an official State award. It was of the same basic design as the standard Luftwaffe Pilot/Observers'

Left: The combined Pilot Observers badge with Diamonds. Made of solid gold, it features a total of 104 individually set diamonds. The craftsmanship shown in this badge is of the highest possible standard. Copies in silver set with sapphires were also manufactured. (F. J. Stephens)

Below: The U-Boat War Badge with Diamonds. Identical in design with the standard badge, this version is struck in solid silver, gilt and has the swastika set with nine small diamonds.

Left: Auxiliary Cruiser War Badge with Diamonds. Struck in 800 silver and with the wreath and eagle gilt, the badge features some fifteen small diamonds. Only one award of this badge has been positively confirmed, though a few original examples are known in private collections.

Badge but crafted in genuine gold and with a total of 104 diamonds set into the eagle and swastika. The following Luftwaffe aces were awarded this beautiful decoration: Oberst Hans-Ulrich Rudel, Oberst Werner Mölders, Generalleutnant Adolf Galland, Hauptmann Hans-Joachim Marseille, Oberstleutnant Werner Baumbach and Major Erich Hartmann.

The U-Boat Badge with Diamonds This badge was instituted by Grossadmiral Karl Dönitz and was presented by him personally. It was identical in design with the standard U-boat badge, but was in genuine silver, gilt, and had a slightly larger swastika set with nine small diamonds. These diamond-studded badges were produced by the Berlin firms of Godet and Schwerin only for top U-boat commanders who had been decorated with the Oakleaves to the Knight's Cross; a total of 29 were awarded.

The E-Boat Badge with Diamonds This badge was instituted by Grossadmiral Raeder and consisted of a solid silver gilt version of the 2nd Pattern E-Boat War Badge, featuring nine small diamonds set into the swastika. Only eight awards of this rare badge were made, to the following E-boat aces: Kapitän zur See Petersen, Kapitänleutnant von Mirbach, Kapitänleutnant Töniges, Korvettenkapitän Feldt, Korvettenkapitän Klug, Korvettenkapitän Kemnade, Korvettenkapitän Christiansen and Oberleutnant zur See Wuppermann.

The Auxiliary Cruiser Badge with Diamonds Instituted by Grossadmiral Raeder, this badge consisted of a solid silver gilt version of the Auxiliary Cruiser Badge having nine diamonds set into the swastika. Assuming that the qualification for this badge was possession of the Oakleaves, a total of four officers should have received it, but only Vizeadmiral Rogge of the famed *Atlantis* is known for certain to have received the badge.

No such diamond-studded versions were produced for any of the Army war badges (with the exception of some known specimens of the Anti-Partisan War Badge with Diamonds, but which are thought never to have been awarded). However, in the case of the Panzer Assault Badge and the General Assault Badge, special numbered pieces, indicating the recipient's participation in 25, 50, 75 or 100 actions, were produced. Any tank crew that had taken part in and survived 100 engagements, could surely consider themselves 'aces'!

The Panzer Assault Badge The original badge was instituted on 20 December 1939 and was awarded to tank crews that had taken part in three separate actions. A bronze grade was also introduced for crews of other armoured vehicles and armoured support units, etc. The badge featured a vertical oval of oakleaves enclosing a tank facing right. At the top of the badge was the national emblem.

In 1943 numbered versions were introduced, being slightly more elaborate and of two-piece riveted construction. At the base was a small box

Left: Numbered Panzer Assault Badges. On the left is the basic pattern for the 25/50 Badge. The tank is attached to the wreath by two small rivets. Both solid and semi-hollow struck versions are known, with makers' marks 'GB' and 'JFS' being most common. To the right is the larger version for the 75/100 Badges. Again the tank is affixed by small rivets and both solid and semi-hollow versions are known. (Malcolm Bowers)

bearing the numbers '25' or '50'. The tank was in black with the rest of the badge in silver or bronze finish as appropriate (some all-bronze versions are known). At the same time, an even more elaborate and larger badge was introduced bearing the numbers '75' or '100' in the box at the base. In this case the tank was in silver or bronze with the rest of the badge in gilt. These 75/100 badges are extremely rare and at the time of writing fetch higher prices even than the Knight's Cross itself. For some time it has been rumoured that there exists a special version of this badge, all in gilt and with the number '200'. This has been discounted by many, but the author has recently confirmed at least one definite award of this '200' Badge to an Oakleaves winner, a Waffen-SS Hauptsturmführer in a Panzerjäger unit.

The General Assault Badge The General Assault Badge was instituted on 1 June 1940, originally as a Combat Engineers Badge, but subsequently the range of potential recipients was widened and included numbers of Sturmgeschütze, Sturm Artillerie and Panzerjäger units. The badge consisted of an oval wreath of Oakleaves containing an eagle and swastika over a crossed bayonet and hand-grenade. It was awarded after participation in three actions.

In parallel with the Panzer Badge, in 1943 more elaborate versions bearing the numbers '25', '50', '75' or 100 were instituted. Like the numbered Panzer Badges, these are extremely scarce, especially the 75/100 pieces, and command very high prices.

Numbered General Assault Badges. Often awarded to crews of Sturmgeschütz, and Panzerjäger units. Method of manufacture was very similar to that for the numbered Panzer badges with the central eagle device being affixed by small rivets.

THE LAND ACES

Although most of the combatant nations of the Second World War had their popular air aces and some had well-known submarine or sub-chaser aces, Germany was unique in the number of tank and assault gun aces she could number in her armed forces. Armoured warfare of course was in its infancy during the First World War, and the few battles involving tanks that did take place were more important for their historical significance, than for their effect on the outcome of the war. Tanks of both sides were dirty, smelly, noisy and extremely unreliable beasts, more of which seemed to be put out of action through mechanical breakdowns than through enemy action. The war ended before tank development could produce a worthy armoured combat vehicle.

During the thirties when the German Army was being rebuilt and expanded, Germany's designers certainly made up for their lack of success during the First World War and produced several excellent vehicles. The Panzerkampfwagen or Pz Kpfw I was a light, fast and reliable tank. Armed only with machine-guns, only a few actually saw service during the Second World War, but its historical significance lies in the fact that it was the first tank manufactured after Hitler's rise to power, and the vehicle with which Germany's first Panzer regiments were initially equipped. The Pz Kpfw II was slightly larger, and carried a 20mm gun. Although still rather light in firepower and armour, these tanks served in the Polish and North African campaigns, and during the early stages of the invasion of the Soviet Union. The Pz Kpfw III, at about 20 tons, carrying a 37mm, 50mm or 75mm gun, and the 23-ton Pz Kpfw IV with its 75mm gun were, however, to be the real backbone of the Panzer forces. The Pz Kpfw III saw front-line service until at least mid-1944, and the Pz Kpfw IV until the end of the war. Both also became the basis for extremely successful assault guns.

Germany's biggest advantage, however, was not so much in its excellent tank design, but in the eagerness with which Hitler embraced the idea of armoured warfare. In Generals such as Guderian and Rommel, the German Army had enthusiastic proponents of the use of tanks in fast assaults with air support. Not for them the outmoded idea of tanks lumbering along with slow-moving infantry and used purely as a support weapon. This is not to say of course that every German General was an enthusiastic supporter of the tank. Germany had its diehard cavalry traditionalists too. However, with Hitler on their side, the armour enthusiasts could hardly lose. Germany therefore went into the war with a marked advantage over the Allies. After rapidly eliminating the Poles and crushing the French, the Panzers threw the British Expeditionary Force back over the Channel and Hitler was the undisputed master of Europe. The Panzers in the full flush of success were then unleashed on the Soviet Union and once again seemed unstoppable. Soviet forces fell back in disarray before the mighty Panzers, but then, incredibly, a tank appeared which was impervious to the Panzers' shells. The Wehrmacht had met the formidable T-34. This caused considerable alarm to the Germans because their tanks had to close to such a short range for their guns to be able to penetrate the T-34s' armour, that they would have no chance against the excellent 76mm gun of the Soviet tank.

Hitler's overconfidence in Germany's ability to win the war quickly had resulted in a stagnation in tank design, and the German war industry had rapidly to come up with a new design to achieve at least parity with the new Soviet tanks if not superiority. At one point it was even suggested that the T-34 be copied. The final result of this situation, however, was the excellent Pz Kpfw V Panther. This formidable vehicle with its high-velocity 75mm gun and well-sloped thick armour soon gave the Germans superiority once again, though teething-troubles caused by too rapid development did plague this tank for some time. It was in this excellent vehicle that many of the Panzer aces in this book achieved their greatest successes.

German heavy tank development had resulted in the equally formidable Tiger tank. This monster, weighing some 56 tons, mounted a development of the superb 88mm Flak gun, and although its success was somewhat limited by its weight and slow speed, in the hands of an experienced commander the Tiger could wreak havoc among any other tanks in existence at the time. Indeed, during the Normandy battles, when the Tiger was used in a defensive role, which suited it perfectly, the Allies regularly expected to lose at least three or more tanks in order to knock out a Tiger. In a good defensive position, the only methods likely to shift this steel colossus were the attacks by rocket-firing fighter-bombers, bombardment from the main armament of warships lying off shore, or mass attacks by Allied tanks where, through sheer weight of numbers, the Tiger being unable to take on all at once, one tank might be fortunate enough to work its way around the Tiger's flanks and fire a disabling shot into the thinner side or rear armour. This method, however, would almost always result in the loss of several Allied tanks.

The same applied to the even more massive 68-ton King Tiger with an improved 88mm gun and even thicker armour. Slow and ponderous it might be, but in the hands of a Panzer ace, the appearance of just one of these tanks on the battlefield could spread panic among the enemy. Indeed it is probably true to say that one of the greatest benefits to infantry units which a Tiger might be supporting, was the panic its appearance could provoke in the enemy. A total of just over 1,800 Tiger and King Tiger models were produced, a tiny number when compared with, say, the M4 Sherman tank which still remains in service with some countries today.

Taking into consideration the excellent training the Panzer crews were given, the high *esprit de corps* prevalent in the Panzertruppen and the power of their awesome weapons, it is perhaps not surprising that some of them managed to achieve some quite incredible scores. If many of the great air aces considered their form of warfare, with its rather outdated notions of chivalry, akin to the honourable combat of the knights of old, surely the Panzer commander in his lumbering armoured steed in the many vast armoured battles in the Western Desert or on the Eastern Front was even more equatable to the armoured knights of antiquity.

There does not seem to have been a laid-down scale of victories required to bring the award of the Knight's Cross; each award was made on the merits of the individual case. Some received the Knight's Cross for scores in the twenties, while others did not receive the award until their score had reached 50 or more. Few of the great Panzer aces considered themselves to be anything other than ordinary soldiers.

In 1987 I had the pleasure of spending an afternoon at the home of one of the great Panzer aces, Ernst Barkmann. As modest as only a true ace can be, Herr Barkmann insisted that he never tried to keep score of his kills, but was interested only in keeping himself and his crew alive and doing his duty to the best of his ability. As he showed me his original Knight's Cross which he had been fortunate enough to retain at the end of war, he reflected on how many of his equally brave comrades had died without being so honoured with this small piece of iron and silver.

No less important than the Panzers were the assault guns or Sturmgeschützen. When the Pz Kpfw III began to be outclassed on the battlefield and increasingly was being replaced by varying marks of the Pz Kpfw IV, it was discovered that the chassis made an excellent base for a self-propelled gun, or Sturmgeschütz; in fact the first versions appeared as early as 1940. By early 1942 the F model of the Sturmgeschütz III was appearing, armed with the excellent long-barrelled 75mm gun. Increasingly the Sturmgeschützen moved from their intended role as assault artillery, to become tank destroyers. Cheaper and easier to produce than a tank, several Panzer units found themselves outfitted with these weapons as a result of tank shortages. With their low profile, making them a difficult target, and their powerful armament, these were excellent weapons. The Pz Kpfw IV also became an excellent Sturmgeschütz. Probably the best of all the self-propelled weapons based on the chassis of a proven tank was the Panzerjäger V Jagdpanther. Designated a tank hunter, this superb weapon boasted an 88mm gun as its main armament. Thankfully for the Allies, this version of the Panther did not see service in significant numbers.

Almost every successful tank found itself being used as the basis for a Sturmgeschütz or Jagdpanzer, even the mighty Tiger II or King Tiger. The Jagdtiger, at 70 tons, was the heaviest vehicle to see service during the Second World War. It featured a powerful 128mm gun, but was hampered by its massive weight and poor manoeuvrability. In addition, its range of operation was limited by the few bridges that could support its weight. Only 70 were built.

One of the most successful of the tank destroyers was the Jagdpanzer 38(t) Hetzer, based on the Czech chassis. Light and fast with a speed of 25mph as compared to 9mph of the Jagdtiger, it carried a 75mm anti-tank gun and was a highly successful weapon in the hands of aces such as Jakob Lobmeyer. Had the German weapons industry been able to concentrate on simple and successful weapons such as the Hetzer, instead of being forced by Hitler's obsession with ever bigger and heavier tanks which were a mssive drain on resources, the Allies would have faced a daunting task in defeating Germany's anti-tank forces.

The heavy tanks of the Panzerwaffe were organized into heavy tank battalions (schwere Panzer Abteilungen), placed under corps level command. They tended to be used as fire brigades, being rushed from sector to sector where the enemy threat was most serious. It is perhaps not surprising then that the Tiger tank aces found themselves in a position where they could achieve such incredible successes.

HAUPTMANN FREIDRICH ARNOLD

Born on 10 May 1919 in Karlsruhe, Friedrich Arnold joined the Army in November 1937 when he was inducted into Artillerie Regiment 41 in Ulm. Promoted to Gefreiter in October 1938, Arnold subsequently joined a heavy 28cm artillery unit using railway-mounted guns. In February 1940 he was promoted to Gefreiter and two months later attended a course for potential officers with schwere Artillerie Ersatz Abteilung 100, a motorized artillery unit. On 9 August 1940 he was promoted to Wachtmeister and on the same day joined a Reserve Officers' course at Rügenwalde, being commissioned Leutnant on 1 September 1940.

On commissioning he was posted to schwere Artillerie Ersatz Abteilung 100 and served with the unit until January 1941 when he was sent for conversion training with the Sturmgeschützen at Artillerie Lehr Regiment 2 in Jüterbog. On completion of this course Leutnant Arnold joined 2 Batterie, Sturmgeschütz Abteilung 201 as a Zugführer. He served with the Abteilung during the opening phase of Operation 'Barbarossa', the invasion of the Soviet Union. He was decorated with the Iron Cross Second Class on 9 July 1941 and the First Class on 29 August 1941. On 1 September 1942 he was promoted to Oberleutnant. Arnold remained with Sturmgeschütz Abteilung 201 until June 1943 when he was transferred to 2 Batterie, Sturmgeschütz Abteilung 237. During his time with Sturmgeschütz Abteilung 201, Arnold had destroyed 29 enemy tanks. After only three months with his new unit his score had risen to 51, and on 16 November 1943 this achievement brought him the award of the Knight's Cross of the Iron Cross. Arnold had been hospitalized because of wounds in September 1943. On his release from hospital he joined Sturmgeschütz Ersatz und Ausbildungs Abteilung 500 in Posen on 21 October 1943 and remained with this unit until the closing stages of the war. On 4 April 1945, he was posted to the Sturmgeschütz School in Burg and served the last phase of the war with Sturmgeschütz Ersatz und Ausbildungs Abteilung 700. He was promoted to the rank of Hauptmann on 20 April 1944. Hospitalized again because of his wounds, Arnold was taken prisoner by the French at the end of the war. Arnold had spent almost the entire war on the central sector of the Eastern Front, and his decorations include the Iron Cross Second and First Classes, the German Cross in Gold, The Knight's Cross of the Iron Cross, General Assault Badge and Wound Badges in Black, Silver and Gold. He lives today in retirement in Gaienhofen.

SS-OBERSTURMFÜHRER ERWIN BACHMANN

Erwin Bachmann was born in Reinhausen on 5 May 1921. His career as an SS soldier began in August 1939 when he was accepted into the SS-

Regiment Germania in Hamburg. Seeing action in the western campaign, and in the opening phases of Operation 'Barbarossa' where he fought at Rostov, Bachmann then attended SS-Junkerschule Tölz from January to June 1942, being commissioned as an SS-Untersturmführer. As the last remaining male member of his family – his brothers had been lost in action on the Eastern Front – he was granted a posting away from the front, at a Reserve Battalion of the Regiment in Arnhem. Unhappy here, however, he volunteered for a return to combat duties and joined SS-Panzer Regiment 10 in the élite 10th SS-Panzer Division Frundsberg in January 1943. At this time the division was newly formed and was initially intended as a Panzer-Grenadier unit. during October, however, it was upgraded to a full Panzer Division.

Bachmann took part in the offensive at Tarnopol in March 1944 where First Panzer Armee had been in danger of annihilation. The timely arrival of the fresh 9th and 10th SS-Panzer Divisions saved the day. Later in 1944, Frundsberg was involved in the defensive battles in Normandy and was badly mauled in action against the invading Allies. Escaping through the Falaise Gap, the division had lost all its tanks and was reduced to barely Battalion strength. Regrouping at Arnhem, the division helped to destroy the British airborne assault in September 1944. Frundsberg was not used in the Ardennes Offensive, but in January 1945 was involved in the attempt to retake Strasbourg. In mid-January 1945, I Abteilung of the Division's Panzer Regiment was involved in combat around the village of Herlisheim, counter-attacking against a strong US armoured push. Bachmann was at this time the Adjutant of the Abteilung.

As the opposing tanks stalked each other through the village streets, Bachmann knocked out a Sherman tank with a Panzerfaust fired from the window of a small house. Spotting two more Shermans in an adjacent street Bachmann ran to warn two of his Panthers and these Shermans too, were quickly eliminated. When the gunfire died down and Bachmann went into the street, an American officer approached and offered to surrender. Soon more than sixty US troops laid down their weapons. Bachmann had expected perhaps the crews of the Shermans which had been knocked out, but these were the crews of other tanks of whose presence he had been unaware. Such was the ferocity of the German attack that they had preferred to surrender rather than fight it out. To Bachmann's delight some twenty German soldiers who had been prisoners of the Americans were thus released and, immediately re-armed, became their former captors' escorts into captivity.

Bachmann now took his two Panthers to the edge of the village where he spotted and quickly destroyed two more approaching Shermans. During this action, nine M4 Shermans had been destroyed and twelve captured. The captured tanks were soon put to good use as the 13 Kompanie of the Panzer Regiment. All this success was due to Bachmann and a handful of his men. For his part in the action he was awarded the Knight's Cross of the Iron Cross on 10 February 1945. In March 1945, Bachmann took command of 1 Kompanie of Panzer Regiment 10 and scored several more kills in the remaining months of the war. He survived these few hectic months and now lives in retirement in Bovenden.

SS-OBERSCHARFÜHRER ERNST BARKMANN

A Holsteiner, Ernst Barkmann is one of Germany's top Panzer aces. Born in the village of Kisdorf in August 1919, Barkmann was a farmer's son. On leaving school in 1935, he too began to learn the family trade, and no doubt would have gone on to become a successful farmer, but in April 1939 he commenced his military service with SS-Standarte Germania in Hamburg. After three months' basic training he was posted to III Bataillon of the Standarte at Radolfszell.

During the Polish Campaign he served with 9. Kompanie as a machine-gunner, and was wounded during house-to-house fighting. During the early days of Operation 'Barbarossa', he was wounded again, near Dnieprpetrowsk, and won the Iron Cross Second Class. On recovery from his wounds he was posted to a training camp in occupied Holland, as an instructor for western European volunteers in the Waffen-SS.

Early in 1942, Barkmann volunteered for a transfer to the Panzertruppe and after completing conversion training joined 2. Kompanie, SS-Panzer Regiment 2, part of the SS Reich Division. The division had been severely mauled before Moscow in February 1942 and was withdrawn to France for rest and refit. At this point it was upgraded to a Panzer Grenadier Division and renamed Das Reich. The regiment was equipped with the Pz Kpfw III medium tank, armed with the 5cm gun. This was a good tank, but was inadequate against the excellent Soviet T-34. During early 1943, Barkmann saw action in the battle for Kharkov, winning the Iron Cross First Class.

Shortly after the battle, SS-Panzer Regiment 2 was re-equipped and now fielded the larger Pz Kpfw IV and Pz Kpfw V Panther tanks, armed with the deadly 75mm gun. With the Panther Barkmann was to become one of Germany's top tank aces. The Panther, however, did suffer initially from teething troubles, brought on, in the main, through over-hasty development in order to rush the tank into action. Once these faults were ironed out the Panther went on to become a formidable weapon and is generally accepted as being one of the finest tanks of the Second World War. Several captured examples were used by the French Army post-war.

In April 1944 the Das Reich Division was pulled out of the Eastern Front and sent to the South of France to counter any attempted Allied landings in that region. When the Allies landed in Normandy, however, this powerful Panzer Division was ordered north. Arriving in Normandy at the beginning of July, it went into action north of St-Lô. Advancing towards Sainteny, I Abteilung of the Panzer Regiment was attempting to halt the advance of the US 9th and 30th Infantry Divisions, and the US 3rd Armored Division. Oberscharführer Barkmann's 4. Kompanie was in the lead in Panther 424. After three long years of war on the Eastern Front,

Barkmann scored his first kill against the Western Allies, an M4 Sherman, on 8 July. It was to be the first of many.

Tank fighting in Normandy was altogether different from that on the Eastern Front. The narrow hedge-lined roads in Normandy were dangerous for tanks, with restricted visibility and little room for manoeuvre. The wide open plains of the Russian steppe with visibility clear almost to the horizon and tank battles taking place at extreme ranges, could hardly be more different from the Normandy battles with opposing tanks stalking one another through the bocage and often firing at almost point-blank range.

On 12 July, Barkmann knocked out two more Shermans of 3rd Armored Division and damaged another. A lull in the fighting followed and gave him the opportunity to ensure that his Panther was well camouflaged, an essential task in view of the damage being wreaked on German tank units by Allied fighter-bombers operating with almost unchallenged air superiority. The next day Barkmann spotted what appeared to be an enemy vehicle moving behind the cover of a hedgerow. Then a Sherman, leading a troop of six came into view. Barkmann immediately opened fire on the first, scoring a direct hit. The damaged tank returned fire, but two more direct hits from Barkmann's Panther soon silenced it. A fourth round penetrated the hull of another Sherman and its crew quickly baled out. While Barkmann was engaging the enemy tanks, the Americans were attempting to outflank him. Warned of this by SS Grenadiers, Barkmann sped off to take them by surprise before they could attack. Bursting through a small wood, Barkmann quickly eliminated a group of enemy infantry with high-explosive shells. An anti-tank gun was also knocked out but a second managed to score two direct hits on Barkmann's Panther, starting a fire, before Barkmann knocked it out also. Barkmann ordered his crew to bale out, then realized that his gun-layer was still inside, so he returned and managed to pull him free. It was then found that the damage was not so severe as he had first thought and the crew tackled the flames with fire-extinguishers and successfully doused them. The damaged Panther was then returned to the Abteilung's Werkstattkompanie.

On 14 July Barkmann set off in command of a group of four Panthers, his task – to secure the recovery of Panthers from his Kompanie which had been cut off. His own tank was still undergoing repairs so he used a spare. He was horrified to find that its interior was still spattered with the blood of its previous commander who had been killed. Despite the sombre reminder of his comrade's fate, Barkmann recovered the missing tanks, destroying three more enemy tanks in the process. In the afternoon of the same day, Barkmann was once again instrumental in the rescue of comrades, in this case wounded SS Grenadiers captured by US infantry. A force of three Panthers commanded by Barkmann quickly secured their release. This eventful day continued when his Panther received a direct hit from an artillery shell. The armour withstood the impact, but the tracks were torn loose and the 45-ton beast was immobilized. His own Panther by now repaired, Barkmann was soon on the move again.

On 26 July, SS-Panzer Regiment 2 was again in action against the

Americans, in the sector formerly held by General Bayerlein's élite Panzer Lehr Division. Panzer Lehr had been decimated and its place in the front was now to be held by Das Reichs' Panzers. Before Barkmann could go into action, however, his tank was hit by mechanical failure of the carburettor. Stranded in the open, his Panther was a sitting duck for prowling Allied fighter-bombers. At the receiving end of a hail of cannon fire, the Panther's engine was hit and set on fire, but working through the night, Das Reichs' mechanics managed to get the tank in running order by dawn. As Barkmann sped towards his unit's anticipated positions, he encountered German infantrymen rapidly retreating. They reported the imminent arrival of strong enemy forces. Two of Barkmann's men went forward to check and soon returned, one wounded, to confirm that the enemy were indeed approaching in strength. Barkmann took his Panther along the road from the village of Lorey, and stopped at the junction of the main road from St-Lô to Coutances. Here, under the cover of a large oak tree, he awaited the enemy. A long column of American vehicles appeared to his left, just 200 metres distant. Barkmann opened fire and soon the road was littered with burning half-tracks, trucks and tankers. Tanks now approached, and soon two M4 Shermans were also blazing. The Americans called up support from artillery and fighter-bombers and Barkmann found himself at the receiving end of a furious bombardment. Two Shermans foolhardy enough to approach too closely were quickly eliminated as the Panther continued to blast at every enemy vehicle within range. Single-handedly Barkmann's Panther had held the junction against overwhelming enemy forces, but now he knew he must withdraw. His Panther had received many hits, none of them fatal. His driver and radio operator were trapped in their seats by jammed hatches. The driver had been wounded in the neck and one of the tank's tracks had been blown off. Despite his wound and the missing track, he managed to coax the battered tank off towards the nearby village of Neufbourg where, using crowbars, the hatches were forced open. Barkmann had knocked out nine Shermans during this hectic battle, as well as a large number of other enemy vehicles. The site was to become known as 'Barkmann Corner'.

Oberscharführer Barkmann made his way to Coutances, reaching it on 28 July. En route he had increased his tally to fifteen tanks in the space of just two days. By 30 July, the American advance had reached Granville. Barkmann and his men were cut off and had to attempt a break out. Towing another disabled Panther from his Kompanie, he succeeded in evading the encircling US forces. However, on 1 August it was decided to destroy the crippled Panther. The tank was set on fire, but when the ammunition inside exploded, Barkmann's trusty 424 was too close and also caught fire. He and his men were forced to abandon their tank and set off on foot, across seven kilometres of the shallows by Avranches, reaching his own lines on 5 August. News of Barkmann's achievements at 'Barkmann Corner' had already reached his unit and unknown to him, he had been recommended for the Knight's Cross of the Iron Cross. It was approved on 27 August and he received his award on 5 September.

Having escaped entrapment in the Falaise pocket, 2nd SS Panzer Division, badly battered and weakened, was withdrawn behind the Siegfried Line for rest and refit. Its next major action was to be in the ill-fated Ardennes Offensive. Das Reich was to be part of Dietrich's Sixth Panzer Armee, its task to act as reserve force on the northern flank. On 19 December the Division passed to Panzer General Hasso von Manteuffel's Command and was used to break through the area held by the US 82nd Airborne Division. As the German advance pushed easily through the surprised and demoralized Americans, Barkmann in his new tank, 401, was moving towards the town of Manhay. His company commander, SS-Hauptsturmführer Frauscher, had gone on ahead and reported that his section had sustained hits from anti-tank guns.

As Barkmann proceeded towards Manhay he spotted what he assumed to be Frauscher's Panther. As he drew alongside he noticed a red interior lamp glow from the other tank – it was a Sherman – Panthers had green lights. As Barkmann's gunner frantically traversed the turret, his gun barrel clanged against the enemy tank. The two were too close for the gun to be brought to bear. The driver quickly reversed far enough for the long-barrelled 75mm gun to be brought into play and the gunner let loose an armour-piercing round which hit the Sherman in the rear. As the tank exploded, two more came into view, but Barkmann was too quick for them and soon they too were in flames. Barkmann went on through the snow covered landscape and on entering a forest clearing was shocked to find it packed with Shermans. With no chance to withdraw, he decided to bluff it out, hoping that the enemy would take the snow shrouded outline of his tank for one of theirs. It worked. Having got his Panther into an advantageous position, he decided to attack the Shermans, only to watch in amazement as the enemy, now realizing that a Panther was in their midst, quickly abandoned their tanks and ran off into the woods.

Barkmann decided to leave the capture or destruction of the Shermans to those following, and continued his bluff, driving on past further columns of tanks and troops who mistook him for one of theirs. Suddenly a Jeep appeared heading straight for his Panther along the narrow road. Barkmann had no choice but to continue and a wild race ensued with the Jeep racing backwards at full speed as the Panther charged after it. Eventually, the 45-ton monster caught the little Jeep and hit it with its right track. The Jeep's crew escaped, but the impact slewed the Panther across the icy road and it slammed broadside into a Sherman and stalled. By now the Americans were alert to the enemy in their midst, and shots were being fired at the Panther. Restarting the engine, 401 roared past even more startled US columns and out of the village. Some quick-thinking Americans took off in pursuit, but Barkmann's turret was traversed to the rear and soon the lead pursuit tanks were in flames, blocking the road to those that followed.

On 25 December, Barkmann was wounded in the head by a shell splinter and lost consciousness. When he came round he found himself in a field dressing station with his head bandaged. On his chest was a label giving his destination as a hospital in Cologne. He would have none of it. He removed the bandage and pulled the splinter from the wound with his fingers, and then calmly walked from the dressing station and hitched a lift back to his unit.

After the end of the Ardennes Offensive, Das Reich was once again refitted to make good its losses and was rapidly sent to the crumbling Eastern Front. In March 1945 Barkmann was back in action with 4 Kompanie, SS-Panzer Regiment 2, near Stuhlweissenberg against Soviet armoured forces. Here Barkmann knocked out four T-34s bringing the divisional kill total for the war so far to an amazing 3,000 tanks. Gradually decimated in non-stop combat against an overwhelmingly superior enemy, Das Reich was little more than a shadow of its former mighty self. Breaking out of a Soviet encirclement in late March 1945, I Abteilung of the Panzer Regiment had only nine battleworthy tanks left, and three of these were soon afterwards lost in combat against some of the new Soviet JSIII super heavy tanks. The remainder finally linked up with the remnant of the Leibstandarte's SS-Panzer Regiment 1 under SS-Standartenführer Jochen Peiper.

By April 1945, *Das Reich* had been thrown into the battle for Vienna and Barkmann was in action just south of the Austrian capital. Leading a troop of three Panthers towards the Regimental Headquarters, his Panther was struck by a *Panzerfaust* projectile. A German grenadier had mistaken his Panther for a Russian tank. Barkmann suffered a number of abdominal wounds from razor-sharp splinters of hot shrapnel, and his arms were lacerated. The gunlayer was blinded in both eyes and the radio operator was also severely wounded. After leaving his two wounded comrades with medics, Barkmann, despite his own wounds, continued on his way, only to have his Panther slide into a huge bomb crater from which it could not be retrieved. He destroyed it to prevent its capture by the Russians. Barkmann survived these last few days of the war and made his way west on foot to surrender to the Western Allies rather than to the Russians, a fate which few Germans, especially Waffen-SS soldiers relished. Barkmann was finally taken prisoner by British troops.

After the war Barkmann returned to farming, and eventually became the Burgomeister of his home town in Schleswig-Holstein. The author had the privilege of meeting Ernst Barkmann at his home in 1987. Looking through his collection of photographs, he often remarked on the fine qualities of many of his comrades, especially his Commanding Officer in the Panzer Regiment, Christian Tychsen, whom he greatly admired. Yet, typically of many great soldiers, he absolutely refuted any suggestion of heroism or ace status. He was, he said, just a soldier doing his duty, perhaps with more good luck than most. Asked about his score of enemy tanks, he replied that he was far too busy trying to best the enemy – but survive himself – to worry about scores.

Despite his protestations, Ernst Barkmann was surely one of the great tank commanders of the Second World War, and a soldier of great personal gallantry. His decorations include the rare Panzer Assault Badges for 25 and 50 engagements with the enemy.

HAUPTMANN HEINZ BAURMANN

Heinz Baurmann was born in Aachen on 11 November 1919. His military career began on 15 November 1938 when, as a Fahnenjunker, he joined Artillerie-Regiment 51 in Fulda. From October 1939 to March 1942, he served with 15 Infanterie Division, seeing heavy fighting on the central sector of the Eastern Front where the division took part in the siege of Mogilev. Baurmann was commissioned Leutnant in April 1940. In June of that year he was awarded the Iron Cross Second Class during the attack on France, and on 17 August 1941, during the invasion of the Soviet Union, this was followed by the Iron Cross First Class.

In March 1942, Baurmann volunteered for service with the Sturm-artillerie and attended training in Jüterbog. During the following month he was promoted to Hauptmann. In June he was appointed Adjutant in the newly formed Sturmgeschütz Abteilung 667 and served on the Eastern Front until he was appointed to command 3 Batterie in September 1942. Still on the Eastern Front, he was decorated with the German Cross in Gold on 16 April 1943.

In July of that year, he took command of 3 Batterie, Sturmgeschütz Ersatz und Ausbildungs Abteilung 600, a post he held for just over a year. In September 1944 he attended a training course for Abteilung Commanders at the Sturmgeschütz School at Burg. On completion of this course he returned to the front to take command of Sturmgeschütz Brigade 322. A mere three months later he was placed on the OKH Reserve, but returned to combat service at the end of March 1945, in command of Sturmgeschütz Brigade 300. The Brigade was in combat alongside 208 Infanterie Division on the southern sector of the Eastern Front, where it was instrumental in blunting many Soviet attacks.

On 21 April 1945, Soviet and Polish troops struck towards Bautzen. A counter-attack was mounted by troops from 20th Panzer Division, Fallschirm Panzer Division Hermann Göring and Sturmgeschütz Brigade 300. Striking north, the German attack liberated Weissenburg and threw the Soviets back from Bautzen. In this closing phase of the war it was to be one of the last German successes. During this counter-attack Baurmann achieved his 38th victory.

On 27 April 1945, Baurmann was seriously wounded in action and suffered the amputation of his right leg. On 4 May he became of the last recipients of the Knight's Cross of the Iron Cross, in recognition of his part in this last great successful counter-attack. On 28 August he was released from hospital and went into US captivity.

Despite his disability, Baurmann returned to military service in 1956 and served in a number of staff positions. He was promoted to Major in 1956 and to Oberstleutnant in 1965. He left military service in 1971 because of his war wounds and is now retired.

SS-OBERFÜHRER GEORG BOCHMANN

Born on 18 September 1913 in Albenau, Saxony, the son of a factory worker, Bochmann joined the SS on 1 April 1934 enlisting into the SS-Totenkopfverbände. He was commissioned SS-Untersturmführer in 1936 and posted to 1 (Oberbayern) Standarte. When the Totenkopfverbände was motorized and upgraded, Bochmann was given command of 14 (Panzerjäger) Kompanie, 1 SS-Totenkopf Standarte. He served in the campaign in the west, winning the Iron Cross Second Class in June 1940. The First Class followed on 8 July 1941 on the Eastern Front, where he served as an SS-Hauptsturmführer and Commander of the Panzerjäger Abteilung of the Totenkopf Division. Under the command of Bochmann, the Abteilung scored heavily against the Soviets. On one memorable day, one of Bochmann's young gunners, SS-Sturmmann Fritz Christen, personally knocked out fifteen Soviet tanks with his 5cm anti-tank gun, winning the Knight's Cross of the Iron Cross. He was the first enlisted man, and the youngest man in the Waffen-SS to win the Knight's Cross.

In April 1942, Bochmann, in command of a Kampfgruppe bearing his name, was given the task of leading a breakout from a Soviet encirclement within the Demjansk area. With his troops already weary and exhausted from constant Soviet attacks, Bochmann struck out for the River Lowat. Often involved in hand-to-hand fighting, Bochmann's group forced their way through, capturing fifteen Soviet artillery pieces. On 21 April, Bochmann and his men finally broke through the encirclement to meet with German troops on the opposite bank of the Lowat. In recognition of his successful leadership of the breakout, despite being severely wounded, Bochmann was decorated with the Knight's Cross of the Iron Cross on 3 May 1942.

Promoted to SS-Sturmbannführer in early 1943, he was given command of Kradschutzen Regiment Thule and commanded the regiment during the fierce combat of the battle for Kharkov. During the first few months of 1943, Bochmann and his men were constantly displaying their aggressive daredevilry, after striking deep behind enemy lines. Alongside his comrade from the Leibstandarte, Joachim Peiper, he was involved in the capture of Bjelgorod.

On 17 May 1943, Bochmann became the 246th recipient of the Oakleaves which he received from the hands of Hitler at a special ceremony at Führerhauptquartier. During the massive tank battles at Kursk, Bochmann commanded SS-Panzer Regiment 3, a post which he held until August 1944 when he was temporarily transferred to command SS-Panzer Regiment 9, in the élite 9th SS Panzer Division Hohenstaufen, replacing its former commander SS-Obersturmbannführer Otto Meyer who had been killed in action.

On 3 January 1945, he was given command of 18th SS-Freiwilligen Panzer Grenadier Division Horst Wessel. This division which, despite his leadership, could not compare in quality with the élite units in which

Bochmann had earlier served, was thrown into action in an attempt to stem the flow of Soviet forces in Silesia. The division was, however, more fortunate than some of its contemporaries in that it was at least well-equipped and at virtual full strength. Encircled by the enemy at Oberglogau, Bochmann once again carried out a masterly breakout and succeeded in bringing his men back to the German lines. On 30 March 1945, he was summoned to Hitler's Headquarters. At a period when any commander who retreated could expect summary justice, Bochmann could be excused for feeling some trepidation at what might await him. However, it was not Hitler's wrath but his pleasure which Bochmann had incurred, and he was invested by Hitler with the Swords to his Oakleaves, the 140th recipient of this award.

Bochmann was now given command of 17th SS Panzergrenadier Division Goetz von Berlichingen which had been constantly in action against the Western Allies since its first committal to battle in the summer of 1944. Bochmann led the division into action against US infantry and armoured units, inflicting heavy casualties. The division surrendered on 8 May 1945 when expressly ordered to so by XIII Armee Korps.

Bochmann ended the war with the rank of Oberführer, a greatly respected and admired soldier. When he died in 1973, his funeral was attended by large numbers of his former wartime comrades, wishing to pay their last respects to this gallant soldier.

LEUTNANT GEORG BOSE

One of the top aces of the Sturmartillerie, Georg Bose was born on 20 October 1921 near Cottbus. After completing his service in the Reichs-arbeitsdienst he began his military career on 26 August 1938 with 3 Kompanie, Bau Bataillon 26, taking part in the invasion of Poland.

On 8 June 1940, Bose became a gunner with 1 Batterie, Flak Ersatz Abteilung 51 in Stettin. Three months later he joined 4 Batterie (a training unit) of the schwere Artillerie Reserve Abteilung 58 in Hamburg. On completion of his training period there, he attended an officer-aspirants' course. He was promoted to the rank of Oberkanonier on 1 June 1940 and in September of that year was posted to 5 Batterie, Artillerie Abteilung 58, seeing action in the French Campaign. The regiment in which Bose served was one of those trained to take part in Operation 'Sealion', the proposed invasion of Great Britain.

Bose saw action during the Yugoslav Campaign before taking part in the opening phase of the invasion of the Soviet Union. Promoted to Unteroffizier on 1 August 1941, some six weeks later he was sent on an officer candidates' course at the Jüterbog Artillerieschule.

On his return to the front he joined 6 Batterie of his old regiment, but in December 1941 applied for a transfer to the Sturmartillerie. This was granted and he joined VI Abteilung of the Artillerie Lehr Regiment 2 in

Jüterbog for conversion training. In January 1943, Bose was promoted to Wachtmeister and posted to the Panzer Aufklärungsabteilung of the Grossdeutschland Division before joining Sturmgeschütz Ersatz und Ausbildungs Abteilung 300 as a trainee. One month later, his conversion training now complete, he was posted to Sturmgeschütz Abteilung 300 as a trainee. One month later he was posted to Sturmgeschütz Abteilung 177 as an assault gun commander. On 15 July 1943 he was granted the Iron Cross Second Class.

Commissioned Leutnant, Bose became the Abteilung Adjutant, and in January 1944 won the Iron Cross First Class. In the summer of 1944, a Soviet breakthrough on the Eastern Front had encircled a large German force in the area between Warsaw and Brest-Litovsk, near the town of Siedlce. Within the pocket, Georg Bose was in command of a troop of three assault guns of his Abteilung, which was attached to 3 Kavallerie Brigade under command of 292nd Infanterie Division.

On the evening of 28 July, Bose and his small force met the full brunt of the attacking Soviet armour by the small village of Radziwilowka to the north of Brest-Litovsk. Stalking the enemy armour through the streets of the village, Bose and his men knocked out eleven of the Soviet T34/85s. Four of these fell to Bose personally, bringing his own score at that point to nineteen tanks destroyed. Not only had Bose blunted the Soviet attack at Radziwilowka, but the entire flank of the 292nd Infanterie Division had been thereby secured as the Soviets withdrew, bloodied and battered.

On his return to his unit, Bose was summoned before the Divisional Commander, Generalleutnant John, who was fulsome in his praise of the gallant assault gun commander . . . 'How can I thank you,' said John. 'You have saved my Division, I congratulate you on your unique achievement!' Generalleutnant John congratulated Bose on his tactical flair and asked his age. Astonished to hear that he was only 22, he continued, 'My God, are you still so young. 22 years old. It seems hard to believe.' On 26 September 1944 he was decorated with the Knight's Cross of the Iron Cross. The official award date was 21 September, but the award could not be made until a suitable pause in the battle.

On 23 March 1945, Bose fell ill and was hospitalized in Pisek, Czechoslovakia. Still there when the war ended, he was captured by US troops who handed him over to the Russians on 11 May. He was held in captivity for more than three years, being released in July 1948. Leutnant Bose had achieved a tally of 44 tanks destroyed before he was invalided out of action. His awards included the Badge for Single Handed Destruction of an enemy tank, using only hand-held weapons. Georg Bose is still alive, and lives in retirement in Einhausen.

MAJOR JOSEF WILHELM SEPP BRANDNER

An Austrian, born in Hohenberg on 1 September 1915, Sepp Brandner began a career as an electrical technician before being conscripted into the

Army in 1936 at the age of 21. Subsequently taken into the German Army after the Anschluss, Brandner joined Artillerie Regiment 102 where, in October 1938 he was promoted to Obergefreiter and in December 1938 to Unteroffizier. After service in the Polish and western campaigns he attended a commissioning course at the Artillerieschule in Jüterbog, being promoted to the rank of Leutnant on 24 July 1940.

Shortly after the invasion of the Soviet Union Brandner joined Sturm-geschütz Abteilung 202. A highly successful assault gun commander, he was awarded the Iron Cross First Class on 16 January 1942 and was promoted to Oberleutnant in June of the same year. On 16 September 1943 he was decorated with the German Cross in Gold in recognition of having destroyed his 45th enemy tank. Further actions during the fighting around Kiev and Tscherkassy and in Roumania saw Brandner's score growing steadily. He was recommended for the Knight's Cross of the Iron Cross after scoring his 50th kill, but on this occasion it was not granted; the recommendation papers appear to have been lost or destroyed by enemy action. In late October 1944 Brandner attended a Brigade Commanders' course at the Sturmgeschütz training school at Burg and on his return to the front took command of Sturmgeschütz Brigade 912. Thrown into the fighting during the Kurland battles, the Brigade performed so well that it was mentioned in an Armed Forces Dispatch in December 1944.

> A south German assault gun Brigade under the exemplary brave and successful
> leadership of its 28-year-old Commander, Sepp Brandner of Vienna, destroyed
> at the beginning of the 3rd Kurland Battle, its 500th enemy tank. The
> Commander himself scored his personal 57th victory.

The fate of Heeresgruppe Kurland hung in the balance in December 1944 as the Soviets with overwhelming superiority sought to fragment and destroy the Army Group. On that day Brandner's brigade was thrown into action. In true daredevil fashion Brandner raced through the enemy barrage and brought much needed morale and material support to the battered German infantry many of whom were on the point of abandoning their positions. A Sturmgeschütz attack against an enemy position without infantry support is very dangerous. The Sturmgeschütz has no defensive machine-gun armament, and unprotected by friendly infantry they make an inviting target for grenades, sticky bombs, Molotov cocktails, etc. Brandner himself narrowly escaped death when, his head exposed above the hatch to direct fire, a grenade exploded on the rear deck of the vehicle. He was unscathed. Brandner's assault guns continued their charge through the enemy lines, scattering hundreds of fleeing Soviet infantrymen. His attack was completely successful. The Soviet armoured spearhead was blunted and their attack plan destroyed.

On 17 March 1945, Sepp Brandner was decorated with his long overdue Knight's Cross following his personal 66th victory. He was to become one of the best-known soldiers in the Kurland pocket as his Sturmgeschütz Brigade served throughout the fourth, fifth and sixth Kurland Battles. By the end of the war it had destroyed more than 600 tanks for the loss of just

38 of its own vehicles. On 26 April 1945 Brandner was decorated with the Oakleaves in recognition of the gallant efforts not only of himself but his entire Brigade. He was also given a battlefield promotion to Major. Heeres Sturmgeschütz Brigade went into Soviet captivity on 9 May 1945 and Brandner was a prisoner until 10 January 1948.

One of Germany's great assault gun aces, Sepp Brandner's decorations include, in addition to the Knight's Cross with Oakleaves, the Eastern Front Medal, the Wounded Badge, the General Assault Badge for 100 engagements with the enemy, the Honour Roll Clasp of the German Army, and the Close Combat Clasp.

OBERLEUTNANT OTTO CARIUS

Otto Carius, one of Germany's top Panzer commanders, was born on 27 May 1922 in Zweibrücken. His career in the Panzertruppe began in 1940 when he joined Panzer Regiment 21, part of 20th Panzer Division. In the summer of 1941, Carius took part in the invasion of the Soviet Union in the central sector of the front, during the push on Moscow. In August 1941, he returned to Germany for officer training which lasted until the spring of 1942 when he returned to his regiment as a Zugführer in 3 Abteilung of Panzer Regiment 21, still in the central sector of the front.

In February 1943, Carius was posted to schwere Panzer Ersatz und Ausbildungs Abteilung 500 in Paderborn for conversion training for the Tiger tank. On the completion of his training he returned to the front, this time as a Zugführer in 2 Kompanie of schwere Panzer Abteilung 502 near Leningrad.

Early in 1944, Leutnant Carius with a battle group from 2 Kompanie of the Abteilung was in support of elements of 11th SS-Freiwilligen Panzer Grenadier Division Nordland in the Narwa bridgehead, where his Tigers were to prove an invaluable asset. Time and again the defence put up by a mere handful of the massive Tigers was enough to blunt huge Soviet armoured assaults which lost about 500 tanks to the deadly 88mm gun of the Tiger.

At the end of April Carius had a narrow escape when his Tiger received a direct hit from a huge Soviet SU152 assault gun. The blast blew off the commander's cupola, wounding Carius. A second hit struck the Tiger between the turret and hull, but the crew managed to escape from the stricken vehicle. On 4 May 1944 Carius was awarded the Knight's Cross of the Iron Cross in recognition of his part in the successes of 502 during this hectic period. In July he was given command of 2 Kompanie which was to find itself employed in a desperate defence of the area around Dünaburg during the Soviet summer offensive. On 21 July, in a series of intense tank battles Carius, along with his Kompanie, saved the day on many occasions where once again the appearance of his Tigers was enough to turn the tables against the Soviets. The battlefield was left littered with destroyed T-34/85 and Josef Stalin tanks and the SU122 heavy assault guns. While on a forward recce with his driver in a motor cycle-sidecar combination, Carius was hit. As he lay unconscious a Russian soldier shot him again three times, one bullet passing through his neck, but without hitting the spinal column. In the nick of time, one of his Tigers appeared on the scene, driving off the enemy, and Carius was evacuated to hospital. While recovering, he was decorated with the Oakleaves to his Knight's Cross in recognition of his personal gallantry and successful leadership. On 1 August 1944 he was promoted to Oberleutnant.

Carius was next posted to schwere Jagdpanzer Abteilung 512. This unit was equipped with the even more massive Jagdtiger, a tank destroyer based on the chassis of the King Tiger tank and weighing in at well over 70 tons. The Abteilung went into action against US forces near Unna, wreaking havoc among the American vehicles with its huge 128mm gun. On 15 April 1945, Carius surrendered his unit to the Americans. He was held as a prisoner of war until 1946. Otto Carius survived to build up his own successful pharmacy business, and wrote the history of his unit entitled *Tiger im Schlamm*. He is still alive.

OBERLEUTNANT HEINZ DEUTSCH

Born on 21 July 1920 in Mutterstadt in the Rhineland, Heinz Deutsch began his military career on 26 August 1939 when he joined the Luftwaffe. In January 1940 he was posted to schwere Flak Abteilung 491 and served in the anti-aircraft defence around the Black Forest area. In October 1940 he was promoted to Gefreiter and one year later to Obergefreiter. In October 1942, by which time Deutsch had risen to the rank of Unteroffizier, he transferred to schwere Flak Abteilung 457, still in the anti-aircraft defence role.

In April 1943, Deutsch was commissioned Leutnant der Reserve, continuing to serve with the Flakartillerie until the spring of 1944 when he transferred to the assault gun branch of the Luftwaffe's Fallschirmtruppe. In 7th Fallschirm Division, he served with Fallschirm Sturmgeschütz Brigade 12 on the Western Front against the advancing British and Canadian forces in the Reichswald area during February 1945.

On the 25th of that month, in a defensive battle against Allied forces with considerable armoured support, Deutsch destroyed two M4 Sherman tanks. On 1 March he was involved in fierce hand-to-hand combat when enemy infantry infiltrated the German positions; the Allied troops were driven off with hand-grenades. Shortly afterwards Deutsch took part in a counter-attack which captured 21 prisoners.

On the following day a further armoured attack was thrown back with three enemy tanks being knocked out, causing the supporting infantry to withdraw. On 3 March, Deutsch was in action again, this time against British armoured infantry units, destroying a half-track and a tank. A day later British infantry pushing towards Sonsbeck ran into Deutsch who knocked out a Cromwell tank and another Sherman, then drove off the accompanying infantry. On the morning of 5 March 1945, Allied tank forces were attacking near Hambt when Deutsch appeared on the scene again and destroyed yet another Sherman. At about noon a heavier attack materialized, and only through the efforts of Deutsch and his Sturmgeschütz was the threat to the infantry of Fallschirmjäger Regiment 22 averted. During 6 March an Allied attack on the Bönninghardt airfield was halted when Deutsch destroyed the two leading tanks, giving the defenders time to regroup.

During the next few days Deutsch and his crew steadily increased their score, each day adding a few more tanks to his tally. Churchills, Shermans, Cromwells, all fell victim to Deutsch and his men. On 30 March in an action west of Külve, Deutsch destroyed five tanks and two other armoured vehicles in a single engagement. Once again Deutsch's action was responsible for the line being held. Despite being a recently formed unit, raised only in September 1944, 7th Fallschirm Division had proven itself to be an excellent combat unit, and Fallschirm Sturmgeschütz Brigade 11 played no small part in its success during the hectic defensive battles.

On 28 April 1945, Heinz Deutsch was decorated with the Knight's Cross of the Iron Cross on achieving his 46th enemy tank destroyed. At the same time he was promoted from Leutnant to Oberleutnant der Reserve. His crew all received the German Cross in Gold. The war for 7th Fallschirm Division ended when the divisional commander, General Wolfgang Erdmann, surrendered his forces to the British. Deutsch survived the war and is still alive. The extent of his achievements in the defence of his homeland can be seen in the Wehrmachtsbericht issued on 14 April 1945 where it was announced that Deutsch had destroyed 34 tanks and two armoured cars in twenty days of combat.

SS-HAUPTSTURMFÜHRER FRANZ-JOSEF DREIKE

Born on 27 October 1910 in Dortmund, the son of a local butcher, Franz-Josef Dreike studied architecture at the Technisches Hochschule in Berlin from 1933 to 1938. Thereafter he became an architect with the construction department of the Reichsnährstandes.

On 1 October 1938 he volunteered for military service and was accepted into Flak Regiment 12 in Berlin. By the outbreak of war in September 1939 he was a Gefreiter and officer-candidate in Flak Reserve Abteilung 129 on home defence duties. Dreike applied many times for front-line duties, but at 29 he was considered too old. Germany had no manpower shortages at this time, and there were any amount of younger men eager and willing for military service.

In January 1940, Dreike volunteered for the Waffen-SS and was accepted for 3 Kompanie Aufklärungs Abteilung of the Totenkopf Division with the rank of SS-Rottenführer. After attending an NCO's training course he was promoted to SS-Unterscharführer. At this time the Totenkopf Division was being reinforced by a considerable influx of captured Czech weapons. Among these were a number of the versatile Skoda 38(t) tanks which were to become the basis of the excellent Hetzer tank destroyer. The Skoda chassis which the Totenkopf Division acquired were re-armed with the 3.7cm Infantry Howitzer. This was to be one of the first Panzer Kompanie of the Waffen-SS.

During the campaign in France, Dreike and his men captured 24 French Somua tanks. For this feat he was, at the conclusion of the campaign, given a commission in the rank of SS-Untersturmführer, and sent on an officers' training course run by the staff of the SS-Junkerschule Bad-Tölz. During the invasion of the Soviet Union in 1941, Dreike served as a Zugführer in 2 Batterie, SS-Flak Abteilung 3. He was in command of twelve 37mm Flak 36 guns, mounted on captured French self-propelled vehicles. Dreike was credited with downing the first Soviet I12 Stormovik, a notoriously difficult aircraft to knock down, being heavily armoured. By the end of the war, the Batterie had accounted for 178 aircraft.

During the battle at Demjansk, the Zug commanded by Dreike was used in a ground defence role. He was seriously wounded during this period and evacuated for hospital treatment. On recovery he was posted to SS-Flak Ausbildungs und Ersatz Abteilung in Arolsen and also attended training at the Luftwaffe's Flakschule in Berlin. After this he became Battery Commander and ultimately Abteilung Commander of 1 Abteilung, SS-Flak Ausbildungs und Ersatz Regiment in Munich. At one point he was Commander of 2 Batterie of SS Flak Abteilung at Berchtesgaden. On 1 June 1944, Dreike took command of 1 Batterie SS-Flak Abteilung 1, part of the élite Leibstandarte Adolf Hitler, serving throughout the Normandy Campaign. During the Ardennes Offensive, he served with SS-Flak Abteilung 2 Das Reich.

With Das Reich during the retreat from Hungary, Dreike and his men found themselves once again used in the ground role. During the defence of Vienna, Dreike was terribly wounded in both hands, the right forearm, left upper arm, both shoulders, the left breast and the head, losing his right eye. He had fought with little regard for his own safety and had paid the price for his reckless gallantry. He was decorated with the Knight's Cross of the Iron Cross on 6 May 1945. He spent two years in captivity at the end of the war, gaining early release because of his disability. After the war, Dreike returned to his peacetime profession as an architect. He died in 1988.

SS-OBERSTURMFÜHRER PAUL EGGER

Panzer ace Paul Egger was born on 26 November 1916, the son of an official in Mautern, Styria. He attended the Volkschule in Mautern-Schladming and after completing his studies at the Gymnasium in 1932, went on to take up employment in the retail trade.

After the Anschluss with Austria in 1938, the Wehrmacht had a vast new pool of manpower available, and in 1938 Egger became one of many Austrians who joined the Luftwaffe. He trained as a pilot and on the outbreak of war flew with Kampfgeschwader 51 as a bomber pilot, seeing action in the polish Campaign and over France and Holland during the attack in the west. Egger also took part in bombing raids over England.

On 1 May 1941, he transferred to the Waffen-SS and was trained as a Panzer soldier, being posted to the newly formed schwere Kompanie of the 2nd SS-Panzer Division Das Reich, equipped with the new Tiger tanks. As a tank commander in Das Reich's 8. Kompanie, he saw intense action in the battle for Kharkov.

The schwere Kompanie of Das Reich was to be the basis for schwere SS-Panzer Abteilung 102, the heavy tank battalion of II SS-Panzer Korps. The Abteilung was thrown into combat on the Normandy invasion front where it took a heavy toll of Allied vehicles, knocking out 250 tanks and tracked/half-tracked vehicles. Ultimately, overwhelming Allied numerical superiority saw the Abteilung being slowly decimated and by the end of August the unit had lost all its tanks. Egger was awarded the German Cross in Gold for his efforts during the Invasion battles, the decoration being awarded on 30 December 1944.

The Abteilung was reformed, now as schwere SS-Panzer Abteilung 502, and went into action on the Eastern Front, having been re-equipped at Paderborn in the winter of 1944/45 with the formidable King Tiger. During a massed Soviet attack on the Oder Front in March 1945, Egger was responsible for blunting the attack and destroying nineteen enemy tanks during the engagement.

502's last great battle was during the Soviet push on Berlin. The Tigers were instrumental in covering the retreat of countless thousands of German troops and civilian refugees from the advancing Russians. Numerous vicious duels were fought between the massive King Tigers, always greatly outnumbered, and the Soviet T-34/85 and J.S.III tanks. Although many localized victories were achieved they were but pinpricks to the vast might of the Red Army, and the Germans were gradually pushed back, their losses irreplaceable, whereas the enemy had a seemingly endless supply of replacement armour available. Every Tiger of schwere Panzer Abteilung 502 fought to the last.

Egger brought his personal score to 113 enemy tanks in the last days of the war. On 28 April 1945 he was decorated with the Knight's Cross of the Iron Cross for his achievements. He was more fortunate than many of his comrades and survived the war. He is still alive.

SS-HAUPTSTURMFÜHRER KARL-HEINZ GUSTAVSSON

Karl-Heinz Gustavsson was one of the aces of the Flakartillerie. Born in Hamburg on 10 February 1915, he joined the civil police in Hamburg on 1

April 1934 and served as a policeman for eighteen months before being
called up for military service in the Wehrmacht. On 16 October 1935 he
joined Infanterie Regiment 16 in Oldenburg as an Unteroffizier. His military
service completed in 1938, Gustavsson was discharged and took up
employment with the railways, the Deutsche Reichsbahn.

After the mobilization of the German Army in 1939, he re-joined the
police and shortly afterwards was transferred to the SS-Verfügungstruppe,
the forerunner of the Waffen-SS. Initially a gun commander in 13
(Infanterie) Kompanie of SS-Standarte Germania, he later became a platoon
leader in SS-Totenkopf Infanterie Regiment 10, and served with this
regiment during the Polish Campaign where he was wounded for the first
time. On 9 November 1939 he was promoted to SS-Scharführer and on 20
April 1940 to SS-Oberscharführer.

During the invasion of the Soviet Union, Gustavsson was again wounded
on 12 December 1941 while his unit was taking part in the attack on
Leningrad. After a period spent with the SS-Freiwilligen Legion Flandern,
he attended, in 1942, an officer candidates' course at the SS Academy at
Bad-Tölz in Bavaria. On 1 July 1942 he was commissioned as an SS-
Untersturmführer, the equivalent of a second lieutenant. Rejoining the
Legion Flandern on the Eastern Front, he was once again wounded in
December 1942. In 1943, after a period of hospitalization, he was posted to
SS-Sturmbrigade Langemarck.

Gustavsson served on the southern sector of the Eastern Front until
March 1944, commanding a battery of the deadly 8.8cm Flak guns. During
these hectic days on the Eastern Front, hand-to-hand combat with Soviet
troops often developed and Gustavsson was decorated with both the Bronze
and Silver Close Combat Clasps. He had been promoted to SS-Obersturmführer in January 1944 and in August of that year was given command of
a Flak battery of the Flakabteilung of the élite 2nd SS Panzer Division Das
Reich.

Gustavsson and his battery were tasked with the defence of the launching
ramps of the V-1 missiles during the preparations for Hitler's Ardennes
Offensive in late 1944. He achieved this task with great distinction. With
no motorized transport and only hand-held anti-tank weapons such as the
Panzerfaust, for support, Gustavsson held off numerous US armoured
attacks until the V-weapons systems and supplies could be evacuated to
safety. Despite his inadequate defensive armament, Gustavsson used his
8.8s to deadly effect and thirteen US tanks and numerous other vehicles
were left blazing on the battlefield. Thanks to his gallantry and exemplary
leadership, the American attempt to capture the V-weapons was defeated.

In recognition of his achievements, Karl-Heinz Gustavsson was decorated
with the Knight's Cross of the Iron Cross on 3 March 1945, the award being
made personally by the Oberbefehlshaber West, Generalfeldmarschall
Walter Model. Gustavsson and his 8.8s served again with distinction in the
defence of the Remagen bridgehead. During this action he was seriously
wounded and had to be hospitalized. The wound led to the loss of his right
leg in 1949.

Having survived the war, this brave Flak commander now lives in retirement in his native Hamburg. Gustavsson's decorations include the Wounded Badge in Black and Silver, the War Merit Cross 2nd Class with Swords, Infantry Assault Badge, Iron Cross 2nd and 1st Classes, Close Combat Clasps in Bronze and Silver, the Eastern Front Medal and the Knight's Cross of the Iron Cross.

SS-HAUPTSTURMFÜHRER WILLI HEIN

Willi Hein was born on 26 April 1917 in Hohenwestedt, the son of a painter. On completing his schooling he worked in the retail trade until April 1939 when he began his compulsory service in the Reichsarbeitsdienst. On the outbreak of war he volunteered and was accepted into the SS Nordland Regiment, in which he served until November 1941 when he was sent on a commissioning course at the SS-Junkerschule at Bad Tölz in Bavaria. In April 1942 he graduated and was promoted to SS-Untersturmführer.

Posted to SS-Panzergrenadier Regiment Wiking which was serving in the southern sector of the Eastern Front, Hein became a Zugführer in SS-Panzer Regiment 5. *Wiking* served during the great tank battle at Kursk, suffering terrible losses. In recognition of his dedication to duty during this famous battle, Hein received the Führer Commendation Certificate. In November 1943 he was promoted to SS-Obersturmführer and Commander of 2 Kompanie of the Regiment and at about this time was also awarded the Honour Roll Clasp of the German Army. This dedicated Panzer officer was further honoured on 30 January 1944 by the award of the German Cross in Gold.

During the battles in the Tscherkassy pocket the divisional supply lines at Olschana came under attack by powerful Soviet forces. Emergency measures were called for and Hein set off to counter-attack with no more than two damaged assault guns which had been hastily repaired. In support were a mere 25 Grenadiers. Hein hurled his meagre force against the might of the Soviet attackers, knocking out three tanks and capturing 200 prisoners. Hein then held his position in support of the supply lines, despite all Soviet efforts to crush his tiny force, until the divisional lines were secured. For his achievement and his own personal gallantry he was decorated with the Knight's Cross of the Iron Cross on 4 May 1944.

The Regiment saw fierce action around Warsaw in the summer of 1944 and suffered considerable casualties. It was subsequently moved south and took part in the relief attempt on Budapest, again taking heavy casualties. In September 1944, SS-Hauptsturmführer Säumenicht, the Commander of I Abteilung of the Panzer Regiment had been killed in action and Hein replaced him, being promoted to the rank of SS-Hauptsturmführer.

Hein received serious leg wounds during the attempted relief of Budapest and ended the war in a Vienna hospital, thus escaping the fate of so many of his comrades when the division was virtually annihilated in April 1945 in the defence of Austria.

LEUTNANT WILLI HEINRICH

Panzer ace Willi Heinrich was born in October 1914. He served during the early part of the war as a Panzer NCO, winning the Iron Cross Class during the campaign in the west and the First Class during the early part of the campaign on the Eastern Front, in July 1941.

While serving on the Eastern Front with 6 Kompanie, Panzer Regiment 4, Oberfeldwebel Heinrich took part in the capture of Kiev and saw fierce combat in the battle for the Caucasus. His regiment was committed to the bitter action in defence of Taganrog and in the Kuban in the winter of 1942–43. Heinrich was decorated with the German Cross in Gold on 13 November 1942.

In 1943 Heinrich attended an officer training course and was commissioned Leutnant in May of that year. In September 1944, he joined the Führer Grenadier Brigade Grossdeutschland, part of the élite Grossdeutschland Panzerkorps. He commanded I Kompanie of the brigade's Panzer Abteilung. Heinrich's Kompanie was equipped with the excellent Pz Kpfw V Panther, a 45-ton medium tank considered by many to have been the best tank of the entire war.

Committed to the battle for East Prussia in the latter part of 1944, the brigade was involved in the defence of Gumbinnen, south of Gross Watlersdorf. A massed Soviet attack had pushed through the German lines towards Gumbinnen on 20 October 1944, and Heinrich's Panther Kompanie was sent in to counter-attack. By this point in the war German losses had much reduced the effectiveness of their forces and the Soviets had a seemingly endless supply of men and material. Heinrich did achieve a local encirclement of the attacking Russians, but this could inevitably be only short-lived.

By 27 October, the Führer Grenadier Brigade had been forced to withdraw and after a further counter-attack in November, which successfully achieved its immediate objective of recapturing Goldap, albeit temporarily, the Brigade was sent into reserve. On 9 December 1944, Leutnant Heinrich was decorated with the Knight's Cross of the Iron Cross in recognition of his command of the Panther Kompanie during these battles.

The Führer Grenadier Brigade was upgraded to full Panzer Brigade status at Cottbus, and was next committed to action during Hitler's ill-fated Ardennes Offensive in December 1944. The Brigade was moved to the Western Front in mid-December and at this stage comprised a Panzer Regiment, Artillerie Batterie, Flak Batterie and Panzer Grenadier Regiment. It went into battle under control of 7 Armee around Heiderscheid. The brigade was decimated during the offensive and at one point average Kompanie strength was as low as only 30 men. During this period Heinrich qualified for the Wound Badge in Silver after being seriously wounded on 28 December in action near Bastogne.

In 1945, the brigade was expanded to divisional status, at least on paper

though it is doubtful if at this late stage in the war enough men and
equipment could be found to make its status a reality. It went into action
near Stargard and at Stettin and was later involved in the defence of the
Kustrin Bridgehead before being withdrawn west for the defence of Vienna
where it eventually surrendered to US forces at Trakwein. It was, however,
handed over to the Russians. Willi Heinrich survived the war, and his
captivity, and now lives in retirement in Wiesbaden.

SS-HAUPTSCHARFÜHRER FRIEDRICH HENKE

Born on 6 January 1921 in Welsede in Lower Saxony, Friedrich Henke
volunteered for service in the SS in September 1939 and was accepted into
the Germania Regiment in Hamburg. In April 1940 he was assigned to the
SS-Nachrichten Abteilung in Unna for training as a signaller before joining
the Sturmgeschütz Batterie of the élite Leibstandarte Adolf Hitler. With
this unit he saw action in the Balkan Campaign where the Leibstandarte
played a major part in the fall of Greece. He was promoted to SS-
Sturmmann in November 1940.

With the Sturmgeschütz Batterie of the Leibstandarte when the German
armies invaded the Soviet Union in the summer of 1941, Henke was
promoted to SS-Rottenführer in October of 1941 and received the Iron
Cross 2nd Class in December. Two months later he qualified for the Panzer
Assault Badge. A proficient NCO, he was further promoted to SS-
Unterscharführer in August 1942.

Henke became as assault gun commander when the Leibstandarte's
assault gun section was upgraded to Abteilung strength. He served as a
commander with 1 Batterie of the Abteilung. He was awarded the Iron Cross
1st Class in July 1943 and again promoted, this time to SS-Oberscharführer,
shortly after having been given command of a Sturmgeschütz Zug in 3
Batterie. At this point in the war the Leibstandarte was heavily involved in
furious defensive battles in the area around Zhitomir on the southern sector
of the Eastern Front. At the end of December the Soviets had pushed
through the German lines on a broad front from Artopol to Bujarka.
Surrounded by overwhelming enemy forces with tanks and supporting
infantry, Henke and his Zug struck out for their own lines. Henke not only
succeeded in reaching safety, but while fighting his way to his own lines,
destroyed 21 enemy tanks and eleven heavy anti-tank guns. For this
achievement as well as for his own personal bravery, Fritz Henke was
awarded the Knight's Cross of the Iron Cross on 12 February 1944.

In November of the same year Henke was promoted to SS-Hauptscharführer at the same time winning the Panzer Assault Badge for 25
engagements with the enemy.

Henke saw further action on both the Eastern and Western Fronts. A
lucky soldier throughout the war, he was wounded only once, and then not

until February 1945. On 15 April 1945 he was awarded the Panzer Assault Badge for 50 engagements with the enemy and five days later received a battlefield commission to SS-Untersturmführer. Fritz Henke survived the war, being taken into captivity on 8 May 1945 and released on 31 December 1946. He is still alive and lives in retirement in Podendorf.

SS-STURMBANNFÜHRER FRITZ HERZIG

A Tiger tank ace, Fritz Herzig was born on 18 July 1915 in Wiener-Neustadt. He left Austria before the Anschluss with Germany and joined the SS in 1934, entering 5 Kompanie, SS-Standarte Deutschland in Munich.

He attended the SS-Junkerschule Braunschweig and was commissioned SS-Untersturmführer in April 1936, being posted to 7 Kompanie of the same Standarte. In 1939 Herzig was promoted to SS-Obersturmführer and by the outbreak of war was with the SS-Artillerie Regiment, serving in the Polish Campaign where he was wounded in action for the first time.

In April 1941, he was promoted to SS-Hauptsturmführer and transferred to the newly formed Wiking Division in which he served as the Commander of 3 Kompanie, SS-Aufklärungs Abteilung 5, winning both the Second Class and First Class Iron Crosses during his time with this Abteilung on the Eastern Front.

A combination of wounds and illness removed Herzig from front-line duties for the first half of 1942 and on his return to duty he joined SS-Panzer Abteilung 2 in the élite Das Reich Division. On 1 September 1944, Herzig was promoted to SS-Sturmbannführer. In December of the same year, Herzig joined SS-Panzer Brigade *Gross* (which was commanded by Knight's Cross winner Martin Gross of the élite Leibstandarte). He was one of the many personnel from Panzer Brigade Gross to be taken into the newly formed 26 SS-Panzer Abteilung when the 26th SS-Panzer Grenadier Division was working-up.

On 6 January 1945, SS-Sturmbannführer Herzig was decorated with the German Cross in Gold and on the 17th was transferred to schwere SS-Panzer Abteilung 503 as its commander. His departure from 26 SS-Panzer Abteilung was timely because it and its parent division were annihilated during the fall of Hungary in early 1945. 503 was the heavy tank battalion of III (Germanisches) SS-Panzer Korps and in January 1945, was equipped with the formidable King Tiger tanks, the most powerful and deadly tank in existence at that stage. In early February Herzig and this Abteilung arrived in Pomerania to shield the evacuation of wounded troops and civilian refugees through Arnswalde. Mid-February found Herzig in action around Danzig which was under great pressure from the inexorable Soviet advance. Split into small groups, part of the Abteilung were attached to support individual infantry units, giving sterling service and fighting to the last round or until all were destroyed.

The remainder of Herzig's Abteilung was removed from battle to be amalgamated with SS-Panzer Abteilung 11 Hermann von Salza, to form SS-Panzer Regiment 11. As the war entered its final stages this powerful force worked near miracles against Soviet attacks with massive superiority in numbers. More than 400 Soviet tanks were knocked out in the last furious battles. SS-Obersturmbannführer Paul-Albert Kausch, the Commander of the Regiment, recommended Herzig for the Knight's Cross in recognition of the heroic efforts of his Tigers, and the award was presented by SS-Brigadeführer Mohnke on 29 April 1945. Herzig survived the war but was killed in a car accident in January 1954.

MAJOR WILLY JÄHDE

Born in Helmsdorf on 18 January 1908, Willy Jähde began his military career in 1927 as a 19-year-old volunteer in the *Reichswehr*. He joined 2.Kompanie 6(Prussian) Kraftfahr Abteilung in Hanover. In 1934 he was commissioned as a Leutnant. On the outbreak of war Jähde served with Panzer Abteilung 66, part of 2nd Leichte Division as an Oberleutnant and Kompaniechef. During late 1940 this division was reformed as 7th Panzer Division and Panzer Abteilung 66 became Panzer Regiment 25. Jähde was promoted to Hauptmann at about the same time.

He served in both the Polish and western campaigns with Panzer Regiment 25. The 7th Panzer Division at this time was commanded by none other than Erwin Rommel and acquitted itself superbly in both campaigns. Jähde won both 2nd and 1st Class Iron Crosses during the Polish Campaign. Throughout 1941 and into 1942 Jähde commanded the Panzer Kompanie at the Army NCO School at Putloss. With the rank of Major, Jähde returned to combat duty with 1 Abteilung/Panzer Regiment 29 in the 12th Panzer Division on the Eastern Front in mid-1942, seeing action around Leningrad and at the battle of Kursk in July 1943.

On 28 October 1943, Willy Jähde was posted to command schwere Panzer Abteilung 502, a Tiger tank unit. From the beginning of November until mid-December the Abteilung was involved in defensive actions around Newel where, in furious combat, it had to break out of a Soviet encirclement. For the first time the Tigers were to meet the formidable Soviet SU152 assault guns. Early in 1944 502 was involved in further desperate defensive actions around Woronowo. On many occasions the appearance of the deadly Tiger tanks on the battlefield saved the day for the battered German formations. On 16 March 1944 Jähde was decorated with the Knight's Cross of the Iron Cross for his skilful command of schwere Panzer Abteilung 502. On 23 February 1944, Major Jähde was able to issue the following Order of the Day.

> The 500th Russian Tank has fallen! Oberfeldwebel Zwetti was the lucky commander . . . The Abteilung has been praised on a Radio broadcast by the Commander-in-Chief of Heeresgruppe Nord, acknowledging the 500th enemy

tank destroyed and expressing his good wishes. Through hard work and
constant readiness for action, through fortitude and bravery, all Abteilung
members have made this possible. Several of our bravest, who have fought
hard for the honour and success of the Abteilung, are no longer with us. They
have made the highest sacrifice . . . It is our duty and our firm resolution to
fight until the end in memory of our fallen comrades. The next number for
us is 1000!

Signed Jähde

502's success was in no small measure due to Jähde's superb leadership.

From May 1944 until the end of the war Jähde commanded the Army
NCO School for Panzer Troops in Eisenach and shortly before the surrender
commanded a Kampfgruppe in the Kassel-Harz area. Taken prisoner by
US forces, Jähde was released in mid-1945 and returned to civilian life to
work as a manager of a company in Eisenach, which was in the Soviet zone
of occupation. In 1961 he and his family escaped to the west and he now
lives in retirement in Tutzing.

CLEMENS GRAF VON KAGENECK

A Berliner born in October 1913, Graf von Kageneck began his military
career in 1934 when he joined the Army, serving with Reiter Regiment 4
at Potsdam. This was one of the first German cavalry units to convert to
tanks and in 1936 were re-equipped with the Pz Kpfw I. As part of 6 Panzer
Regiment in 3rd Panzer Division, Graf von Kageneck served during the
Polish Campaign as a Zugführer with 6 Kompanie of the Regiment. during
the campaign in the west he served as unit Signals Officer.

In March 1942, von Kageneck was given command of 4 Kompanie of the
Panzer Regiment which he led on the Eastern Front in the drive through the
Caucasus and the retreat on the southern sector of the front after the defeat
at Stalingrad. In June 1943 this experienced and highly regarded Panzer
officer was given command of schwere Panzer Abteilung 503 which, with
the rank of Hauptmann, he commanded during the Battle of Kursk. During
this furious tank conflict 503 was equipped with a full complement of 45 of
the dreaded Tiger tanks. Although the offensive failed, 503 acquitted itself
well and in recognition of his successful command of the Abteilung he was
decorated with the Knight's Cross of the Iron Cross in 1943. During the
fighting Graf von Kageneck was seriously wounded and was evacuated to
Germany where he spent several months in hospital before returning to the
Abteilung in the autumn of 1943. As part of Heeres Gruppe Sud, 503 was
slowly forced westwards in defensive actions culminating in the withdrawal
over the Dnieper at the end of the year.

In early 1944, 503 became, on the orders of General Hube, the major
component of a new super heavy independent Panzer Regiment. Strengthened by a 46-strong Abteilung of Panther tanks it became Panzer

Regiment Bäke named after its commander, Oberstleutnant Dr Franz Bäke. The Tigers of 503 were utilized in many furious actions often being used to break through to an encircled German force, or to lead a breakout from encirclement. In one action near Balabanowka on 26 January 1944 the Regiment spent five continuous days and nights of combat against overwhelming Soviet armoured forces. A total of 267 enemy tanks were destroyed. German losses amounted to just one Tiger and four Panthers, and at the end of the action two Soviet Armies had been encircled. For his command of 503 during this action von Kageneck was awarded the Oakleaves to the Knight's Cross on 26 June 1944.

At the end of January 1944 Graf von Kageneck was once again seriously wounded and evacuated for hospital treatment. On his recovery he was posted to command the Tiger instructional unit at the Panzertruppenschule at Bergen near Munsterlager. Here his considerable experience was to be invaluable in the training of future tank crews. Clemens Graf von Kageneck survived the war and now lives in retirement in Bad Homburg.

SS-OBERSTURMBANNFÜHRER PAUL-ALBERT KAUSCH

Paul-Albert Kausch was born on 3 March 1911 to a land-owning farmer, Dietrich Kausch, in Jädersdorf, Pomerania. He attended the State School in Potsdam and on completion of his studies attended the Gymnastics School in Berlin-Spandau. In 1933 at the age of 22 he enlisted into the Leibstandarte SS Adolf Hitler in Berlin. In April 1935, Kausch was sent to the SS-Junkerschule Braunschweig for a commissioning course, and was thereafter promoted to SS-Untersturmführer. Kausch then spent some time in attachments to various Army and SS units, and on the outbreak of war was serving with the SS Totenkopf Division.

During the western campaign, Kausch, by now an SS-Hauptsturmführer, was in command of 5 Batterie, SS-Artillerie Regiment 3, in the Totenkopf Division and won both the Iron Cross Second and First Classes for his successful command of the Batterie. After the successful conclusion of the campaign, Kausch became Divisional Adjutant of the élite Wiking Division, serving with the Divisional Staff on the southern sector of the Eastern Front, after the German invasion of the Soviet Union in 1941. Shortly thereafter, he returned to the Artillery and commanded 1 Abteilung, SS-Artillerie Regiment 5 in the Wiking Division in the battles around the Terek.

Towards the end of 1942, Kausch retrained for service in the Panzer-truppe and then attended a Battalion Commanders' course with the Army in Paris. In March 1943 he took command of the Panzer Abteilung of 11th SS-Freiwilligen Panzer Grenadier Division Nordland. With this Panzer Abteilung, named Hermann von Salza, Kausch saw action on the northern sector of the Eastern Front. For his successful command of his sector, and his personal gallantry during the battles on the Narwa, SS-Obersturmbannführer Kausch was awarded the Knight's Cross of the Iron Cross on 23 August 1944. Kausch had been seriously wounded in this battle and had to be evacuated to Estonia for hospital treatment.

Towards the end of the war, Panzer Abteilung 11 was combined with schwere Panzer Abteilung 503 to form SS-Panzer Regiment 11, with Kausch in command. It took part in the battles in defence of Berlin as the might of the Red Army fell upon the beleaguered city. Kausch and his regiment put up a ferocious defence in and around the east of Berlin, destroying nearly 500 enemey tanks. On behalf of Hitler, SS-Brigadeführer Joachim Ziegler presented Kausch with the Oakleaves to his Knight's Cross on 23 April 1945. He was the 846th recipient of this coveted award. Two days later, during a breakout attempt, he was seriously wounded. Unable now to escape he was taken prisoner by the Russians on 2 May 1945. Kausch was held in various prison camps, including Minsk and Stalingrad, for more than ten years, being released in January 1956. He is still alive.

OBERFELDWEBEL ALBERT KERSCHER

Albert Kerscher was born on 29 March 1916 in Woppmannsdorf. He was to become one of Germany's top Tiger tank aces and one of less than thirty Army NCOs to win the coveted Oakleaves to the Knight's Cross.

Kerscher's early war career was spent in service with 2nd and 13th Panzer Divisions with which he saw action in the Polish Campaign, the fall of France and the early part of Operation 'Barbarossa'. At this point Kerscher was serving with the divisional supply services. In 1942 he became a Panzer crewman and served as a tank commander in Panzer Regiment 4 of the 13th Panzer Division, on the southern sector of the Eastern Front. At the end of 1943 however, Kerscher joined the unit in which he became one of Germany's top tank aces, schwere Panzer Abteilung 502. As a tank commander with 502, Kerscher quickly became an accomplished ace. On 23 October 1944 after just one year's service with Tigers, Feldwebel Kerscher was decorated with the Knight's Cross of the Iron Cross in recognition of his sixtieth enemy tank destroyed. At this time 502 fought with great distinction during the defensive battles against the great Red Army counter-offensives. It was to be during the closing months of the war on the northern sector of the front, however, that Kerscher was to achieve real glory.

On the morning of 13 April 1945, Kerscher was located in a defensive position near Norgau. An enemy offensive was expected and Kerscher with his own, and one other Tiger, commanded by his comrade Unteroffizier Baresch, was to attempt to halt the enemy advance in his section. After a barrage of horrendous intensity, heavy tanks approached. Kerscher ordered his gunner to open fire, and soon more than twenty Russian tanks were ablaze. Once the element of surprise was lost, however, the enemy soon located the positions of the Tigers and supporting heavy assault guns were soon manoeuvring to engage the Tigers. Kerscher's gunner blasted at the assault guns with his mighty 8.8cm cannon, but the massive frontal armour of the vehicles survived the blow. Unnerved by the accuracy of the German fire, however, the Russians withdrew; their first attempt to break through had been stopped by just two Tigers.

As Kerscher moved off towards Norgau he encountered a further Soviet armoured column only a short distance away. After a short engagement in which several tanks fell victim to Kerscher's Tiger, he broke off the engagement to resupply with ammunition. In action again towards evening Kerscher, in conjunction with another Tiger, came up against a column of twelve heavy assault guns and destroyed all of them. On that day fifty tanks and assault guns had been destroyed.

A few days later, in defensive positions near Pillau covering the evacuation of thousands of wounded German soldiers, Kerscher was supported by a King Tiger from schwere Panzer Abteilung 505, a Panzer Mk IV and two Hetzer tank destroyers. After heavy artillery and aerial bombardment a massive Soviet armoured attack began. The defenders took a heavy toll, but soon the Mk IV was knocked out and the King Tiger had to withdraw, its ammunition expended. The two Hetzers were hit shortly afterwards and only Kerscher was left to hold back the Soviet attack. For his heroic efforts in defending the evacuation of Pillau during which he scored his own personal 100th victory, Albert Kerscher was decorated with the Oakleaves to his Knight's Cross on 21 April 1945 and was shortly thereafter promoted to Oberfeldwebel.

In an Order of the Day, Generalleutnant Lorenz of the élite Grossdeutschland Panzergrenadier Division stated:

> Schwere Panzer Abteilung 511 commanded by Hauptmann von Foerster, which has been fighting as part of our Division, has destroyed 102 Russian tanks between 13 and 20 April 1945.
>
> In the ranks of this Abteilung Feldwebel Kerscher ·has been especially distinguished through his exemplary bravery. On 21 April 1945 he destroyed his 100th enemy tank. My thanks and appreciation go to him also. The Division is proud to have fought alongside schwere Panzer Abteilung 511.
>
> signed Lorenz

Note. 502 and 511 Abteilungen were merged in the closing stages of the war.

The following day, Kerscher's Tiger was still in position. Leaking fuel tanks had flooded the Tiger with petrol and dangerous fumes. All hatches had to be left open to ventilate the tank. The Soviets attacked again and Kerscher and his crew were forced to go into action in a tank which was lierally a time bomb. Even a near miss could cause an explosion. Luck was with him, however, and the last of the attackers was destroyed. Kerscher's crew could at last breath a sigh of relief. The remaining days of the war were a constant struggle for the Abteilung mechanics to keep the few remaining Tigers in action. Kerscher was fortunate in that a wound received in the last days of the war required his evacuation and he thus escaped capture by the Russians when the war ended.

Taken into British captivity in Schleswig-Holstein in May 1945, Kerscher was treated with the respect that such a highly decorated front-line soldier deserved. His captors even went so far as to allocate him a room of his own in POW quarters as a mark of respect and he was released only two months later. It was fitting that one of Germany's greatest tank heroes, whose exploits not only destroyed so many of his enemies but were crucial to the survival of so many of his wounded comrades, was treated so well. Albert Kerscher also served in the Armed Forces of the West German Federal Republic where he rose to the rank of Oberstabsfeldwebel in the Bundesheer. This modest soldier is still alive and now lives in retirement in Ingolstadt.

LEUTNANT HEINRICH KÖHLER

Heinrich Köhler was born on 3 July 1922 in Hemeln. His military career began on 3 October 1941 when he joined 1 Batterie, schwere Artillerie Abteilung 49 in Dessau. After attending an officer candidates' course in Magdeburg he joined Panzer Artillerie Regiment 19, an element of 19th Panzer Division, on the Eastern Front. Köhler saw extensive combat action around Taropez-Bieloy and Smolensk during the winter of 1942.

On 1 April 1943, Köhler was promoted to Fahnenjünker and attended an officers' commissioning course at the Artillerieschule in Marmelon near Reims in France. In August of the same year he attended yet another course at the Sturmgeschützschule in Burg. In October 1943 he was commissioned Leutnant before joining Sturmgeschütz Abteilung 322 at Azay-le-Rideau near Tours. Köhler remained with this Abteilung during its working-up period and was then transferred to the Eastern Front in March 1944. On 25 March 1944 Köhler received the Iron Cross Second Class and on 1 August the First Class. He saw action around Zloczow-Brody and Kowel in eastern Poland and here claimed his first enemy tank destroyed.

January 1945 found Köhler and his Abteilung with Panzer Korps Nehring cut off by the Red Army at Kielce. As German losses mounted the remaining elements of Sturmgeschütz Abteilung 322 were merged with the remnants of Sturmgeschütz Abteilung 201 to form a new unit, Sturmgeschutz Brigade 210. With this brigade Köhler saw action in the bridgeheads at Schwedt, Küstrin and Stettin, covering the retreat from East Prussia. Köhler was in command of 1 Zug/3 Batterie of the brigade when it was in action around the bridgehead Altdamm-Stettin. Elements of the brigade were located at Willstock, Klebow and around Wintersfelde, Ferdnandstein and Untermühle on 16/17 March 1945. Köhler and his 1 Zug were responsible for beating back three separate Soviet armoured attacks. The Russians used M4 Sherman tanks supplied by the USA. Köhler's Zug destroyed fifteen of the attackers and his crew personally scored six destroyed. This brought Köhler's score to 21 and on 20 April 1945 his achievements brought him the award of the Knight's Cross of the Iron Cross. From Stettin

Köhler's brigade retreated through Mecklenburg, Schwerin and into Schleswig-Holstein where it was captured by British troops on 8 May 1945. Köhler remained in captivity until 22 June 1945 when he was released. Heinrich Köhler lives today in retirement in Emmerthal.

MAJOR NORBERT KUJACINSKI

Born in Berlin on 11 July 1920, Norbert Kujacinski was the son of a coppersmith. On completing his schooling in April 1938, he entered his local government finance department as a tax inspector, until his military career began in August 1939 when he was called up into the Army.

After service in the French campaign Kujacinski was posted to the army weapons school near Jüterbog and after completing a training course for armoured warfare was promoted and commissioned as a leutnant. Kujacinski served with 1/Panzer Regiment 23, part of 23rd Panzer Division on the Eastern Front. The division fought at Kharkov and the Terek during the spring of 1942. Fighting on the southern sector of the front at the end of that year it narrowly escaped being caught up in the débâcle at Stalingrad. It subsequently became part of the force used by 4th Armee in an attempt to relieve the beleaguered Stalingrad forces. By January 1943 the division had been virtually decimated, having only twenty tanks left. During this difficult period, Kujacinski had been awarded both the Second Class and First Class Iron Cross.

After refitting the division took part in the summer defensive battles and was heavily involved in the fighting around the Dnieper at the end of the year. Kujacinski was decorated with the German Cross in Gold in November 1943. In early 1944 the division broke out from an encirclement near the Dnieper though by this time it had been reduced by losses to Kampfgruppe size. This Kampfgruppe fought in Poland and in Hungary in late 1944 where the Germans inflicted a serious defeat on the Russians during the attack on Nyiregyhaza from 23 to 29 October, more than 600 armoured vehicles being destroyed or captured. For his part in this success Norbert Kujacinski was awarded the Knight's Cross of the Iron Cross on 18 November 1944.

The Kampfgruppe acquitted itself well during the remainder of the battle for Hungary. As the Red Army continued its inexorable advance, 23 Panzer Regiment withdrew into Austria where it was still fighting when the war ended. Kujacinski and his men were taken into US captivity. Ending the war as a major in command of 4 Kompanie Panzer Regiment 23, Kujacinski's decorations include the wound badge in Gold and the Panzer Assault Badge for 75 engagements with the enemy. Released from captivity in July 1945, Kujacinski returned to civilian life, but rejoined the military and served with the Bundeswehr where he reached the rank of Oberstleutnant der Reserve before his retirement.

OBERLEUTNANT WOLFGANG KOLTERMANN

Wolfgang Koltermann began his career as a Tiger tank commander in September 1943 on the formation of Heeres schwere Panzer Abteilung 507 in Vienna. This new heavy tank unit was formed from a cadre of experienced soldiers from 13th Panzer Division. Koltermann was to become the Adjutant of the new Panzer Abteilung which saw its first major action around Tarnopol and Brody in the spring of 1944 where its powerful Tigers were to prove their worth time and time again. By late autumn Koltermann had become commander of 3 Kompanie of the Abteilung.

From November 1944 until mid-January 1945, 507 lay in reserve at the Narew bridgehead. On 14 January, the Red Army launched a massive offensive on the Narew. Marshal Rokossowski's 2nd White Russian Front was hurled against the sector in which 507 was located. 507's massive Tigers, with infantry support from 7 Infanterie Division were able, after two days of the most vicious combat, to blunt the Russian advance and regain their original positions, having destroyed more than sixty tanks without loss. Soviet strength was so massive, however, that the losses they had suffered were soon made good.

On the following day, Koltermann's positions were the subject of a major artillery and air bombardment, but once again the Tigers were lucky and not one was lost. The positions on 507's flanks were penetrated and the Abteilung had to pull back. In the battle which ensued, the Tigers were able to increase their score to 136 tanks, still incredibly, without loss. Such achievements were rare at this stage of the war when Germany's fortunes were at a very low ebb. In recognition of this, the Abteilung was praised in a special Wehrmachts Bericht, and Oberleutnant Koltermann was decorated with the Knight's Cross of the Iron Cross on 11 March 1945 for his part in the action (as were Oberleutnant Wirsching and Oberfeldwebel Ratajczak).

The Abteilung's successes continued until the unit was evacuated from the Eastern Front when many of its Tigers were destroyed so as to avoid their capture by the Russians. 507 was at Paderborn training grounds being re-equipped with King Tigers when, in March 1945, Allied forces closed in. Koltermann, still in command of 3 Kompanie, took all the King Tigers he could assemble and in conjunction with elements of schwere SS-Panzer Abteilung 501, prepared to meet the enemy.

Koltermann's King Tigers engaged the attacking US Sherman tanks at a range of some 850–900 yards and within minutes the deadly fire of their 88mm guns had completely destroyed the two leading platoons of the enemy force, and the advance had halted. The Tigers of 2 Kompanie now joined battle, cutting off and destroying a further US task force. Well over twenty US tanks and numerous armoured vehicles had been destroyed and once again Koltermann's 3 Kompanie had played a leading role in a major action without a single loss. Ironically, Koltermann was nearly killed when, on returning to his own lines in a captured American Jeep, he was accidentally fired on by his own side. Koltermann had once more brought his men back safe and sound. They were very lucky; some 100 Waffen-SS Grenadiers who surrendered to the Americans were slaughtered out of hand. Wolfgang Koltermann is still alive.

SS-HAUPTSTURMFÜHRER JAKOB LOBMEYER

Born in Lachen on 12 October 1918, Jakob Lobmeyer joined the SS-VT in 1936 and completed his basic military training with 2 Kompanie SS-Standarte Deutschland. He attended the SS-Junkerschule at Bad Tölz in Bavaria, and was commissioned SS-Untersturmführer in June 1939. Lobmeyer served with the Standarte Deutschland during the Polish Campaign, and with the SS-Artillerie Regiment during the campaign in the west, where he was decorated with the Iron Cross Second Class. Both regiments were part of the SS-Verfügungsdivision.

Subsequently, Lobmeyer transferred from the Artillerie to the Sturmgeschützen and served in the Sturmgeschütz Batterie Das Reich, seeing combat in the Balkan Campaign and in the early part of Operation 'Barbarossa', winning the Iron Cross First Class in July 1941. Wounded at Jelna, he was evacuated to hospital and on recovery from his wounds was transferred to the Sturmgeschütz Batterie of 5 SS-Panzer Division Wiking with which he saw almost a full year of combat on the southern sector of the Eastern Front. Wounded again in April 1942, he was once more evacuated for hospital treatment. On recovery he was posted to the élite Leibstandarte where he served with the Sturmgeschütz Batterie during the battle for Taganrog and the capture and subsequent re-capture of Kharkov. During the winter of 1942–43 he was again wounded in action on two occasions.

On recovery Lobmeyer was yet again posted to a new unit, this time SS-Sturmgeschütz Batterie 505. A few months later he became adjutant of SS-Aufkläungsabteilung 505 with the rank of SS-Obersturmführer, and two months after this, in July 1944, came a short period as Orderly Officer on the Staff of V SS-Gebirgs Korps before being posted as an instructor to the Sturmgeschütz School at Burg. In September 1944 Lobmeyer moved to the SS-Junkerschule in Prague as a tactics instructor. On Christmas Day of 1944, SS-Obersturmführer Lobmeyer was given command of the Sturmgeschütz Batterie of the 15th Waffen Grenadier Division der SS (lettisches Nr. 1), and went into action around the Danzig area. Lobmeyer's first action was an attempt to halt a Soviet armoured thrust towards Frankfurt-on-Oder. Equipped with the small but deadly Jagdpanzer 38(t) Hetzer tank destroyer, Lobmeyer succeeded in his task. On 15 February, Lobmeyer's Batterie was merged with SS Jagdpanzer Abteilung z.b.v. 562 and he was promoted to SS-Hauptsturmführer. This new fast reaction force came under the direct command of Heeresgruppe Weichsel.

Following a Soviet breakthrough on 18 February, Lobmeyer's Hetzers were tasked with the protection of the Army Group's right flank. In the wooded area east of Güben, his tank killers stalked and destroyed more than thirty T-34s. Accompanying assault troops destroyed eight more tanks with magnetic mines. The total tally for the day came to about 50 tanks and more than 100 guns destroyed. Lobmeyer was decorated with the German Cross in Gold on 15 March and the Close Combat Clasp in Bronze on 16 March. Shortly afterwards the Abteilung was pulled back and held in reserve for the awaited enemy push on Berlin. On 16 April the Soviet attack began, and broke through the German lines south of Frankfurt. The Abteilung was thrown into action again in a desperate attempt to hold back the overwhelming Soviet onslaught. On 16 April, Lobmeyer was appointed commander of Kampfgruppe Lobmeyer, under command of V SS-Gebirgs Korps. With a total strength of about 2,000 men, the Kampfgruppe went into action to the south of the Frankfurt–Berlin highway, effecting a link-up between V SS-Gebirgs Korps and XI SS-Panzer Korps operating to their north. On 30 April 1945 SS-Hauptsturmführer Lobmeyer was decorated with the Knight's Cross of the Iron Cross.

As the Abteilung withdrew westwards it inflicted heavy losses on the pursuing Russians. The unit then met up with the remnant of schwere SS Panzer Abteilung 502 near Halbe. Even the presence of 502's mighty Tiger Tanks, however, could make little difference at this late stage of the war. The total breakdown of the supply system meant that whenever an otherwise serviceable vehicle ran out of fuel or ammunition it had to be destroyed to avoid capture. Such vehicles were irreplaceable at this point. On 28 April 1945, the award of the Oakleaves to Lobmeyer was approved, but the chaotic military situation meant that the award was never actually presented.

On 1 May, the Abteilung destroyed the last of its vehicles and withdrew on foot, its survivors reaching the Elbe on 9 May. Here they were captured by Russian troops but escaped by swimming the Elbe. On reaching the west bank the group split up, each making for his own home. Lobmeyer's decorations included the Silver Close Combat Clasp, the Badge for single-handed destruction of an enemy tank, and the Army Honour Roll Clasp; he is one of the few – possibly the only known – recipients of the exceptionally rare Panzer Assault Badge in Gold for 200 engagements, a badge the very existence of which has often been doubted.

SS-STURMBANNFÜHRER ERWIN MEIERDRESS

Erwin Meierdress was born on 11 December 1916 in Wesel, the son of a customs official. He joined the SS in 1934 as a volunteer in the Leibstandarte SS Adolf Hitler. After attending Junkerschule Braunschweig he was commissioned as an SS-Untersturmführer. By September 1939 Meierdress was serving as the Adjutant to 1 Abteilung, SS-Totenkopf Artillerie Regiment. He won the Iron Cross Second Class in November 1939 during the Polish Campaign, and remained with the Abteilung until the early part of 1941, when he was posted to the newly formed Sturmgeschütz Batterie within the Division.

When Totenkopf was upgraded to the status of a Panzer Division, Meierdress was given command of 1 Abteilung, SS-Panzer Regiment 3. During the period February 1941 to April 1942, the Totenkopf Division, as part of II Armee Korps was encircled in the Demjansk pocket. The combined efforts of three Soviet armies could not defeat the stout defence offered by the encircled Germans. The Soviets had eighteen divisions tied down in the attempt to crush the German defenders. Many heroic acts of valour by German soldiers were rewarded by the Knight's Cross of the Iron Cross. Meierdress was one of those so honoured.

At the time SS-Obersturmführer Meierdress was in command of a small battle group of just 120 men. For several days, enemy units had been attacking around Bjakowo. The desperate defenders, incurring surprisingly few fatalities, put up a ferocious fight which cost the attackers dear. At one point, however, Meierdress had only thirty unwounded men. Cut off from the other encircled German units in the Demjansk cauldron, Meierdress continued his stout defence against overwhelming odds until he himself was severely wounded and had to be evacuated by air. On 13 March 1942 SS-Obersturmführer Meierdress was decorated with the Knight's Cross of the Iron Cross in recognition of the heroic defence of Bjakowo by him and his men. He had already received the Iron Cross First Class in January of the same year. When the Bjakowo battle group finally broke out, only 85 men had survived of whom 55 had been wounded to some degree.

While recovering from his wounds, Meierdress was promoted to SS-Hauptsturmführer and on his return to duty in the autumn of 1942, was given command of the newly formed SS-Panzer Regiment 3 Totenkopf. Meierdress commanded the Abteilung throughout the winter of 1942–43 and was involved in the fierce fighting around Kharkov. From spring to September 1943 Meierdress was in constant action. At Bjelgorod, Kursk, at the Oka, the Mius and the Heights of Augustowo his men acquitted themselves with distinction, destroying great numbers of Soviet tanks and guns in the process. Meierdress was again wounded, for the fifth time, in September 1943 and was evacuated from the front.

For his command of the Abteilung SS-Hauptsturmführer Meierdress was decorated with the Oakleaves on 12 October 1943. He was the 301st recipient of this award. On returning to duty, he saw action in the battle for Kielce during the Soviet summer offensive, as the German armies retreated through Poland. While serving with the Abteilung in Hungary in January 1945, Meierdress was leading five of his Panthers in an attack on a Soviet-held position, when he was surprised by a force of T-34s which opened fire at almost point-blank range. His tank received a direct hit in the turret from the T-34's 85mm gun and he was killed outright.

Erwin Meierdress is a prime example of the gallantry shown by many Panzer officers. In this terrible and deadly form of warfare, he showed constant courage and fortitude over a sustained period rather than having scored a high tally of tanks destroyed, like Michael Wittmann, but he was an ace nevertheless and a deserving winner of some of his country's highest awards.

SS-OBERFÜHRER KURT MEYER

One of the most famous of all of the Panzer commanders of the Waffen-SS, Kurt Meyer was born on 23 December 1910 in Jerxheim, the son of a factory worker. His career began in 1929 when he became a police officer in Mecklenburg. In 1934 he became a Zugführer in the Leibstandarte Adolf Hitler, and like so many Waffen-SS officers, spent a period of attachment to the Army to gain first-hand military experience. In Meyer's case he was attached to the Panzertruppe.

In October 1936 he was given the task of forming an anti-tank or Panzerjäger company for the Leibstandarte, with the rank of SS-Obersturmführer. Meyer commanded the Panzerjäger unit of the Leibstandarte during the Polish Campaign but on its conclusion was transferred to the Kradschutzenkompanie with the rank of SS-Hauptsturmführer. These motor-cycle recce troops were the spearhead of the division and in command of this unit Meyer was in his element. He led them with great *élan* during the campaign on the Western Front, winning both Second and First Class Iron Crosses. He was rewarded with the command of the Aufklärungs-abteilung when the Leibstandarte was enlarged in 1940.

During the Balkan Campaign, Meyer was to enhance his daredevil reputation even further during the assault on the Klissura Pass. Meyer, then an SS-Sturmbannführer, was in command of the Aufklärungsabteilung when the attack was bogged down. With machine-pistol in hand, Meyer rallied his men and led them forward to capture the enemy positions. On 18 May 1941, Meyer was awarded the Knight's Cross of the Iron Cross for his actions in the Greek Campaign. He was the ideal character to lead the Aufklärungsabteilung, which was always the first into action. Always in the thick of it, Meyer set an example of fearless courage to his men, never asking them to take risks he would not take himself.

Meyer and his Abteilung continued to excel in the Eastern Campaign; at Shitomir, Kriwoj Rog, Mariupol, Taganrog, Rostov and all along the Leibstandarte's route of march, the Recce troops were in the forefront of the action.

In the first quarter of 1943, when the Leibstandarte was heavily involved in the battle for Kharkov, Meyer again proved his worth. His Panzer Aufklärungsabteilung along with the Panzer Abteilung commanded by Max Wünsche, spearheaded the successful attack and threw back the VI Soviet Guards Cavalry Corps. For this achievement Meyer was decorated with the Oakleaves on 23 May 1943. The award was made personally by Hitler at a ceremony at the Führerhauptquartier. He was the 195th recipient of this award.

The year 1943 also saw the formation of a new division of the Waffen-SS. A Panzer division was to be raised from members of the Hitler Youth organization. For the training of these politically indoctrinated young fanatics it was decided that only soldiers of the highest calibre should be used as cadre personnel and where better to look for such soldiers than the finest unit of the Waffen-SS, the Leibstandarte Adolf Hitler. Many well-known Leibstandarte veterans such as Fritz Witt, Max Wünsche, Gerd Bremer, Hein Springer and of course Kurt Meyer were to find their places in this new division. Meyer was sent on a Regimental Commanders' course at the Army Panzertruppenschule at Wunsdorf and was then appointed SS-Standartenführer and Commander of SS-Panzer Grenadier Regiment 25, in the 12th SS-Panzer Division Hitlerjugend.

Meyer was an extremely tough, hard-bitten officer, but was renowned for being fair. His men revered him, as despite his harsh exterior he had a soft spot for his Grenadiers. On one occasion when a homesick young lad went absent without leave, Meyer, after giving him a severe dressing down, let the fortunate lad off with no more than a box on the ears; many officers would have had the boy shot for desertion. His men obeyed his orders without question and with reckless disregard for their own safety. Despite their inexperience, the Hitlerjugend Grenadiers fought ferociously and within a few short months of its formation, the division had become one of the élite units in the German Armed Forces.

The tendency of many senior Waffen-SS commanders to wish to remain always at the front with their men often cost them lives. Such was the case for the Hitlerjugend Commander, Fritz Witt. An Allied barrage landed on the Division's Forward Headquarters and he was killed outright on 14 June 1944. The Waffen-SS had lost one of its best commanders.

Kurt Meyer was promoted to SS-Oberführer and appointed Divisional Commander. On 27 August 1944 he became the 91st recipient of the Swords. The award never reached him because he was captured by Belgian partisans on 6 September. Handed over to the Allies, he was charged with war crimes in that personnel under his command were said to have executed Canadian prisoners. Indeed it is now known that such excesses were committed – but by both sides. He was found guilty and sentenced to death though this was commuted to life imprisonment. Meyer was visited in prison by Chancellor Konrad Adenauer who shook his hand and wished him well. Released in late 1954, Meyer wrote his biography Grenadiere, and devoted his time to fighting for civil rights for former Waffen-SS men, branded as criminals and treated as social pariahs. Meyer's health deteriorated and in December 1960 while celebrating his 50th Birthday he suffered a fatal heart attack. Large numbers of his former Grenadiers and brother officers attended his funeral.

SS-STANDARTENFÜHRER JOHANNES RUDOLF MÜHLENKAMP

Top Waffen-SS Panzer Commander Johannes Mühlenkamp was born on 9 October 1910 in Metz, the son of a local government official. A soldier's soldier, his military career began in September 1934 when he volunteered for service and was accepted into SS-Standarte Germania. After a year's military experience in the ranks, he attended SS-Junkerschule Braunschweig and was commissioned as an SS-Untersturmführer. During 1936, Mühlenkamp spent time on attachment to the Army's 2nd Panzer Division. The experience gained during this formative period in his career was to be invaluable in later years. Mühlenkamp returned to his unit to command the Kradschützen Kompanie and with this element of the regiment he took part in the Polish Campaign in 1939, winning the Iron Cross Second and First Classes.

Subsequently, as the Germania, Deutschland and Der Führer Regiments were formed into the SS-Verfügungsdivision, under SS-Gruppenführer Paul Hausser, he became the Divisional Adjutant. Service in the western campaign and in the Balkans followed, with Mühlenkamp commanding the division's Aufklärungs Abteilung. In combat near Jelnja he received a severe head wound and while recovering was decorated, on 2 January 1942, with the German Cross in Gold for his leadership of the Abteilung and his own personal gallantry.

A further honour awaited Mühlenkamp, however, as he was chosen to command the first Panzer Abteilung of the Waffen-SS. Originally intended for the Das Reich Division, the Abteilung ultimately joined the élite 5th SS-Panzer Grenadier Division Wiking. In July 1942 Mühlenkamp took his Abteilung through its baptism of fire during the attack on Rostov. Together with its Army neighbours 13th and 22nd Panzer Divisions, Wiking acquitted itself well. Mühlenkamp was always to be found with his men in the thick of the fighting. Many photographs of that period show him, dirty, unshaven, smeared with oil, but smiling, happy to be with his lads. Not for him the soft life of one who leads from the rear. An unbreakable bond of admiration and respect was formed between Mühlenkamp and his Panzertruppen which lasted until the day he died! Mühlenkamp's Panzers forged southwards and to the east, through Bataik and Kagalnizkaja. On 3 September 1942 Mühlenkamp was decorated with the Knight's Cross of the Iron Cross in recognition of his command of the Panzer Regiment during this successful period in its history.

The reputation of the Wiking Division grew steadily thanks in no small measure to Mühlenkamp's inspired leadership of his beloved Panzers. In 1943 the Abteilung was enlarged to Regimental strength, and by 1944 Mühlenkamp had reached the rank of SS-Standartenführer. When Wiking's successful commander, SS-Gruppenführer Herbert Otto Gille, a commander of the highest standard, was promoted to take command of IV SS-Panzer Korps, Mühlenkamp was the logical successor, and he became Divisional Commander in July 1944.

On 8 July, the Soviets launched a massive offensive against the Kowel area. A total of ten infantry divisions and three armoured brigades were thrown against the front held by 26th and 342nd Infanterie Divisions. Into this inferno Mühlenkamp threw his Wiking Division. The lead Soviet elements had already began to roll back the German front when the Panthers of SS-Panzer Regiment 5 arrived and in the ferocious battles which ensued more than 100 tanks were destroyed, bringing the enemy advance to a halt.

By August, Soviet forces were closing in on Warsaw, and once again Wiking was there to meet them. During the period from 4 August to 3 September, Wiking destroyed 151 enemy tanks, 19 assault guns, 13 armoured personnel carriers, 176 guns, 94 machine-guns and shot down five enemy aircraft. The Russians received such a bloody nose that the advance had to be halted. In recognition of his, and his division's gallantry and success during this period, Mühlenkamp became the 596th recipient of the Oakleaves on 21 September 1944. Even an officer of such high rank as he, was still to be found in the turret of his tank, at the front, with his men.

During the first few weeks of 1945, Mühlenkamp was tasked with the formation of a new division, 32nd SS-Panzer Grenadier Division 30 January, named after the date on which the Nazi Party came to power. Mühlenkamp subsequently found his superb tactical knowledge and leadership recognized by his appointment as Inspector General of SS Panzer Troops, a post in which he remained to the end of the war.

Mühlenkamp had served with Wiking for two and a half years and his name is forever linked with that of his élite division. He maintained close links with his men after the war, and many soldiers from the ranks of his former enemies visited him in his home in Langelsheim to pay their respects to the retired Panzer genius. A Wikinger to the end, Mühlenkamp died in retirement in September 1986. The quality of Mühlenkamp's leadership is well reflected in the fact that some fifteen of his Panzer officers went on to become Ritterkreuzträger themselves, successful pupils of a great leader.

OBERSTLEUTNANT ALFRED MÜLLER

Born in Kaltensandheim on 23 November 1915, Alfred Müller had a long career of service to his country. Joining the Army in April 1935, he finally retired from military service in April 1969, as a Brigadegeneral in the Bundeswehr.

Müller's military career began when he joined the Reichswehr's Artillerie Regiment München. Commissioned as a Leutnant on 20 April 1937, by the outbreak of war he had reached Oberleutnant and was serving as Adjutant with Artillerie Regiment 74 in Vienna. On 1 May 1940, Müller was given command of Sturmgeschütz Batterie 666 in which post he served until November 1941, when he was allocated to the Reserve of the Oberkommando des Heeres. On 7 June 1942, Müller, now a Hauptmann, was appointed Commander of 8 Batterie, Artillerie Lehr Regiment 2. In December of that year, this unit became Sturmgeschütz Lehr Batterie 901 which saw heavy fighting on the southern sector of the Eastern Front around Stalingrad with its companion unit Infanterie Lehr Regiment 901.

The summer of 1943 found Müller in command of a rearguard unit around Starobjelsk. From 20 to 23 June his men destroyed three T-34 tanks and scattered an attacking infantry force. A few days later, his small force was responsible for breaking through the Russian lines to rescue an encircled German infantry combat group. For this achievement he was decorated with the Knight's Cross of the Iron Cross on 20 February 1943.

On 28 March Müller was given command of Sturmgeschütz Brigade 191 which fought at Noworossisk and the Kuban bridgehead, destroying 95 enemy tanks. Müller's brigade covered the evacuation of the Kuban, halting the Soviet advance at Eltingen and Bulganak. Throughout the hard-pressed withdrawal Müller's brigade excelled itself and Müller himself was decorated with the Oakleaves on 15 December 1943 in recognition of this. A communiqué by Heeresgruppe Sud-Ukraine stated:

> 'Sturmgeschütze Brigade 191, in the battle in the Crimea has destroyed a total
> of 137 tanks, 48 anti-tank and anti-aircraft guns and a great number of
> weapons and vehicles, under the command of Oakleaves winner Major Müller.
> This Brigade, which has proved itself particularly proficient during the long
> battles in the Kuban bridgehead destroyed its 445th enemy tank on 12 May
> 1945, proving its outstanding bravery.'

On 1 July 1944, Major Müller was appointed Commander of the Tactical Instruction Staff at the Sturmgeschütz School in Burg, and one month later became the Commander of the school itself. On 1 April 1945, Müller was promoted to Oberstleutnant and on 10 April formed a Kampfgruppe from the Sturmgeschütz School staff and Sturmgeschütz Ersatz und Ausbildungs Abteilung 700, which went into action against the Americans around Magdeburg before being sent to the Eastern Front.

In the very last days of the war, Müller was promoted in the field to Oberst, by General Wenck and given command of an *ad hoc* division, Ferdinand von Schill. Divisional strength only on paper, it still had some bite, and Müller's Sturmgeschützen left many Russian tanks burning on the battlefield. On 7 May 1945, the remnant of the division crossed the Elbe and surrendered to American troops. Müller's decorations included both Classes of Iron Cross, the Knight's Cross, the Oakleaves, the Kubanschild, and the Roumanian Order of Michael the Brave.

On 1 February 1956 Müller rejoined the Army and served as an Oberstleutnant in the Bundeswehr. By 1961 he had been promoted to Oberst and in April 1964 he took command of Panzer Brigade 33. In October 1968 Müller was given command of the Panzer Lehr Brigade in Münster. Promotion to Brigadegeneral came in April 1969 and six months later he was given command of Kampftruppenschule II in Münster. Brigadegeneral Müller was decorated with the Bundesverdienstkreuz in February 1973. He retired in April 1975 and is still alive.

SS-HAUPTSTURMFÜHRER KARL NICOLUSSI-LECK

Karl Nicolussi-Leck was born in Pfatten, South Tirol on 14 March 1917, the son of a farmer. On completion of his schooling he attended Padua

Above: A fine portrait study of Sturmgeschütz ace, Hauptmann Friedrich Arnold, who was decorated with the Knight's Cross in November 1943 as a Zugführer in 2./Sturmgeschütz Brigade 237. Note the particularly fine wreathed cockade on the band of his peaked cap, and the hand-embroidered eagle and swastika. Basic quality caps had these insignia in metal.

Above right: SS-Obersturmführer Erwin Bachmann, Adjutant of I Abteilung, SS-Panzer Regiment 10 Frundsberg. This photograph was taken just after the award of his Knight's Cross in the Gamsheim Bridgehead in February 1945. Despite the late stage of the war Bachmann's Panzerjacke still features the silver cord collar piping. (Erwin Bachmann)

Right: A rare photograph, taken in action on the Eastern Front, showing Panzer ace Ernst Barkmann in the turret of his Panther tank. In comparison to the smart black Panzerjacke, this shows the more comfortable leather jacket often worn by tank crewmen for everyday wear. The shoulder-straps indicate the rank of SS-Scharführer. Barkmann served with 4 Kompanie, SS-Panzer Regiment 2 Das Reich. (Ernst Barkmann)

Above: Major Heinz Baurmann. As Commander of Sturmgeschütz Brigade 300(Feld), Baurmann was one of the last recipients of the Knight's Cross in the closing days of the war. The award was made on 3 May 1945 by General-Feldmarschall Schörner, Commander of Heeresgruppe Mitte. (Heinz Baurmann)

Above: Austrian Assault Gun ace Major Josef Sepp Brandner. In this portrait study he wears the field grey version of the Panzerjacke. His decorations include the Knight's Cross with Oakleaves, the Honour Roll Clasp of the Army, the Close Combat Clasp, Iron Cross 1st Class, Wound Badge and General Assault Badge. On the lower left sleeve is the rare Kurland cufftitle and just visible on the original print is the German Cross in Gold just below the breast eagle. Brandner was Commander of Sturmgeschütz Brigade 912. (Sepp Brandner)

Left: SS-Oberführer Georg Bochmann. As Commander of 18 SS-Panzer Grenadier Division Horst Wessel, Bochmann was decorated with the Swords in March 1945. Here he is seen receiving his Oakleaves from Hitler in May 1943. On his black Panzerjacke, Bochmann wears the distinctive Deathshead collar patches of the élite Totenkopf Division in which he had commanded the Panzerjäger Abteilung. (J. R. Angolia)

Above: Leutnant Georg Bose, Zugführer in Sturmgeschütz Abteilung 177. Bose was awarded the Knight's Cross in September 1944. In this photograph, recently discovered in East Germany and returned to Herr Bose, he poses in full regulation Sturmgeschütz dress. On his left breast is the Iron Cross First Class together with the Wound Badge in Black and General Assault Badge. Just visible on his right sleeve is the badge for single-handed destruction of an enemy tank. (Georg Bose)

Above right: Oberleutnant Otto Carius. Commander of 2 Kompanie, schwere Panzer Abteilung 502, Carius was decorated with the Oakleaves in July 1944. This photograph was taken while he was in hospital recovering from wounds; his own Panzer uniform was not available so the white summer uniform seen here was borrowed for the occasion. The breast eagle on the tunic is the silver wire, hand-embroidered version on black backing for Panzer officers. (Otto Carius)

Right: Hans Deutsch, seen here as a Leutnant, wearing the standard officer's field blue service dress of the Luftwaffe. Deutsch was serving with 1 / Fallschirmsturmgeschütz Brigade 12 when he won his Knight's Cross in April 1945. Normal field dress would have been the popular Fleigerbluse or a field grey or field blue version of the Panzerjacke with Luftwaffe insignia. (Josef Charita)

Left: SS-Hauptsturmführer Josef Dreike, Commander of SS-Flak-Abteilung 2 in the élite Das Reich Panzer Division. Dreike was awarded his Knight's Cross on 6 May 1945. In this photograph he is wearing standard Waffen-SS officers' field dress. Unlike his Army counterparts who wore red artillery piping to their caps, Dreike is almost certainly wearing white piping; coloured piping, though utilized, was rare in the Waffen-SS. His shoulder-straps, however, would feature red underlay between the matt silver braid and the black wool base. (Josef Charita)

Right: SS-Hauptsturmführer Karl-Heinz Gustavsson. As Commander of 3 Batterie SS-Flak-Abteilung 2, he was awarded the Knight's Cross on 3 March 1945. This interesting photograph was taken while Gustavsson was on home leave in his native Hamburg in June 1944. Taken before the award of the Knight's Cross, the photograph shows the Iron Cross First Class, as well as the Infantry Close Combat Clasp and Infantry Assault Badge, a reminder of his earlier service with SS-Totenkopf Infanterieregiment 10. The Army Stabsfeldwebel wearing the old-pattern tunic with tresse to the top rather than bottom of the collar is Gustavsson's uncle. (Karl-Heinz Gustavsson)

Left: SS-Obersturmführer Paul Egger with two of his crew members pose next to their Tiger tank. The wearing of one-piece overalls was widespread by tank crews as these were more comfortable than the black Panzerjacke. The wearing of insignia on these overalls was unofficial, but widely practised. Note the anti-magnetic Zimmeritt paste which has been applied to the Tiger. (Paul Egger)

Right: SS-Hauptsturmführer Willi Hein, Commander of 2 Kompanie, SS-Panzer Regiment 5 Wiking. This photograph was taken when he was an SS-Obersturmführer just after the award of his Knight's Cross on the Eastern Front in May 1944. Compare Hein's peaked cap, complete with its officer's chincords, with that worn by Hans Sailer. (Willi Hein)

Left: Leutnant Willi Heinrich. Serving with the Führer-Grenadier-Brigade, Heinrich nevertheless continued to wear the 'GD' monogram of the parent Grossdeutschland Panzerkorps. He wears the old pattern officer's field cap with soft leather peak and metallic thread-woven insignia. The black Panzerjacke is rarely seen buttoned up to the neck as here. (Willi Heinrich)

Below left: SS-Oberscharführer Fritz Hencke, Zugführer in 3/SS-Sturmgeschütz Abteilung 1, part of the élite Leibstandarte Adolf Hitler. Henke wears NCO tresse on the collar of his field grey Panzerjacke, a practice which was not normally permitted on either field grey or black patterns of the Panzerjacke, but this restriction was overlooked in the case of the Leibstandarte. Henke also wears the old-pattern field cap with soft peak and regulation woven insignia. (Fritz Henke)

Right: Major Willy Jähde. As Commander of schwere Panzer Abteilung 502, Jähde was one of Germany's top Tiger tank aces. Seen here on the Eastern Front, he wears a sheepskin jacket, very necessary protection during the Russian winter, over his black Panzerjacke. Jähde wears the officer's version of the black M38 Feldmutze, with silver piping to the crown and scallop. The chevron over the cockade on the front of his cap is in rose-pink Panzer Waffenfarbe. (Willy Jähde)

Right: Clemens Graf von Kaganeck. Major Kageneck was one of the most successful Tiger commanders of the German Army. This photograph was taken in late 1944 when he was Commander of schwere Panzer Abteilung 503. He wears the typical late war Panzerjacke without collar piping, and the officer pattern M38 Feldmutze (field service cap) with silver cord piping. (Graf Kageneck)

Left: SS-Sturmbannführer Fritz Herzig. As Commander of schwere SS-Panzer Abteilung 503, equipped with King Tigers, on the Eastern Front, Herzig was awarded the Knight's Cross on 27 April 1945. In this photograph he wears the officers' version of the M-43 Panzer Einheitsfeldmutze, with silver piping to the crown and silver wire woven Totenkopf to the front of the cap. The SS eagle is worn on the side.

Opposite page

Top left: SS-Obersturmbannführer Paul Albert Kausch. He was Commander of SS-Panzer Regiment 11. This photograph was taken in the winter of 1944 after the award of the Knight's Cross but before he received the Oakleaves. (Paul Albert Kausch)

Top right: Oberfeldwebel Albert Kerscher. In this photograph, taken prior to the award of his Oakleaves, he wears the typical dress of a Panzer soldier from the latter part of the war. Below his Iron Cross First Class on the left breast is the Panzer Kampfabzeichen for 50 engagements with the enemy. Kerscher was one of the most highly decorated NCOs in the Panzerwaffe. (Albert Kerscher)

Bottom left: Leutnant Heinrich Köhler, Zugführer in 3 Heeres Sturmgeschütz Brigade 210. Köhler won the Knight's Cross in April 1945. This photograph shows the standard pattern officers' M36 Field Bluse particularly clearly. Note also once again the General Assault Badge usually worn by combat-experienced assault gunners. (Heinrich Köhler)

Bottom right: Oberleutnant Wolfgang Koltermann. Commander of 3 Kompanie, schwere Panzer Abteilung 507. Koltermann won his Knight's Cross in March 1945. Small in stature, but a soldier of great courage and personal gallantry, Koltermann commanded his Tigers until the last days of the war, always willing to attack against overwhelming odds. (Wolfgang Koltermann)

Above right: Major Norbert Kujacinski. In this view Kujacinski is wearing the rarely seen open neck style jacket, his status as a Panzer officer being indicated by the rose-pink underlay to his shoulder-straps, and central stripes to his collar bars. Just visible on the pocket below the breast eagle is the tip of his German Cross in Gold. The Iron Cross First Class is on his left breast pocket. (Norbert Kujacinski)

Right: SS-Hauptsturmführer Karl Nicolussi-Leck, Commander of 8. Kompanie of SS-Panzer Regiment 5 Wiking. Seen here in front of his Panther tank, on the Eastern Front, he wears the Officer's version of the M43 Field Cap with silver piping, as well as officer's silver piping to the collar of his Panzerjacke. Of interest is the Hitler Jugend Badge of Honour with gold rim, worn next to his Iron Cross First Class. (Karl Nicolussi-Leck)

Above left: SS-Hauptsturmführer Jakob Lobmeyer, Commander of SS-Jagdpanzer Abteilung 561. Lobmeyer won both the Knight's Cross and the Oakleaves in the space of one week in April 1945. He was also one of only a tiny handful of recipients of the exceptionally rare Panzer Assault Badge for 200 engagements. In this photograph his peaked cap, though fitted with chincords, has the soft leather peak and woven insignia of the old-pattern field cap. (Jakob Lobmeyer)

Above right: SS-Sturmbannführer Erwin Meierdress. This photograph shows Meierdress as an SS-Obersturmführer in 1942 as a Baterie Kommandeur in an SS-Sturmgeschütz unit in the Totenkopf Division. On his field grey Panzerjacke he wears the mirror image pattern Totenkopf collar patches so that his rank is shown only on his shoulder-straps. Interestingly he appears to have artillerie red Waffenfarbe to his SS peaked cap, a rare feature.

Left: SS-Brigadeführer Kurt Meyer seen when he was an SS-Obersturmbannführer in Command of SS-Panzeraufklärungsabteilung 1 in 1943. One of the most dashing of the Waffen-SS senior officers, he was a divisional commander when only 34 years of age. He was known to his men as 'Panzermeyer'.

Right: Johannes Mühlenkamp. Father of the Waffen-SS Tank forces, and one time Commander of the élite 5 SS-Panzer Division Wiking, Mühlenkamp became one of the most highly esteemed soldiers of the Waffen-SS. This photograph was taken in late 1944 when he held the rank of SS-Standartenführer. The original print shows signs of the Oakleaf collar patch of his rank having been touched out, but his rank can be confirmed by the two pips on his shoulder-boards. His cap, though bearing a metal SS Totenkopf on the cap band, has a silver wire on black, Army pattern Panzer officer's cap eagle. (Johannes Mülenkamp)

Right: Oakleaves winner Obersleutnant Alfred Müller won his Oakleaves as a Hauptmann commanding Sturmgeschütz Abteilung 191 with Heeresgruppe A on the Eastern Front in December 1943. In this photograph he is wearing the officer's piped field service dress which featured the red piping of the artillery, visible here around the collar and down the front of the tunic. The bright silver bullion embroidered collar patches and shoulder-straps also feature red underlay. The Oakleaves wreath on his cap band is also in fine hand embroidery. (Josef Charita)

Above left: Panzer ace SS-Standartenführer Joachim Peiper is seen here as an SS-Obersturmbannführer, before the award of his Swords. He is wearing the officer's version of the SS-Pattern Panzerjacke, with silver cord piping to the collar. On his left breast is the Infantry Close Combat Clasp and on his right sleeve is just visible, the braid badge for single-handed destruction of an enemy tank.

Above: Oberwachtmeister Hugo Primozic, one of Germany's top Assault Gun aces. This original wartime propaganda postcard photograph is captioned for Leutnant Primozic, because he was later commissioned, but the photograph shows him wearing NCO's shoulder-straps. Primozic won his Oakleaves as Zugführer in 2./Sturmgeschütz Abteilung 667 in January 1943. (Paul Anderson)

Left: SS-Hauptsturmführer Rudolf von Ribbentrop. An SS-Obersturmführer at the time this photograph was taken, von Ribbentrop was serving as Commander of 6. Kompanie SS Panzer Regiment 1. He is wearing the standard field grey service dress tunic with the gilt 'LAH' monograms clearly visible on his shoulder-straps. His arm eagle is of the heavy silver wire hand-embroidered type. (Rudolf von Ribbentrop)

Right: SS-Obersturmführer Wilfried Richter, Batterie-Führer in SS-Sturmgeschütz Abteilung 3 of the élite Totenkopf Division. Richter won his Knight's Cross in April 1942. In this photograph bearded Richter wears a well-battered, old-style field cap with soft leather peak and devoid of the usual chinstrap. The cap eagle used appears to be an actual arm eagle, and the Totenkopf on the cap band seems to have been cut from a collar patch. Such curiosities were by no means rare in the Waffen-SS where any number of non-regulation insignia were utilized.

Left: Johann Sailer, here an SS-Obersturmführer, wears a late pattern Panzerjacke without the officer's piping to the collar. His cap has had the chincords and wire brim stiffener removed, a very popular practice. On his left breast is the Close Combat Clasp as well as the Iron Cross First Class and Panzer Assault Badge. (Johann Sailer)

Left: Major Hans Sandrock. A former Army Panzer officer, Sandrock won the Knight's Cross as Commander of III (Sturmgeschütz) Abteilung, Fallschirm Panzer Regiment Hermann Göring. Sandrock wears a typical mixture of uniform clothing including standard officers' Luftwaffe blue forage cap, field grey Sturmgeschütz pattern Panzerjacke with standard army pattern pink piped collar tabs, and black Panzer issue shirt. The piping to his jacket collar is silver twist cord. (Hans Sandrock)

Below: Crack anti-tank gunner, SS-Sturmmann Remy Schrijnen, is shown here immediately after the award of his Knight's Cross in October 1944. Marching alongside him are his Commander, Conrad Schellong, and the unit adjutant, Willy Teichert. Schellong was also to become a Knight's Cross winner four months later.

Right: Major Fritz-Rudolf Schultz. A major and regimental commander at the age of just 27, this dashing young Panzer officer was decorated with the Knight's Cross in 1940, and the coveted Oakleaves in October 1944. He became a staff officer in the High Command of the German Army.

Right: Emil Seibold, here an SS-Hauptscharführer, served as a Zugführer in 8 Kompanie of the elite SS-Panzer Regiment 2 Das Reich, operating in captured Soviet T-34 Tanks. The photograph has been retouched at some time to add the Knight's Cross. Seibold's award was made in the closing days of the war and of course no time was available for his decoration to be presented. (Emil Seibold)

Left: SS-Hauptsturmführer Paul Senghas. This photograph was taken when he was an SS-Untersturmführer and has been retouched at some time because his Knight's Cross was not awarded until December 1944 when he held the rank of SS-Obersturmführer. His German Cross in Gold can be clearly seen on the right breast of his Panzerjacke. (Paul Senghas)

Right: Hans Siegel. In this photograph, taken in August 1944 just after the award of his Knight's Cross, Siegel wears the rank badges of an SS-Hauptsturmführer. He later rose to the rank of SS-Sturmbannführer. In his buttonhole he wears both the Iron Cross Second Class and East Front Medal ribbons and just visible on his lower left breast is the Panzer Assault Badge for 25 engagements with the enemy. (Hans Siegel)

University in the north of Italy, studying economics and jurisprudence. With the outbreak of war he broke off his studies and in January 1940, volunteered for military service in the SS. Accepted, he joined the motorized Infantry Regiment Deutschland in July 1940 and saw action in the Balkan Campaign.

Following the invasion of the Soviet Union, Nicolussi-Leck was in action with his regiment on the Central Sector of the Eastern Front until November 1941 when he was assigned to the SS-Junkerschule at Bad Tölz on a commissioning course, and in the spring of 1942 was promoted to SS-Untersturmführer and posted to 5th SS-Panzer Division Wiking.

At the end of March 1944, Wiking was located near Kowel, in the Pripet Marshes. This was an important road and railhead and contained several field hospitals housing more than 2,000 wounded soldiers. A massive Soviet armoured push succeeded in surrounding Kowel and cutting the road and rail links. Nicolussi-Leck, in command of 8. Kompanie, Panzer Regiment 5, was tasked with breaking through the encirclement. Because of the strength of the enemy forces, and the terrible terrain, snow-covered bog, the breakthrough was to be costly and protracted. At about midnight, ten hours after he had started, only half the distance had been covered, with the loss of about one-third of the unit strength. The prospects for the breakthrough seemed slim indeed. In the full knowledge of the seriousness of the situation for his encircled comrades, Nicolussi-Leck decided to press on over the treacherous bogs, under cover of darkness.

Thanks to concealment by near blizzard conditions, after eighteen hours of combat and with only half his tank strength remaining, Nicolussi-Leck reached the outskirts of Kowel in the early hours of the following morning. Here he held his positions for eight days until a Panzerkorps could break the Soviet encirclement and the thousands of German wounded be evacuated to safety. For his part in the rescue of the encircled Germans, SS-Obersturmführer Karl Nicolussi-Leck was decorated with the Knight's Cross of the Iron Cross. The award was announced in a Regimental Order of the Day:

SS-Panzer Regiment 5   Kowel, 15.4.44
2a/Kdr/Eg

Regimental Order of the Day

The Führer has awarded the Knight's Cross of the Iron Cross to SS-Obersturmführer Nicolussi-Leck, Commander of 8. Kompanie.

SS-Obersturmführer Nicolussi-Leck resolutely succeeded, under difficult circumstances, in breaking through to the encircled city of Kowel on 30 March 1944. He gave the garrison critical support. With his 8. Kompanie he played a special part in the garrison holding out.

The Regiment is proud to hear of this well-deserved award to one of its old members.

We wish a soildier's good luck shall stay with him always.

sig. Mühlenkamp

In the summer of 1944, Nicolussi-Leck was promoted to SS-Hauptsturm-führer and given command of II Abteilung of the Regiment during the retreat by Warsaw and at the end of 1944 in Hungary. By the beginning of March 1945, the Regiment had lost all its tanks and the crews, with little more than their personal small arms, were ordered to Paderborn to be re-equipped.

With 70 new Panthers, the Regiment was to entrain for the Eastern Front once again, but events overtook the Wiking Panzer men. Oberbefehlshaber West, Generalfeldmarschall Model had committed suicide, and his replace-ment, General Oberst Student, ordered Wiking's tanks into battle in the line around Bielefeld-Münster. Had the attacking Allies realized they were up against the hardened Wiking veterans of the Eastern Front they would perhaps have been less confident. As it was, when US armoured forces attacked near Celle, Wiking troops equipped with seven Ferdinand assault guns destroyed more than sixty US tanks and armoured vehicles. On 22 April 1945, Nicolussi-Leck was captured by the Americans. Released in 1948, he returned to his native Tyrol where he lives to this day, running a small fruit farm.

A fine soldier by any standards, Karl Nicolussi-Leck's greatest personal achievement was in saving so many of his wounded comrades from almost certain death at Kowel. To this day he still receives letters of thanks from these grateful survivors of that terrible battle.

SS-STANDARTENFÜHRER JOACHIM PEIPER

One of Germany's most notorious Panzer commanders, Joachim or *Jochen* Peiper was born in Berlin on 30 January 1915. His family had a military tradition and it is not surprising that he gravitated towards a military career. His father Waldemar had been a captain in the Imperial German Army and had fought in the East African Campaign. A very intelligent young man, Peiper nevertheless failed his school-leaving examination, though this was through lack of application rather than lack of ability. This did mean however that many avenues into professional careers were closed to him. Peiper was a member of the Berlin SS Reitersturm in whose ranks were numbered some of Berlin's top citizens, and indeed two Hohenzollern princes. In early 1934, therefore, Peiper decided to try to make a career for himself in the SS and applied for full membership in the hope of obtaining a commission in Hitler's élite force. In early 1935 he was called to the SS Junkerschule Braunschweig to begin his cadet training. Peiper passed his course and in April 1936 was commissioned as an SS-Untersturmführer and posted to the Leibstandarte Adolf Hitler.

Almost from the start Peiper was seen as an ambitious high-flyer. Although not a social mixer he was well respected by his peers and in July 1938 was assigned to the personal staff of Reichsführer-SS Heinrich Himmler. Although this was a good career posting for the ambitious young officer, when war broke out in 1939 it meant that he was far from the fighting. Peiper was well aware of the possibilities for accelerated promotion in a combat unit. His pleas for a combat posting were eventually granted and in 1940 he was re-assigned to the Leibstandarte as it prepared for the assault on France and the Low Countries. Peiper enjoyed his combat duties and indeed won both the 2nd and 1st Class Iron Crosses during the campaign in the west. This was followed by service in Greece at the close of which he had attained the rank of SS-Hauptsturmführer.

It was to be during the campaign in Russia that Peiper would begin his real rise to fame. His reckless daring often resulted in high casualty rates though this was true of the Waffen-SS as a whole. However, his willingness to expose himself to the same dangers as his men rather than lead from the rear, as some did, earned him the growing respect and admiration of his tough soldiers.

By early 1943, Peiper held the rank of SS-Sturmbannführer and commanded III Bataillon/SS Panzer Grenadier Regiment 1. The Soviet victory at Stalingrad had demoralized the Germans and the enemy offensive had left many isolated German units cut off. One such unit was 320 Infanterie Division at the town of Stary Oskol. With more than 1,500 wounded men, the division was ordered to try to withdraw to the River Donetz. Burdened with so many wounded it would have little chance of success. The Leibstandarte's commander, Sepp Dietrich, tasked Peiper with the rescue of this unit, and Peiper was soon on his way deep behind enemy lines with just one battalion of armoured infantry. On meeting the withdrawing columns of the 320th, Peiper's medics toiled through the night to ease the suffering of the most seriously wounded. The next morning the column set off for German lines with Peiper's half-tracks guarding the flanks. Peiper intended to make the crossing of the Donetz at Udy where a small bridge was held by German troops. On arrival he found that the bridge had been destroyed by an attacking Soviet force which had killed most of the defenders and slaughtered many of the wounded. Peiper's furious grenadiers tore into the Russians and in a fierce battle lasting several hours in which no quarter was given, the enemy were wiped out.

Peiper's men made makeshift repairs to the bridge so that the wounded and the stragglers from the 320th could cross. The rickety bridge however would never take the weight of his heavy armoured personnel carriers. Rather than abandon his vehicles and make good his escape together with the forces he had rescued, Peiper turned back into Soviet-held territory, travelling many miles before he located a suitable crossing-place, and succeeded in getting his entire force home without the loss of a single vehicle.

Dietrich was delighted with Peiper's achievement and immediately recommended him for the award of the Knight's Cross of the Iron Cross. This was approved and the decoration was awarded on 9 March 1943.

As the year progressed Peiper was involved in the furious battles for Kharkov which changed hands several times. At one point his HQ was cut off and a force of Tiger tanks was sent to rescue him. Before the Tigers could reach his location, Peiper had taken the initiative and broken clear without help.

Following the débâcle at Kursk in July 1943, the Leibstandarte was sent to Italy. As the fortunes of war turned against the Axis powers, Mussolini's regime tottered. Partisan forces were becoming a problem and the Leibstandarte was to find service in a so-called allied country to be no rest cure. In September 1943, two of Peiper's NCOs were kidnapped by partisans in the town of Bovec. Peiper sent in a Company of Panzergrenadiers to effect their release, but these rescue forces themselves came under heavy fire. Peiper himself set off for Bovec and soon he too was coming under disconcertingly accurate fire; his radio-operator slumped dead, hit by a burst of machine-gun fire. The NCO next to Peiper was wounded and Peiper himself had a narrow escape, bullets passing through his tunic sleeve without hitting him. Peiper's self-propelled artillery was brought into action against the partisan-held town and they soon fled. In the battle 33 civilians were killed and the Communist partisans were soon crying 'war crime'. Needless to say the Partisans did not see anything wrong with using an innocent civilian location as cover for their attack. For the first time then, Peiper's name was to be linked to an alleged war crime.

Returning to the Eastern Front in the winter of 1943 Peiper, despite three years of gruelling combat, had lost none of his flair. In December he took part in a night attack against the Soviet-held town of Pekartschina. His attack was carried out with such determination and ferocity that the enemy were quickly eliminated and in the following two days Peiper was responsible for the capture of more than 2,000 prisoners, and the scattering of the Combat Headquarters of three entire Soviet divisions. In recognition of his leadership during these days he was decorated with the Oakleaves to his Knight's Cross on 27 January 1943.

In January 1944 the Leibstandarte was transferred to France for rest and refitting. Thrown into the battle for Normandy following the Allied invasion of Europe in June 1944, it fought gallantly but suffered terrible casualties. Peiper, now with the Panzer Regiment, was to feel the full effects of Allied air superiority as his tanks were pounded by rocket-firing fighter-bombers. On one occasion Peiper's own tank was hit, and he risked his life to save his radio-operator who had been blinded. Peiper was among those fortunate enough to escape the Allied encirclement of the German armies in Normandy, breaking out through Chambois in August 1944.

Refitted and rested once again, the Leibstandarte was to be in the forefront of Hitler's last desperate gamble for success on the Western Front, the Ardennes Offensive in December 1944. It was during this offensive that Peiper was to gain the fame and notoriety which was ultimately to cost him his life. None of the German commanders had any real hope of success for this offensive and Peiper was no exception. However, he was still a supremely loyal soldier and would do his utmost to achieve his mission.

Kampfgruppe Peiper was to be a spearhead Panzer unit, tasked to break through to the River Meuse and capture the bridge at Huy. Peiper knew the impracticality of taking a heavy Panzer unit through the narrow, twisted steep roads through the Ardennes, roads which he claimed were only fit for bicycles. The impatient Peiper soon found his worst fears fully realized as his tanks could hardly move along the congested roads. Cross-country travel was hardly any better as the preceding infantry units had failed to clear enemy minefields and Peiper lost several vehicles with tracks blown off. By the time he reached the village of Lanzerath, three tanks and five half-tracks had been lost.

On 17 December 1944 came the event which was to have such tragic consequences. A group of captured US soldiers were being held in a field by the Baugnez crossroads on the road to Malmédy. The exact sequence of events may never be fully known, but German troops guarding the prisoners fired at them and at least eighty were killed.

A number of scenarios have been postulated to explain the tragedy, but whatever the full facts may have been one thing was certain, as the men involved in the massacre were from Kampfgruppe Peiper, he was held responsible. Though there has never been any firm evidence to suggest that Peiper had given any orders for the execution of prisoners and he himself was more than twelve miles away at the time of the massacre, his name was once again linked to a serious war crime. It should also be pointed out that following the discovery of the massacre, many unarmed German soldiers were murdered by US soldiers after surrendering, in revenge for the Malmédy Massacre as it came to be known. In fact the Headquarters of the US 328th Infantry Division issued an order stating that no SS or Paratroops were to be taken prisoner but were to be shot on sight.

Peiper, however, oblivious to this furore, continued his advance and reached the river Ambleve at Trois Ponts where he could only watch in frustration as US Combat Engineers blew the bridge over the river in front of his very eyes. Turning from Trois Ponts Peiper made for la Gleize which he quickly captured. US Engineers once again frustrated his advance by blowing the bridge at Habiemont just outside la Gleize. Peiper's way was now barred. The trapped Germans came under heavy fire from US 155mm guns and Peiper's force was slowly decimated. With no fuel left Peiper destroyed his tanks and broke out under cover of darkness, safely reaching his own lines. His part in the Ardennes Offensive was over.

Peiper served through the last hectic months of the war on the Eastern Front, in Hungary, Czechoslovakia and Austria. He was captured by US troops in Bavaria as he attempted to reach his home and family. Peiper, however, could not look forward to a return to a peaceful civilian life. His name was inexorably linked to a major war crime and on capture he was put on trial. In July 1946 he was found guilty and sentenced to death. The trial itself, however, was to become the cause of a great scandal. It had been established that confessions had been extorted from the German defendants, of whom Peiper was only one, by illegal methods including beatings, fake executions, bribes and threats. Several Americans spoke up for Peiper and a campaign led by Senator Joseph McCarthy led to the quashing of the death sentence and Peiper's eventual release. He was never to find peace, however. His past followed him like a sinister shadow. Each time he appeared to be settled in a successful career his past would rise up and the thought of employing such a notorious person would lead to his dismissal. In 1972 he finally moved to the village of Traves in France, with the full knowledge of the authorities and led a quiet life translating books. In 1976, however, Communist agitators discovered Peiper's identity and a threat campaign was mounted against him. Peiper was too much of a soldier to be intimidated by such threats, but did send his wife to safety. On the night of 14 July 1976, Jochen Peiper was murdered by unknown terrorists. The local priest who blamed Peiper's death on Communist agitators was himself threatened with death. The perpetrators have never been apprehended.

To this day Peiper remains an enigma. Undoubtedly brave in battle with little regard for his own life, the one-time member of Himmler's staff, who was not even a member of the Nazi Party, intervened to save the lives of a Jewish family in Italy who were about to be deported by the local fascists to a concentration camp. During the Ardennes Offensive he treated an American prisoner, Major McCown, with great chivalry. At his trial when many of his comrades abandoned him, he willingly accepted responsibility for the atrocities committed by his men though he himself had not been involved, knowing that this would surely mean the death sentence. The notoriety his military career brought him will probably mean that his positive qualities will never be truly appreciated. In a book dealing with military achievements, however, he must surely qualify as one of Germany's great soldiers.

LEUTNANT HUGO PRIMOZIC

Probably the most famous of all the great assault gun aces, Hugo Primozic was born on 16 February 1914 in Backnang, Baden-Wurttemberg. After completing his Reichsarbeitsdienst service, he joined the Army in April 1934 and was taken into Artillery Regiment 5 in Ludwigsburg. In April 1935 he was promoted to Gefreiter, and in October 1936 to Obergefreiter when he joined Artillery Regiment 51 in Hanau.

By the outbreak of war in 1939, Primozic held the rank of Unteroffizier and was serving with Artillerie Regiment 152, a newly formed unit which was part of 52nd Infanterie Division. His regiment fought in the Polish and French Campaigns before Primozic, in April 1941, volunteered to transfer to the Sturmartillerie. He attended training with Sturmgeschütz Abteilung 200 in Schweinfurt before being posted, in May 1942, to the newly created Sturmgeschütz Abteilung 667 in Jüterbog.

Primozic arrived on the central sector of the Eastern Front in July 1942, seeing action at the Chleppen bridgehead along with the élite 5th Panzer Division. Thereafter he saw combat on the northern sector at Cholm and at Gredjakino. On 1 September 1942 he was decorated with the Iron Cross Second Class and promoted to Oberwachtmeister. On 13 September 1942 the Iron Cross First Class followed and two days later Primozic scored his first great personal victory when, during an attempted Soviet breakthrough near Rschew, he destroyed 24 tanks, bringing his personal score at this point to 45. For this achievement Primozic was decorated with the Knight's Cross of the Iron Cross on 19 September 1942 and, in a special Order of the Day by Generaloberst Walter Model, was praised for his part in throwing back the enemy attack.

A further Soviet breakthrough in mid-December saw Sturmgeschütz Abteilung 667 thrown into the counter-attack. In one single engagement Primozic destroyed seven tanks. He fought to his last round of ammunition than calmly called down an artillery barrage on to his own position with total disregard for his own safety. By the end of the month his personal score had reached 60, bringing him, on 25 June 1943, the award of the Oakleaves. Primozic was the first NCO of the German Army to win the coveted Oakleaves which were personally presented by Hitler at a ceremony in the Führerhauptquartier at which his entire crew were awarded the German Cross in Gold.

As with many aces from all branches of the armed forces, it was decided that Primozic would be of more value at a training establishment where the benefit of his extensive combat experience could be put to good use in training future Sturmgeschütz crews. On 1 February 1943, he was commissioned Leutnant and posted as an instructor to the Sturmgeschütz School at Burg, and in April 1944 to the Sturmgeschütz Reserve and Training Battalion Schieratz. Finally in February 1945 he was posted as a Battery Commander with Sturmgeschütz Reserve and Training Battalion 700.

As the Allies inexorably closed in on the shrinking Reich, these Sturmgeschütz Reserve and Training units were mobilized for front line combat duties. The assault guns were formed into a Kampfgruppe under Major Alfred Müller, himself an Oakleaves winner. Leutnant Primozic's last actions were against advancing US armoured units around Magdeburg and it was here on 8 May 1945 that this great ace was finally captured. He was released in August 1945.

SS-HAUPTSTURMFÜHRER RUDOLF VON RIBBENTROP

Rudolf von Ribbentrop was born on 10 May 1921 in Wiesbaden, the son of German Foreign Minister Joachim von Ribbentrop. He was educated in Berlin and spent some time in London when his father was Ambassador, before completing the usual period of obligatory service in the Reichsarbeitsdienst.

On the outbreak of war, Rudolf von Ribbentrop was already a serving member of the SS-Verfügungstruppe. He served with 11 Kompanie of SS-Regiment Deutschland during the campaign in the west, winning the Iron Cross Second Class. With the rank of Sturmmann he was sent to the SS-Junkerschule Braunschweig whence he was commissioned as an SS-Untersturmführer in April 1941. Von Ribbentrop then saw service on the Northern Front in Finland as a platoon commander with a reconnaissance unit. Wounded in action and hospitalized, on his recovery he was posted to the élite Leibstandarte SS Adolf Hitler to serve in the Panzer Abteilung.

During the attack on Kharkov in early 1943, von Ribbentrop was wounded in action for the third time, winning the Iron Cross First Class. He also saw action during the massive tank battle at Kursk where he commanded 6 Kompanie of the Panzer Regiment. On 9 July 1943, near Teterewino, his Kompanie encountered a strong column of 40 or more Russian tanks. Immediately attacking, six enemy tanks were destroyed and the remainder fled in disarray, their attempt to outflank the German position thwarted.

On 12 July, von Ribbentrop was ordered to support infantry units in their area, against advancing Russian armoured forces. With only seven tanks from his Kompanie, von Ribbentrop awaited the inevitable attack. It came between 08.00 and 09.00, between Prochorowka and Teterewino, with more than 150 tanks involved. Two of von Ribbentrop's Panzers were quickly knocked out, but the remainder stood firm. The battle raged at almost point-blank range, as one Russian tank after another was hit. When the Russians finally withdrew, the field was littered with knocked out enemy tanks and dead infantry. In this single engagement, von Ribbentrop had personally destroyed fourteen tanks. In recognition of his cool and audacious defence, SS-Obersturmführer von Ribbentrop was decorated with the Knight's Cross of the Iron Cross on 15 July 1943.

Rudolf von Ribbentrop commanded 3 Kompanie of SS-Panzer Regiment 12 in Normandy. He was one of many veterans of the Leibstandarte transferred to this new unit. Wounded in a strafing attack by Allied fighter-bombers a few days before the invasion of 6 June, he was hospitalized. Knowing that his comrades were in the thick of battle, and despite being unfit for action, his arm still in a sling, von Ribbentrop discharged himself from hospital and immediately returned to his unit.

On 25 August 1944, he was decorated with the German Cross in Gold in recognition of his command of the Kompanie during these difficult battles. In September 1944 he was appointed Regimental Adjutant of SS-Panzer Regiment 12 in which post he served until the Ardennes offensive when, following the death of SS-Sturmbannführer Jürgensen, himself a Ritter-kreüzträger von Ribbentrop was given command of I Abteilung of the Regiment.

Following the end of the disastrous Ardennes offensive, the division was reformed near Cologne towards the end of January. In February it was transferred to Hungary, participating in the offensive near Lake Balaton, in the attempt to recapture Budapest. During this period, von Ribbentrop received the Wound Badge in Gold having been wounded in action yet again. SS-Hauptsturmführer von Ribbentrop commanded I Abteilung of the Panzer Regiment as the division was withdrawn into Austria where it surrendered to US forces. Despite having a father who was one of the Nazi chiefs, von Ribbentrop's progress was achieved entirely by his own skill and endeavours. A brave and dedicated soldier, his Ritterkreuz was richly deserved. He is still alive.

SS-HAUPTSTURMFÜHRER WILFRIED RICHTER

Born in Pforzheim on 9 May 1916, Richter joined the SS in 1937 when he was accepted into 15 Kompanie, SS-Standarte Deutschland. He attended the SS-Junkerschule Braunschweig and after commissioning as an SS-Untersturmführer, he was posted to the SS-Totenkopf Division. In August 1940, Richter was posted to the division's Sturmgeschütz Batterie and saw action with this unit in the Western Campaign, and also in the opening phases of Operation 'Barbarossa'. In September 1941 he was awarded the Iron Cross Second Class and on 22 October 1941, the First Class.

The *Totenkopf* Division was one of the major German units cut off in the pocket at Demjansk in early 1942, on the northern sector of the Eastern Front. The division's elements were mostly formed into small Kampfgruppen fighting alongside their Army comrades. Richter's Kampfgruppe was located at Kalitkino on the west bank of the River Robja. During early February, heavy Soviet artillery fire had reduced the village and its surroundings to a barren sea of rubble and smoking ruins. Despite the ferocious barrages, the accompanying infantry assaults were thrown back with considerable loss to the attackers. It was to this dangerous situation that Richter arrived to take command. He rapidly re-organized the defences, strengthening the strong-point against inevitable attacks to come. On 5 April the expected Soviet attack materialized. Without the warning of an artillery barrage, the enemy attacked at daybreak with sixteen T-34 tanks and massed infantry support. After knocking out the defenders' anti-tank guns, the enemy established a hold on the northern edge of the strong-point, but not before six of the T-34s had been knocked out.

Totenkopf grenadiers were quick to react to the danger and immediately attacked with Teller mines. The attackers lost five more tanks to these deadly mines. At this point Richter risked bringing down an artillery barrage on his own position.

In the relative safety of their bunkers the Germans sheltered while the artillery shells fell upon the attackers, knocking out one more T-34 and killing many Russian infantrymen. As soon as the barrage ended, Richter stormed out of his bunker at the head of his men, launching into the remaining attackers. A frenzy of hand-to-hand combat ensued in which no quarter was given. Fighting raged until all the attackers had fled or been killed. The gallantry of the German defenders had driven off an attacking force vastly superior in numbers and caused the enemy heavy casualties in men and tanks. For his leadership during this battle and his own personal gallantry, Richter was decorated with the Knight's Cross of the Iron Cross on 21 April 1942, and promoted to SS-Hauptsturmführer.

After spending one month on the Führerreserve of the Oberkommando des Heeres, Richter was posted as a Zugführer to schwere Kompanie, SS-Panzer Regiment 3, equipped with the formidable Tiger Tank. On 1 May 1944 Richter became deputy Training Group Commander at SS-Junkerschule Tölz and ultimately a Battalion Commander in 38th SS Grenadier

Division Nibelungen. This division was formed in the closing stages of the war from the students and staff of Junkerschule Tölz. In reality it never exceeded regimental strength. It went into action on the southern sector of the Eastern Front, commanded by former Führeradjutant and Leibstandarte veteran, SS-Obersturmbannführer Richard Schulze.

Wilfried Richter survived the war, but died in April 1981 from a heart attack, after a long illness. This daring and popular soldier was laid to rest in a ceremony attended by many of his wartime comrades.

SS-OBERSTURMFÜHRER JOHANN SAILER

The son of a butcher, Johann Sailer was born in Wildon on 23 December 1921. He began his military career in 1940 as a 19-year-old, and by the end of the following year was an experienced soldier having served on both the Balkan and Eastern Fronts. After serving for a period on the Eastern Front with an SS-Panzerjäger unit, he attended SS-Unterführerschule at Radolfzell on the Bodensee. Returning to the Eastern Front in 1943, he served as a senior NCO during the battle of Kharkov.

By the summer of 1944, Sailer was serving in SS-Panzerjäger Abteilung 9, in the recently formed 9th SS-Panzer Division Hohenstaufen. As Zugführer in 3 Kompanie of the Abteilung, Sailer served with distinction during the Normandy battles and the battle for the Falaise Gap where his unit destroyed at least 53 Allied tanks and armoured vehicles. Sailer remained with the Abteilung throughout the retreat and was with Hohenstaufen at Arnhem when the British airborne assault was made. The division played a major role in the defeat of the British paras before being withdrawn to Münstereifel for refitting in October 1944.

The division had reached approximately 75 per cent of its nominated strength when it was allocated to the Ardennes Offensive. Sailer's Abteilung could boast approximately 21 Jagdpanzer IV and 30 Sturmgeschützen. Despite the best efforts of Sailer and his comrades, the offensive was doomed from the start; the great effort that had been made to rebuild the division had come to naught. During the offensive Sailer was seriously wounded, the seventh time he had received wounds in action.

In early 1945 Hohenstaufen was transferred to the Eastern Front where it was heavily involved in the defence of Hungary before being transferred once again, ending the war in combat against US forces where his Kompanie exacted a heavy toll of enemy vehicles. On 19 March 1945 Sailer was decorated with the German Cross in Gold and on 4 May he received the Knight's Cross of the Iron Cross. His Kompanie had destroyed a total of 600 tanks and vehicles and more than 200 guns. Sailer survived the war and is still alive.

MAJOR HANS SANDROCK

Hans Sandrock was born in Saarbrücken on 20 April 1913. His father was an official at the Air Ministry in Berlin and it was in the capital city that Sandrock was raised. He attended school in Berlin-Steglitz, followed by a year's mechanical engineering apprenticeship at the Piechatzek factory in Berlin prior to commencing a 4-year course in engineering studies at the Berlin Techniches Hochschule.

His military career began at the age of 21 when he volunteered for the Army and was taken into the Driving Instructional Unit at Zossen on 1 September 1934. Seven months later he was promoted to the rank of Gefreiter and nominated as a potential officer. With the development of the German Army, Sandrock's unit was absorbed into a Panzer regiment and after completing a course at the Hanover Kriegsschule in 1936, he was commissioned as a Leutnant and returned to his unit, Panzer Regiment 5.

Leutnant Sandrock became a platoon commander with 2 Kompanie of the Panzer regiment. In this position he served during the occupation of the Sudetenland and ultimately of Czechoslovakia. Promoted to Oberleutnant just prior to the outbreak of the war, and transferred to 1 Kompanie of the Regiment, Sandrock took part in the Polish Campaign, winning the Iron Cross 2nd Class on 22 October 1939. Service during the campaign in the west followed, during which Oberleutnant Sandrock qualified for the Panzer Assault Badge.

On 10 March 1941, Panzer Regiment 5 was sent to North Africa as part of Rommel's Afrika Korps. It had, in late 1940, been withdrawn from 3rd Panzer Division to become the basis for 5th Light Division. The Regiment took part in the push to Tobruk, suffering heavy casualties. Oberleutnant Sandrock was decorated with the Iron Cross First Class on 18 April 1941. During the summer of 1941, the regiment was re-formed with 21st Panzer Division, and Sandrock saw action during the capture of Benghazi, the Battle of Gazala and the push to El Alemein. On 1 June 1942, Hauptmann Sandrock, who had been promoted from Oberleutnant in February of that year, was decorated with the German Cross in Gold. Severely wounded in November 1942 when the British forces opened their 'Supercharge' offensive, Sandrock was evacuated to Germany for hospitalization.

On 25 July 1943, fully recovered from his wounds, Sandrock returned to the Mediterranean front, but this time to the III (Sturmgeschütz) Abteilung, of Fallschirm Panzer Regiment Hermann Göring. Together with a number of fellow Army Panzer officers, Sandrock had been transferred to the Luftwaffe, as Göring's personal combat force continued its growth. Sandrock fought in Sicily and the evacuation to the Italian mainland across the Straits of Messina. During the Allied advance through Italy, the Hermann Göring Division saw action in almost every major battle. On 9 December Sandrock qualified for the Panzer Assault Badge for 25 engagements with the enemy and on 1 February 1944 was promoted to Major.

After the fall of Rome, the Hermann Göring Division was transferred to the Eastern Front as part of Hitler's promised reinforcements for Model's summer offensive of 1944. The division was used in conjunction with 19th Panzer Division and 5th SS-Panzer Division *Wiking* to defend Warsaw in a counter-offensive which decimated the Soviet III Tank Corps.

In October 1944, the Hermann Göring Division was battling against overwhelming Soviet armoured forces north of Radom in Poland. Major Sandrock and his Abteilung were responsible for blocking a Soviet attempt to break through the German lines, and for destroying all the Soviet armour that penetrated the German-held areas. During this action Sandrock and his Abteilung achieved a score of 123 tanks and armoured vehicles destroyed. For this achievement he was decorated with the Knight's Cross of the Iron Cross, and on 21 October 1944 the award was presented together with the superb solid silver Luftwaffe Salver of Honour, by General Weidlich, Commander of XXXI Panzer Korps.

Wounded again in the spring of 1945, Sandrock was once again evacuated to hospital and on his release joined the Reserve Abteilung of Hermann Göring in Oranienburg. On 8 May 1945, he was captured by the Western Allies, but escaped just ten days later and managed to make his way to his family in Bonn. Hans Sandrock is now the Treasurer of the Ordensgemeinschaft der Ritterkreuzträger and lives in retirement near Cologne.

SS-UNTERSCHARFÜHRER REMI SCHRIJNEN

Remi Schrijnen, the first Belgian to win the coveted Knight's Cross of the Iron Cross was born in Kumtich in Flanders on Christmas Eve, 1921. As a volunteer in the Waffen-SS he served with Freiwilligen Legion Flandern on the Eastern Front. From 1942 to the end of May 1943 he fought on the northern sector of the front, seeing action around Leningrad. At the end of May the Legion was withdrawn from the front and sent to Czechoslovakia to a training depot where it was strengthened by the influx of new personnel from Flanders. With the addition of a Finnish SS volunteer unit, the new formation reached brigade strength and was renamed SS-Freiwilligen Sturm Brigade Langemarck. At the end of 1943 it returned to the front in the region of the Ukraine.

Schrijnen served with the brigade as a gunner with a heavy 7.5cm anti-tank Kompanie. Only five days after reaching the front Schrijnen was involved in fierce combat with attacking Soviet tank units, supported by large numbers of infantry. In this first engagement he personally destroyed three T-34 tanks. The ferocity of the combat can be gauged by the fact that by 3 March Schrijnen had been wounded seven times. He was awarded the Iron Cross Second Class on 28 May 1944 and the First Class on 3 August of the same year.

On 21 September 1944, SS-Sturmmann Remi Schrijnen was decorated for an act of singular skill and gallantry. A ferocious artillery barrage on the

German positions had been followed by a massive armoured breakthrough on 26 June. The SS-Grenadiers had been overwhelmed. Schrijnen calmly waited in his position as the enemy tanks rolled even closer. Opening fire, Schrijnen knocked out four T-34s and disabled two others. The enemy push continued however and gradually the German losses grew until Schrijnen's entire gun crew were killed and all the German infantry had withdrawn from their positions. Schrijnen was also ordered to pull back but refused and, determined to stop the enemy, loaded, aimed and fired the 7.5cm anti-tank gun himself. When the supporting Soviet infantry surged forward there was no German infantry to stop them. Among the thirty-plus attacking enemy tanks were five of the new super-heavy Joseph Stalin models. Schrijnen destroyed three of these and four T-34s before a direct hit from yet another Stalin only thirty metres from his position blew his gun up and flung Schrijnen away from his position.

A dying German radio-operator managed to call down an artillery barrage on the SS positions, desperately trying to blunt the Soviet attack. This succeeded and when the counter-attacking German forces recovered the position, the battered and bleeding body of Remi Schrijnen was found amid the wreckage of a dozen of the best tanks the Soviets could field, all destroyed by this gallant soldier. Schrijnen, on recovering from his wounds, went on to serve in Pomerania with his Belgian comrades. By this point the Brigade had been expanded to Divisional strength, but it was slowly decimated during the remaining months of the war.

A hero to the Germans, Schrijnen was, however, considered a traitor by the liberated Belgians at the end of the war. He was imprisoned and held in extremely harsh conditions for ten years. Released in 1955, he moved to West Germany where he lives today in retirement near Hagen.

MAJOR FRITZ-RUDOLF SCHULTZ

The son of an Army officer, Fritz-Rudolf Schultz was born in Munich on 19 February 1917. His military career began in 1935 when he became a Fahnenjunker with an Army signals unit. He was commissioned Leutnant in 1937 and joined Panzer Regiment 3.

On the outbreak of war in 1939 Schultz served as a Regimental Staff orderly officer with Panzer Regiment 35 and saw service in the Polish and western campaigns. His commander at this time, Heinrich Eberbach, was himself to become one of Germany's great Panzer leaders. He was decorated with the Knight's Cross of the Iron Cross on 21 April 1940.

During the campaign on the Eastern Front, Schultz impressed his superiors as a quiet but efficient soldier. In 1942 he became Regimental signals officer in Panzer Regiment 35. The short-barrelled 50mm and 75mm guns of the early Panzer Mks III and IV which had wreaked havoc among the disorganized Soviet forces in the summer of 1941 were soon to be shown as totally inadequate against the Soviet T-34 tanks with their 76mm and later 85mm guns, and their well-sloped armour. German tanks had to get much closer to have a chance of eliminating these tanks, and often these excellent Soviet weapons were only halted by the determined bravery of individual soldiers taking on the enemy tank with a satchel charge, or blowing its tracks off with a Teller mine. Schultz distinguished himself in this way on many occasions.

Promoted to Hauptmann in 1943, Schultz commanded 1 Kompanie of Panzer Regiment 35, equipped with the Panzer IV during the defence of Warsaw against the huge Soviet offensive in 1944.

In May 1944, Schultz and his men were given leave prior to a planned counter-offensive. The Allied invasion of Normandy put paid to the well-earned rest of the exhausted Panzer men and they were ordered to the front. A furious Schultz made so much fuss about his men's leave being stopped, even trying to overrule the orders, that he ended up being arrested by the Feldgendarmerie and was sentenced to seven days' close arrest. This was a perfect example of the close bond of comradeship, forged in battle, betwen this popular officer and his men.

In late 1944, as the northern sector of the Eastern Front crumbled under the Soviet onslaught, Panzer Regiment 35, as part of 4th Panzer Division, was located around Preekuln with 11th SS-Freiwilligen Grenadier Division Nordland and 30th Infanterie Division as its neighbours. At this time Schultz, as Major and temporary Regimental Commander, was instrumental in throwing back a Soviet attack which threatened the German flanks. His Panzers acted as a fire brigade, rushing from crisis point to crisis point, throwing back enemy attacks. For his part in this, Schultz was decorated with the Oakleaves to his Knight's Cross of the Iron Cross on 28 October 1944. The award was presented by Reischsführer-SS Heinrich Himmler at Trossingen.

Following his award, Schultz was given leave and was advised that he had been posted to the staff of Heeresgruppe A. At the surrender he was taken into US captivity, but was held for a mere seven days before being released. After the war, he went into politics and became an FDP Member of the Bundestag.

SS-HAUPTSCHARFÜHRER EMIL SEIBOLD

Emil Seibold was born on 26 February 1907 in Basle, Switzerland. He volunteered for military service with the Waffen-SS in the spring of 1940 and was initially posted for training to SS-Totenkopf Regiment 10. After completing his basic military training he was assigned to Panzer Grenadier Division Das Reich where he served as a dispatch rider with 3 Kompanie of Das Reich's Panzerjägerabteilung.

In the summer of 1943, a large number of captured Soviet T-34/76 tanks became available to the division, and an Abteilung of these T-34s was formed in SS-Panzer Regiment 2, along with several hundred captured

Russian engineers who were put to work under German supervision. This was a dangerous business because, although repainted with large German crosses on the side of the turret, these captured vehicles were always liable to fall victim to German anti-tank gunners who, recognizing the shape of the T-34, would take no chances but fire first and ask questions later.

On 4 June 1944, just before the Allied invasion of Normandy, Seibold was decorated with the German Cross in Gold in recognition of his service on the Eastern Front with his Kompanie of captured tanks. He was also promoted to SS-Oberscharführer. Seibold went on to serve in SS-Panzer Regiment 2 with great distinction. By the end of the war, his personal score of enemy tanks destroyed had reached 69. Unbeknown to him, his Commander had recommended him for the Knight's Cross of the Iron Cross and this had been approved on 6 May 1945. The war ended before Seibold learned of the award and it was not until many years after the war that he found out that he was a Ritterkreuzträger. Emil Seibold is still alive.

SS-STURMBANNFÜHRER HANS SIEGEL

One of several tank aces whose achievements during the hectic Normandy battles brought them the Knight's Cross of the Iron Cross, Hans Siegel was born on 25 July 1918 in Böckau/Erzgebirge. Like most young Germans of his generation, Siegel entered the Reichsarbeitsdienst for a compulsory period of Labour service after leaving school and before commencing his military career. In 1938 he volunteered for the SS and was accepted into the Leibstandarte SS Adolf Hitler.

Initially serving in the infantry, Siegel saw action during the Polish Campaign with 12 (Maschinengewehr) Kompanie of the Leibstandarte. On the successful conclusion of the campaign, he was sent to the SS-Junkerschule at Bad Tölz in Bavaria where after approximately one year's training he was commissioned as an SS-Untersturmführer. Following his commissioning, Siegel served with the Training and Reserve Battalion of the Leibstandarte in Berlin.

On the opening day of the campaign against the Soviet Union, Siegel served as a Zugführer in the Sturmgeschütz Abteilung of the Leibstandarte. He remained with this Abteilung until the recapture of Kharkov in March 1943. During this period he was wounded in action three times and spent six months in hospital. On his recovery he was posted as a Company Commander to the Sturmgeschütz training Abteilung.

In 1943, a new SS Division, the 12th SS-Panzer Division Hitlerjugend, was formed. The bulk of the division's personnel were from the Hitlerjugend as the divisional title suggests. When drawing up a cadre of experienced personnel as a core for the new division, the Leibstandarte was to furnish the new unit with many of its best men. Thus the fanatically keen Hitlerjugend grenadiers were to be trained and led by some of the toughest soldiers in the world.

In 1944 Siegel was transferred to the new division to command 8 Kompanie of the Panzer Regiment. His Company was part of II Abteilung of the Regiment which was equipped with the Panzerkampfwagen IV. Following the Allied invasion of Normandy the 12th SS-Panzer Division was thrown into battle and Siegel's Panzers found themselves in the thick of the furious fighting around Caen. Despite the spirited defence offered by the young Grenadiers, Allied air superiority and overwhelming superiority of ground forces soon saw the new division decimated. On 27 June Siegel's Kompanie had only four tanks left to face Allied armoured attacks around Cheux. Despite this, four Allied attacks were driven back with heavy losses. Siegel's tank was hit and he suffered severe burns to his hands and face. His wounds were severe enough to warrant hospitalization. In recognition of his gallantry in action against overwhelming enemy forces, Siegel was awarded the Knight's Cross of the Iron Cross on 23 August 1944.

On his return to the division, having recovered from his wounds, Siegel was given command of II Abteilung of the Panzer Regiment, in which post he remained until the end of the war. He saw much further action in the Ardennes Offensive and in Hungary during the closing stages of the war.

Siegel ended the war with the rank of SS-Sturmbannführer commanding the Panzer Regiment. His gallantry in action is attested to by his Knight's Cross and his Gold Wound Badge for having been wounded on no less than nine separate occasions. Hans Siegel survived the war and returned to a civilian career as an architect. He now lives in retirement in Herrenberg.

SS-HAUPTSTURMFÜHRER PAUL SENGHAS

Born on 31 January 1916 in Böttingen, the son of a senior police officer, Paul Senghas applied to join the SS on completion of his schooling and further education in 1935. He served during the Polish Campaign and the campaign in the west where he was decorated with the Iron Cross Second Class. When the invasion of the Soviet Union began in the summer of 1941, Senghas was posted to 5th SS-Panzer Grenadier Division Wiking, serving on the southern sector of the Eastern Front. In December 1941, he was promoted to SS-Scharführer and decorated with the Iron Cross First Class.

By now Senghas was becoming an accomplished tank commander and by the summer of 1943 he had been promoted to SS-Hauptscharführer. On achieving his 30th enemy tank destroyed he was decorated with the German Cross in Gold on 9 January 1943. He was also commissioned to SS-Untersturmführer. About eighteen months later, in December 1944, Senghas, by now an SS-Obersturmführer, was decorated with the Knight's Cross of the Iron Cross for his continued success and gallantry as Commander of 1 Kompanie, SS-Panzer Regiment 5 during the battles near Warsaw in August of that year.

On 20 January 1945, Paul Senghas was given a battlefield promotion to the rank of SS-Hauptsturmführer for gallantry in the face of the enemy.

During the retreat on the Eastern Front in April 1945, he was seriously wounded. Hit in the arm, thigh and foot, he was evacuated to a military hospital in Westphalia. Taken prisoner by the Americans, he was held in captivity until the summer of 1946 before being finally released. He is still alive.

HAUPTMANN BODO HEINRICH FERDINAND OTTO SPRANZ

Assault gun ace Bodo Spranz was born on 1 June 1920 in Nordhausen. On completion of his education he entered the Reichsarbeitsdienst in April 1938 for the usual six months' obligatory service. On 1 November after his release from Labout Service he joined the Army as an officer cadet with Artillerie Regiment 12, and served with this unit during the Polish Campaign. From late October 1939 until the end of January 1940 he attended a training course for potential officers at the Artillerieschule in Jüterbog, joining, on completion of the course, Artillerie Regiment 209 with the rank of Wachtmeister. With this new regiment he served in the French Campaign, winning the Iron Cross Second Class. In the summer of 1940 Spranz attended a further course at Jüterbog for conversion from towed artillery to assault guns. By the time he completed this course he had been commissioned Leutnant.

Awarded the Iron Cross First Class during the invasion of the Soviet Union in the summer of 1941, Spranz served with Sturmgeschütz Abteilung 185 as a battery commander. In March 1943 he was promoted to Oberleutnant and two months later was decorated with the German Cross in Gold. In August of that year, Spranz proved his gallantry in the face of the enemy by winning four awards for the single-handed destruction of a tank, using Teller mines and satchel charges.

In June 1943, Oberleutnant Spranz was posted as Commander of 1 Batterie, Sturmgeschütz Abteilung 237, still on the Eastern Front. In the space of just six days' intense fighting at the end of August 1943, he and his battery destroyed 61 tanks. In the battles around Smolensk in September 1943, Spranz and his Battery distinguished themselves in numerous defensive actions. He had already been nominated for the Knight's Cross of the Iron Cross when, in mid-September, he destroyed his 76th tank. This, along with his contribution to the battles around Jelnja, was considered sufficient justification for the recommendation for the Oakleaves. The Knight's Cross was approved on 3 October and the award was made a day later. The Oakleaves were also awarded on 8 October with approval backdated to 3 October. The two decorations were presented at the same time, making this one of the extremely rare occasions when a soldier was presented with a Knight's Cross and Oakleaves, rather than with a set of Oakleaves to go with an existing Knight's Cross. At the same time Spranz was also promoted to the rank of Hauptmann.

In April 1944, Hauptmann Spranz was posted as an instructor to the

Sturmgeschütz School at Burg, an appointment he held until December of that year when he was transferred again, this time as a staff officer at the Oberkommando des Heeres. In May 1945 he was taken prisoner by the Western Allies, but held for only five months before being released.

SS-OBERSTURMBANNFÜHRER CHRISTIAN TYCHSEN

One of the great tank heroes of the Waffen-SS, Christian Tychsen was born on 3 December 1910 in Flensburg in Schleswig-Holstein, the son of a cabinet-maker. At the age of 24 he entered I Bataillon, SS-Standarte Germania in Hamburg. He attended SS-Junkerschule Braunschweig and was commissioned as an SS-Untersturmführer.

By the outbreak of war Tychsen had been promoted to SS-Obersturm-führer and was serving with the Aufklärungs Abteilung of the Deutschland Standarte. He took part in the campaign in the west with the Kradschutzen-kompanie of the Abteilung, in the SS-Verfügungsdivision. During this period he won the Iron Cross Second Class, in May 1940 and the First Class in July. His Kompanie was then absorbed into the newly formed Kradschutzenbataillon of the SS Reich Division. By the time of the invasion of the Soviet Union in the summer of 1941, Tychsen had reached the rank of SS-Hauptsturmführer. His unit, as part of the division's reconnaissance arm was always in the forefront of the advance. Constantly in the thick of the action, Tychsen was wounded several times, earning the Wound Badge in Gold and receiving on 13 May 1942 the German Cross in Gold.

In the summer of 1942, the division was posted to France for rest and refitting and was renamed Das Reich. Tychsen's Kompanie was to be absorbed into the new SS-Panzer Regiment 2, which Tychsen was to command with his new rank of SS-Sturmbannführer. He led the Panzer Regiment with great success during the advance to Kharkov and again during its recapture in March. In recognition of his skilful leadership of the Regiment during this period he was decorated with the Kight's Cross of the Iron Cross on 31 March 1943.

Following the unsuccessful Operation 'Zitadelle' at Kursk, Soviet counter-attacks had recaptured Kiev and Kharkov and by November a fresh German counter-offensive was desperately trying to regain the initiative and halt the Soviet advance. Numerous localized battles raged with each side trying to gain the advantage. In early November massive Soviet attacks broke through the units on the flanks of the Das Reich Division. Tychsen, with a formation of his Panzer Regiment, took on the defence of the right flank to prevent its penetration by the Soviets. Only five tanks could be spared for this daunting task, but Tychsen had no hesitation, and contact with the enemy was soon made. A formation of three T-34 tanks appeared, of which Tychsen himself quickly accounted for two. His accompanying Combat Pioneers went into the attack and Tychsen added a further six T-34s to his tally. Holding his position against the Soviets until reinforcements arrived the next day, Tychsen played a leading role in the securing of the divisional flanks and displayed great personal courage. On 10 December, he was decorated with the Oakleaves to his Knight's Cross as the 353rd recipient of this distinction.

July 1944 found Tychsen and his regiment at Normandy, and on 28 July while on a recce trip his vehicle came under enemy fire. His driver was fatally wounded and his escaping orderly officer thought that Tychsen too had only been wounded. Assuming him to have been captured, Das Reich Division offered their American opponents twenty of their captured men in return for Tychsen. The enemy, however, knew nothing of his whereabouts and Tychsen was posted missing in action, a state of affairs which lasted for many years before his death was officially confirmed.

A cool, daring and indisputably brave front-line officer, adored by his men, Tychsen died a soldier's death on the field of battle in the service of his country.

LEUTNANT WILHELM WEGNER

Wilhelm Wegner was born on 21 October 1914 in Niederbarnim near Potsdam. He volunteered for military service and was accepted into Artillerie Regiment Schwerin in October 1934. After attending a training course for Army aerial observers he joined Artillerie Regiment 48 in Güstrow on 28 September 1939. Shortly afterwards he was transferred to Artillerie Lehr Regiment Jüterbog on a training course for conversion to assault guns, and subsequently joined Sturmgeschütz Batterie 640 on the Western Front. Wachtmeister Wegner earned the Iron Cross Second Class on 3 July 1940 on the Western Front and added the First class on 25 July 1941. On 30 November 1941 he was promoted to the rank of Oberwacht-meister.

While serving with 16 (Sturmgeschütz) Abteilung of the Infanterie Regiment Grossdeutschland on the Eastern Front, Wegner was decorated with the German Cross in Gold in April 1942. In March 1943, Wegner was serving as an Assault Gun Commander in the First Troop of the 1st Batterie of Sturmgeschütz Abteilung Grossdeutschland in the area around Kharkov. His unit was attacking towards Stamowje and came into contact with a superior force of T-34 tanks. Wegner determined to carry forward his advance despite the overwhelming enemy strength. Six T-34s fell to Wegner's gun as his unit cleared the way for troops of the Aufklärungs-abteilung to enter the town. Wegner held back the Russian tanks until his last round of ammunition was expended then retreated to resupply with ammunition and immediately returned to the fray. Once again his assault gun was instrumental in holding back the attacking tanks, reckoned to be at least forty strong, until relief in the form of a Tiger Tank unit arrived that evening. For his decisive part in the success of the operation, Wegner was recommended for the Knight's Cross of the Iron Cross. The award was approved and Wegner joined the ranks of the Ritterkreuzträger on 13 June 1943. Wegner remained with 1. Batterie until October 1944 when he was sent on an officer candidates' course and was commissioned Leutnant on 1 November 1944. That same month he was posted back to the Sturmgeschütz Brigade Grossdeutschland, this time to 3. Batterie. Panzerkorps Grossdeutschland was heavily involved in the defensive battles of 1944/45 on the Eastern Front and suffered dreadful casualties though the fighting spirit of this élite organization never faltered.

On 31 January 1945 Leutnant Wegner was seriously wounded and evacuated from the front. He was awarded the Golden Wounded Badge on 27 March 1945 and was taken into British captivity on 17 July 1945. He is still alive and now lives in retirement in Emsdetten.

SS-OBERSTURMBANNFÜHRER HANS WEISS

Born on 28 August 1911 in Vöhringen, Weiss was the son of a brewery worker. After leaving school he too went into the brewing trade before joining the SS in 1933. Commissioned SS-Untersturmführer in 1935, on the outbreak of war he served in the Polish Campaign in an SS-Aufklärungsabteilung, winning the Iron Cross Second Class. During the invasion of France in 1940, Weiss served in the SS-Verfügungsdivision, winning the Iron Cross First Class. In the Balkan Campaign, he commanded the Panzeraufklärungskompanie in SS-Aufklärungsabteilung 2. The Verfügungsdivision ultimately evolved into 2nd SS Panzer Division Das Reich with which Weiss served on the Eastern Front.

In early 1943, Weiss took part in the battle to recapture Kharkov, by now as SS-Hauptsturmführer in command of the Aufklärungsabteilung. In recognition of his part in this successful battle, Weiss was awarded the Knight's Cross of the Iron Cross on 6 April 1943. During the battle Weiss and his men had captured six tanks, 30 heavy artillery pieces and numerous anti-tank weapons.

The heavy Kompanie of SS-Panzer Regiment 2 evolved into an independent schwere Panzer Abteilung, numbered 502. During the battles following the Allied invasion of Normandy, Weiss, by this time an SS-Obersturmbannführer, commanded this Abteilung, equipped with the Tiger tank. During the battle for the Falaise pocket, on 19 August 1944 Weiss suffered a severe head wound. At the same time a bullet perforated his lung and yet another bullet damaged his pelvis. He was subsequently taken prisoner by the British and survived the war. Weiss died in August 1978.

HAUPTMANN MAXIMILIAN WIRSCHING

Born on 23 November 1919 in Altenschonbach, Max Wirsching completed his education in March 1939 and after his service period in the Reichsarbeitsdienst began his military career when he joined Panzer Regiment 4 on 1 September 1939, as a Fahnenjunker. Panzer Regiment 4 was a component of 2nd Panzer Division, which was originally raised in 1935 and was composed mainly of Austrians.

In 1940 the division, which had suffered considerable losses during the Polish campaign, became part of Guderian's XIX (motorized) Korps in the attack on France. Wirsching saw his first combat action with the division at this time as a tank commander. The division achieved great success in its drive through France, capturing Abbeville and reaching the English Channel in May 1940.

In the latter part of 1940, after the fall of France, several of the Panzer divisions were reorganized. Panzer Regiment 4 was transferred to 13th Panzer Division, located in Roumania. The regiment took part in the invasion of the Soviet Union in the summer of 1941, and saw constant heavy combat action.

On 14 July 1941 Wirsching, who had now been commissioned as a Leutnant, was awarded the Iron Cross Second Class. He served as Zugführer and Regimental Orderly Officer, seeing action at Kiev and Rostov, before the defensive battles following the Soviet winter offensive of 1941–2. On 17 September 1941 Wirsching won the Iron Cross First Class. During 1942 the regiment was on the offensive again during the drive through the Caucasus.

On 2 February 1943, Wirsching was promoted to Oberleutnant and it was during 1943 that he joined the recently formed schwere Panzer Abteilung 507. Raised in Vienna in September 1943, this unit drew many of its cadre personnel from 13th Panzer Division. 507 was equipped with the deadly Tiger tank and saw its first combat action around Tarnopol and Brody in the spring of 1944. When the Soviet summer offensive of 1944 broke with all its fury on Heeresgruppe Mitte, the Abteilung played an important role in the defence of the central sector of the Front, fighting alongside 4th Panzer Division. The commander of 4th Panzer Division, Generalmajor Clemens Betzel, was fulsome in his praise of the Abteilung's efforts, sending a special communiqué to the division, which he concluded with the following message: 'I wish schwere Panzer Abteilung 507 soldierly good luck for the future and express to Major Schmidt, the Commander, and all his brave crews, my and my Division's thanks and appreciation.'

On 7 July 1944, Max Wirsching was decorated with the Honour Roll Clasp of the Army following the addition of his name to the Roll of Honour for his dedicated service during this period. From November 1944 to mid January 1945 507 lay in reserve on the Narew bridgehead. On 14 January the Soviets launched a massive offensive on that sector of the front. Marshal Rokossovsky's 2nd White Russian Front fell upon the 7th Infanterie

Division which 507 was supporting. While deep penetrations were made in other areas, the sector held by 507 remained firm and a ferocious two-day battle threw the Soviets back. The Tigers of 507 knocked out 66 enemy tanks. On the third day a massive artillery and air attack still failed to move the Germans. Eventually, only a deep penetration of the flanks forced a withdrawal by 507. Even now, during the retreat, the Tigers claimed 70 enemy tanks bringing a total of 136 victories in three days.

On 19 January 1945, an Army Communiqué was released: 'The schwere Panzer Abteilung 507 has, under the leadership of Oberleutnant Wirsching, in the area Zichenau-Praschnitz in three days of fighting, destroyed 136 enemy tanks, including 66 in the last two days alone, without losing a single Tiger.' Command had passed to Wirsching on the serious wounding of the Abteilung commander, Hauptmann Fritz Schöck.

For his action Max Wirsching was decorated with the Knight's Cross on 7 February 1945, although the award was not actually received until 4 April. On 1 March 1945 Wirsching was promoted to Hauptmann and appointed deputy commander of a schwere Panzerjäger Abteilung. At the end of April, he was wounded for the ninth time and hospitalized. Still in hospital when the war ended, Wirsching escaped from the Soviet Zone in July 1945 and safely reached the west. From 1946 to 1950 he studied dentistry, qualifying as a Doctor of dental medicine and now has his own practice.

As well as his Iron Crosses, MaxWirsching was decorated with the Wound Badges in Black, Silver and Gold and the Knight's Grade of the Order of the Crown of Roumania with Swords.

SS-HAUPTSTURMFÜHRER MICHAEL WITTMANN

The greatest tank ace in history, Michael Wittmann, was born on 22 April 1914 in Vogelthal, Oberpfalz. His father, Johann Wittmann, was a local farmer and after completing his education, Michael worked for his father for a short time. In February 1934, he joined the Freiwilligearbeitsdienst or FAD. This was the forerunner of the compulsory Reichsarbeitsdienst. After six months' labour service he returned to his father's farm until October when he enlisted in the Army, joining Infanterie Regiment 19. After completing his two years of military service he was discharged in September 1936 with the rank of Gefreiter.

Wittmann volunteered for the SS on 1 April 1937 and was accepted into the élite Leibstandarte Adolf Hitler. As a trained soldier the military aspects of the training posed no problems for Wittmann. The stress on comradeship between all ranks during his SS training no doubt contributed greatly to the moulding of the young Wittmann's character.

On the outbreak of war in 1939 Wittmann was an SS-Unterscharführer and saw action in the Polish and western campaigns in an armoured unit. When Hitler's armies invaded the Soviet Union in June 1941, Wittmann was serving in the Sturmgeschütz Abteilung of the Leibstandarte. Under

XIV Panzer Korps on the southern sector of the front, the Leibstandarte was in the thick of the action and Wittmann's Sturmgeschütz Abteilung saw heavy action where he quickly gained a reputation for being cool-headed and determined. Earning the Iron Cross Second Class on 12 July 1941, a few weeks later he was wounded for the first time, winning the Wound Badge in Black on 20 August 1941. The Iron Cross First Class followed shortly afterwards, on 8 September, and on 21 November 1941 he qualified for the Panzer Assault Badge.

During one engagement when he came under attack from eight enemy tanks, Wittmann coolly dispatched six of them. This sort of determined courage was not to go overlooked and Wittmann was selected to attend an officer candidates' course at the SS-Junkerschule Bad Tölz in Bavaria in July 1942. Successfully completing his training he was commissioned in December 1942 as an SS-Untersturmführer.

At the beginning of 1943 Wittmann was assigned to 13 (schwere) Kompanie of SS Panzer Regiment 1. He had exchanged his Sturmgeschütz for one of the world's most deadly weapons, the Tiger tank. He applied the same skills and determination in his command of a Tiger as he had with his Sturmgeschütz. On the first day of the great tank battle at Kursk alone, Wittmann knocked out eight enemy tanks and seven artillery pieces. By the end of that ill-fated offensive, Wittmann had added 30 enemy tanks and 28 guns to his ever-mounting score.

One one day in late autumn 1943, Wittmann destroyed ten tanks in a single engagement, bringing his score to 66 tanks destroyed. The Press release which was issued at the time of the award of the Knight's Cross of the Iron Cross to Wittmann on 14 January 1944 refers to Wittmann and his troop of Tigers preventing the breakthrough of an entire Soviet Armoured Brigade on 8/9 January 1944. Many of Wittmann's comrades felt that his award had been long delayed, but if he had waited over long for the Knight's Cross, the Oakleaves were much quicker in coming. On 31 January 1944 Wittmann received a telegram informing him that the Oakleaves had been awarded on the previous day. It read: 'In thankful appreciation of your heroic actions in the battle for the future of our people, I award you, as the 380th soldier of the German Wehrmacht, the Oakleaves to the Knight's Cross of the Iron Cross. Adolf Hitler.' Wittmann was also granted a much-deserved promotion to SS-Obersturmführer. In April 1944, he became Commander of 1 Kompanie schwere SS-Panzer Abteilung 501.

It was during the Allied invasion of Normandy in June 1944 that Wittmann was to earn his place in military history. His name has become so much associated with his formidable weapon that one can hardly mention the Tiger tank without thinking of this great ace.

The Tiger tank, designed by Professor Ferdinand Porsche, was a formidable weapon. Its low speed and poor manoeuvrability made it a rather inadequate offensive weapon, but in defence, as a form of mobile pillbox, it was nearly invincible. None of the standard Allied tanks in Normandy was a match for this monster. Its frontal armour was all but impenetrable. In the hands of an ace such as Wittmann, the Tiger was truly an awesome weapon. Allied tank troops would become almost paranoid in their fear of this terrible beast.

Stationed at Beauvais at the time of the invasion, schwere SS-Panzer Abteilung 501 did not reach the front until 12 June. On 13 June Wittmann took a force of four Tigers and a Panzer Mk IV on a reconnaissance of the battle area. At Villers-Bocage he spotted a number of armoured vehicles advancing towards the German lines. Wittmann entered the town from behind the British vehicles and quickly knocked out three of four Cromwell tanks he encountered. Passing through the town he encountered Sherman Firefly tanks armed with the fearsome 17-pounder gun. Seeing that he was outnumbered, Wittmann withdrew through the town only to find that the remaining Cromwell had been stalking *him*. Two shots at almost point-blank range from the Cromwell merely bounced off the Tiger's thick armour plating and Wittmann coolly eliminated the Cromwell.

After rejoining the rest of his force and replenishing his ammunition, Wittmann moved against a British armoured column at the far end of the town. Approaching under cover of a wood, he knocked out the lead and tail vehicles and then calmly proceeded to destroy the entire column of about 25 armoured vehicles. He then withdrew through Villers-Bocage with the rest of his force, but British tanks were lying in ambush and succeeded in getting in a flank shot against his Tiger, disabling it. Wittmann and his crew were able to escape on foot. The British poured petrol over Wittmann's Tiger and set it on fire to prevent its recovery.

Wittmann's actions on that day prevented the British armoured thrust which threatened to encircle Panzer Lehr Division. Its commander, General Fritz Bayerlein, immediately recommended Wittmann for the award of the Swords to his Knight's Cross. The original recommendation document for the Swords was signed by the Commander of the Leibstandarte Adolf Hitler, SS-Obergruppenführer und Panzer Genral der Waffen-SS, Sepp Dietrich, and included the following report on the action:

'Headquarters 1 SS Panzer Korps   Korps Field HQ 13 June 1944
Leibstandarte
On 12 June 1944, SS-Obersturmführer Wittmann was ordered to secure the left flank of the Korps near Villers-Bocage, because of growing reports that British armoured forces had broken through and were pushing to the south and south-east. Wittmann set off at the appointed time with 6 Tigers. In the night of 12/13 June 1944 Wittmann's Kompanie had to change its position several times due to heavy artillery bombardments, but in the early hours of 13 January Wittmann had 5 Tigers ready for action by Hill 213 north-east of Villers-Bocage.

At 0800 hrs a report reached Wittmann that a strong column of enemy armour was proceeding along the Caen to Villers-Bocage road. Wittmann with his Tiger concealed under cover 200m south of the road knew that the British armoured battalion would be accompanied by armoured personnel carriers.

The situation required immediate action and Wittmann struck right away, firing on the move, into the British column. His swift action trapped the British column. From a distance of 80m he destroyed 4 Sherman tanks than travelled along the length of the column at a distance of only 10 to 30m and succeeded in destroying a further 15 enemy armoured vehicles. A further 6 tanks were hit and their crews forced to abandon them. The leading armoured personnel carriers were quickly destroyed. The accompanying tanks from Wittmann's Kompanie took 230 prisoners.

Wittmann then raced ahead of his Kompanie into the village of Villers-Bocage. In the town centre his tank was struck by an enemy anti-tank shell and disabled. Nevertheless he destroyed all enemy vehicles within range before abandoning his tank. He and his crew struck out on foot approximately 15km north towards the Panzer Lehr Division where he reported the action to the Divisional Staff Officer . . . Through his determined act, against an enemy deep behind his own lines, acting alone and on his own initiative with great personal gallantry, with his tank he destroyed the greater part of the British 22nd Armoured Brigade and saved the entire front of the 1 SS-Panzer Korps from the imminent danger which threatened. The Korps at the time had no reserves available.

With today's battle, Wittmann has destroyed a total of 138 enemy tanks and 132 anti-tank guns.

> signed Dietrich
> SS-Obergruppenführer
> und Panzer General der Waffen-SS

The Swords were awarded on 22 June 1944 and a few days later Wittmann was promoted to SS-Hauptsturmführer. Offered a transfer to a non-combatant post at a training school, where the benefit of his vast experience could be passed on to future Panzer soldiers, Wittmann refused, preferring to remain with his comrades.

On 8 August the Abteilung, attached to the remnants of the battered 12th SS-Panzer Division Hitlerjugend, was ordered to capture the village of Cintheaux in order to protect the Division's flank. Engaging M4 Shermans of the Canadian 4th Armoured Division, a battle ensued which lasted several hours until Panthers from 12th SS Panzer Division arrived and Cintheaux was finally captured. That evening Wittmann was reported missing and eyewitness accounts report that he had engaged five Shermans at one time and had taken hits from all sides. Even the mighty Tiger could not withstand such punishment. Wittmann's Tiger exploded and he and his entire crew were killed. Wittmann's remains were undiscovered until 1987 when a road-widening operation uncovered his unmarked grave. He is now buried at the Soldatenfriedhof at La Cambe.

Michael Wittmann was the most successful tank commander in history and had the honour of receiving the Knight's Cross, Oakleaves and Swords all within five months. His total recorded score was 138 tanks and 132 guns in a period of less than two years.

Never the flash, daredevil type, Michael Wittmann was a quiet, thoughtful man much admired and esteemed by his comrades and very highly regarded by his superiors. His unquestionable skill and personal gallantry have assured him a well-deserved place in the annals of military history.

Mention should also be made of Wittmann's gunlayer, Balthasar Woll. In no small way did Woll contribute to Wittmann's success, so much so that he was awarded the Knight's Cross on 16 January 1944. At the time of Wittmann's death Woll had command of his own Tiger. He survived the war and is still alive at the time of writing.

THE AIR ACES

Although Germany could boast a considerable number of great U-boat aces and many superb Panzer and assault gun aces, there can be no doubt that it is the air ace who captured the imagination of the public. These young daredevils, often fighting in solo combat against their adversaries, seemed to recapture the ideals of medieval chivalry, and indeed, in the early part of the war there may have been some chivalry; some pilots might decline to administer the *coup de grâce* to an opponent whom they knew was finished.

During the Second World War Germany's great air aces exceeded all previous records of combat success and set new goals which may never be surpassed, except perhaps by the Israelis. The greats such as Hartmann, Barkhorn, Marseille, Graf, Gollob and Galland achieved scores which are almost unbelievable. Indeed, for several years after the war, serious doubts were expressed over the scores these aces had claimed, and it has been thought that they had been artificially inflated for propaganda purposes. Post-war research and comparison with admitted Allied losses has shown that some of these claims were accurate, and in some cases possibly understated.

The German system of verifying kills was far more stringent that that used by any of the Allies, so accepting that the Luftwaffe's kill claims were accurate, how is that the claims of the Luftwaffe aces exceeded those of the Allies? More than 5,000 German pilots were considered to be aces, having shot down at least five aircraft. There are in fact several contributory factors which can be considered.

The aircraft
There is no doubt that the Luftwaffe fielded some of the finest aircraft in the world at that time. In 1939 the Me 109E could outmatch any aircraft in the world with the possible exception of a Spitfire in the hands of a first-rate pilot. As the war progressed, the Me109 evolved through the F, G and K Marks. As the aircraft of the Allies improved, so did the Me 109. It was nearing the end of its day, however, and there was a limit to how much it could be improved, many of the top aces preferred the Me 109 to any other aircraft including the Me 262 jet. Likewise the Focke-Wulf Fw 190A, a formidable fighter in its own right, was further developed into the magnificent 190D long-nosed version, which few Allied fighters could match, and ultimately into the Ta 152, a high-altitude interceptor. Had Hitler refrained from interfering in aircraft production, it is likely that even more advanced types would have seen service. As it was, the most important aircraft to emerge from the war, the Messerschmitt Me 262 jet, was virtually

completely wasted. A magnificent aircraft, far superior to anything at that time, its deployment was subjected to Hitler's erratic moods. With Hitler's insistence that it be used to carry two 550kg bombs, its superior speed was so reduced that any advantage it had over Allied piston-engined aircraft was completely negated. By the time that Hitler relented and allowed its use as a fighter, it was too late. Although the first Marks flew as early as 1941, it did not come into operational service until 1944. Had development been concentrated on the basic fighter model and the aircraft put into production earlier, the Luftwaffe might well have regained control of the skies over Europe. As it was, those that did reach service, although they performed superbly, were much hampered by lack of fuel and insufficient pilot training. If fuel was short for combat operations, it was even scarcer for training flights. It must be said that at almost any point during the war, on a one to one basis, an experienced Luftwaffe pilot flying any of the major fighter types, was the equal of any of his Allied counterparts. The Luftwaffe ace was rarely let down by the quality of his aircraft.

Combat service
The average Luftwaffe pilot did not have the advantages of a tour-of-duty type service. The majority spent almost the entire war on front-line duty, broken only by short periods of home leave as and when they could be spared, which was seldom indeed. Occasionally a decision would be made to withdraw a particularly successful ace from front-line service and transfer him to a post as an instructor when it was felt that the disadvantage to national morale in a famous ace being killed would outweigh the advantages of his staying in combat service. Few such aces could adapt to such a posting, however, and most managed to arrange a return to their units. Of course towards the end of the war, desperate shortages of trained pilots meant that every man was needed at the front. Clearly though, for whatever reason, the average Luftwaffe fighter pilot flew far more combat missions that his Allied counterpart.

The pilots
Logically, taking into consideration a pilot flying a top-quality aircraft, on a far larger number of combat missions than his Allied counterpart, it seems quite likely that he would have the opportunity to achieve more kills. This, however, cannot even begin to explain scores such as Hartmann's 350 on the Eastern Front or Galland's 104, all scored on the Western Front. Clearly, a great deal of the credit must go to the quality of the training received by the Luftwaffe's pilots and of course to the pilots themselves. At the end of the day it is difficult to avoid the conclusion that the average Luftwaffe pilot was quite simply *better* than his adversaries.

The Luftwaffe's system of verifying kill claims was very strict indeed and precluded any large-scale exaggeration of claims. Each victory was supposed to be verified by at least one ground and one air witness, unless of course the kill took place over German-held territory and the wreckage of the downed aircraft provided irrefutable proof that a kill had been made. Alternatively, if the pilot or crew of the enemy aircraft succeeded in baling out and safely reaching the ground and were taken prisoner, this would also be acceptable evidence that a kill had been made. Each victory claim, with its supporting paperwork had to be submitted to the Air Ministry for final confirmation. The pilot's Geschwader would then be advised that the claim had been approved, and the pilot advised of his confirmed kill. No one could accuse the Luftwaffe of not being thorough.

Similarly, where two aircraft combined to shoot down an enemy, only one could be credited with the kill. There was no such thing as a shared kill in the Luftwaffe. In the case of dispute, the Geschwader itself rather than the individual pilot, would be given credit. With reasonable certainty, therefore, that only one credit was ever given for one plane destroyed, and no shared kills or probables being credited, it is in fact more likely that many scores claimed and approved were in fact understated rather than exaggerated.

It is significant that from 1939 to 1945, German fighters claimed approximately 25,000 victories against the Western Allies. Admitted Allied losses, however, were in the region of 40,000. Clearly then, German kill claims were *not* exaggerated in any way. On the Eastern Front, about 45,000 kills were claimed. No official enemy loss figures are available, but some sources suggest that at least 75,000 may have been lost from 1941 to 1945.

The losses sustained by the Jagdwaffe or Fighter Force during the period towards the end of the war were quite horrendous. Due to lack of manpower, poorly trained pilots were rushed into combat before they were anything like ready, having very few flying hours to their credit. Lack of fuel precluded extensive flying training. Even worse, during the closing stages of the war, lack of fuel for combat operations meant that many pilots were squandered in infantry operations, in vain attempts to hold back the ever-advancing Allies.

A total of about 25,000 fighter pilots were either killed, wounded or reported missing in action, and well over twice that number of aircraft lost. In view of these factors it is little short of astonishing that aces such as Hartmann could continue to fly combat missions and achieve such a level of success right up to the closing days of the war. With more than 5,000 German pilots entitled to the status of ace, having scored five or more victories, clearly it would have been impossible for the Ritterkreuz to be awarded for this achievement alone. This high decoration was retained for much greater feats. During the first two years of the war when the bulk of the combat flying by the Luftwaffe's pilots was against the tough opposition of the RAF with its excellent Hurricane and Spitfire fighters, the number of victories required for the Knight's Cross reflected the difficulty of these combat encounters in comparison with what was to come. A score of about twenty victories was normally required at this time.

Following the invasion of the Soviet Union where, in the early days at least, victories were easily had, many pilots were able to run up exceptionally high scores. Clearly, a retention of the twenty score to bring the Knight's Cross would result in a severe devaluation of its status. The score was raised, initially to 25 and by the end of 1941 to 40. The difficulties faced by pilots still based on the Western Front were recognized by the retention of the twenty score requirement in this theatre of operations. Nearly ten times as many aces qualified for the Knight's Cross on the Eastern Front, indicating perhaps that even the 40 level might be considered rather easy.

By the end of 1942, the requirement had risen to 50 kills on the Eastern Front and anywhere between 30 and 40 in the west; but nearly ten times as many awards were still being won by the fighter pilots in the east. During the course of 1943, the requirements reached an all-time high of 100 on the Eastern Front, though this was subsequently lowered again to 75, a sign perhaps that more confident and accomplished Russian opponents were making victories harder to achieve. Soviet aircraft types were also much improved compared to those of 1941, and of course the Soviet forces could boast overwhelming numerical superiority. In addition, many pilots were being withdrawn from the Eastern Front to take part in the defence of the Reich from ever-increasing Allied bomber raids. The result was that, in 1943, less than half the number of awards made in 1942 were approved.

From 1943 onwards the situation was made even more confusing by the introduction of a points system. Obviously the shooting down of a heavily laden 4-engined bomber was of more benefit to Germany than the destruction of a single enemy fighter. For knocking out a 4-engined bomber or *Viermot*, three points were awarded as well as one victory. For crippling an enemy bomber and knocking it out of its formation, two points plus a kill were awarded, on the basis that such a disabled bomber flying over enemy territory was unlikely to reach safety. Finally, for administering the *coup de grâce* to a disabled enemy bomber, one point was given, but no kill. A total of 40 points was required for the award of the Knight's Cross. For example, by shooting down ten bombers and crippling five more, a pilot would achieve fifteen kills, but more importantly would acquire 40 points thus bringing the Knight's Cross. This may help to explain why pilots with a seemingly small total of kills were awarded the Knight's Cross, as the significant factor now was the type of aircraft downed. It should be borne in mind, however, that a tight formation of say, B-17 Flying Fortresses could put up a tremendous defensive crossfire and even shooting down one of these aircraft was a considerable achievement.

The rather glamorous image of the fighter pilot may well lead one to think that they may have received more than their fair share of the awards, and the limelight. In fact a total of only 538 awards of the Knight's Cross were made to fighter pilots as compared to 640 to bomber and assault pilots. Clearly the Knight's Crosses of the fighter arm were hard won and richly deserved. For night fighter pilots, the required score started at ten and gradually rose to a maximum of 25, indicating the difficulty of this form of combat as compared with day fighting.

The Oakleaves to the Knight's Cross required a score of 40 during the Battle of Britain period, rising to 60–70 in 1942, at which point the figure remained static. On the Eastern Front however, the figure rose to as high as 150. For the Swords, pilots on the Western Front initially required a score of 70, rising ultimately to about 100. On the Eastern Front, however, between 200 and 250 victories were required. The ultimate award, the Diamonds, was given for figures ranging from 94 and 101 victories (Galland and Mölders) to 172 and 301 (Graf and Hartmann). Each award recognized what was, at the time, an exceptional score. Strangely, however, Gerd Barkhorn, with a score of 301, surely deserved the Diamonds, but never received it.

The bomber/assault aces

In this category are included the bomber, dive-bomber and ground-assault pilots, who played an extremely important part in the fortunes of the Luftwaffe and accordingly numbered a considerable proportion of Knight's Cross winning aces in its ranks.

The dive-bomber and assault pilots certainly played a leading role in the opening battles of the war. The image of the predatory Stuka dive-bomber has become synonymous with the *Blitzkrieg* and, although obsolete even then, its effectiveness both actual and psychological was considerable. As early as the Norwegian Campaign in 1940, Stuka pilots were receiving the Knight's Cross for their contribution.

During the Battle of Britain, however, the slow and ungainly Stukas were easy prey for British fighters, and losses were so great that they had to be withdrawn from the battle. The Stuka was, however, used to considerable effect on the Eastern Front and during the Mediterranean Campaign. Indeed, the most highly decorated pilot in history, Hans Ulrich Rudel, flew a Stuka for most of his combat career, and the conversion of later Marks into successful tank-busters proved the versatility of this venerable aircraft. Later in the war, most of the Stuka units were re-equipped with the superb Focke-Wulf Fw 190 fighter-bomber.

The assault pilots (*Schlachtflieger*) flew low-level ground support missions and were initially equipped with such aircraft as the Henschel Hs 123 biplane, achieving considerable success in the Polish and French Campaigns. Later, squadrons of Me 109 fighters and the twin-engined Henschel Hs 129 were added, and used to good effect during the great tank battle at Kursk.

By 1943, the *Schlachtflieger* were being re-equipped with the Focke-Wulf Fw 90 fighter-bomber which, with the Hs 129 tank-buster, made a deadly combination. Although the principal role of both the dive-bombers and assault pilots was in ground attack and close support, several pilots also achieved considerable numbers of aerial victories, some even exceeding the score of 100 aircraft destroyed.

Germany's bomber pilots began the war with aircraft which could certainly hold their own in comparison with Allied types. The Heinkel 111, Junkers Ju 88 and Dorner Do 17 all giving sterling service in one guise or another. During the night assault on Great Britain, however, it became clear that these aircraft had an inadequate bomb-carrying capability. While the Allies developed superb heavy bombers, such as the Lancaster, Halifax,

Flying Fortress and Liberator, which were to wreak such terrible havoc on Germany, German bomber design stagnated.

The excellent Focke-Wulf Fw 200-C Condor proved itself to be an excellent maritime reconnaissance bomber, but was not suitable for the type of night-bombing raids with massive payloads which the Allies could deliver. The only purpose-built heavy bomber to be put into service was the huge Heinkel He 177 Greif. A promising type with many innovative features, it had many teething troubles including an alarming tendency for its engines to catch fire. Germany did have a greater level of success in anti-shipping strikes with, in addition to the excellent Condor, the Junkers Ju 88 giving excellent service.

Clearly, a bomber or dive-bomber pilot would be unlikely to achieve ace status in the sense of shooting down enemy fighters, though as stated, some *Schlachtflieger* did, thanks mainly to their excellent Fw 190s. Bomber and dive-bomber pilots therefore tended to be rewarded for completing a particular number of successful missions. No hard and fast number seems to have been set, and occasionally, awards would be made for, for example, sinking a large enemy ship in the same way as a successful U-boat ace might be awarded the Knight's Cross for sinking a single important enemy.

An overall view was taken of the successes achieved by an individual pilot in conjunction with the number of combat missions flown. Initial awards tended to be to unit commanders in recognition of the achievements of their Geschwader. However, as individual pilots began to run up sizeable tallies of missions flown, these were taken into account. Most Knight's Cross winners in the first half of the war had flown somewhere between 100–300 missions.

Again, on the Eastern Front the bomber pilots found things easier than on the Western Front and found themselves flying many more missions before winning the Knight's Cross. By 1944, most Knight's Cross winners had flown between 500–600 missions.

For those flying tank-busting missions, a score of between 50 and 60 tanks destroyed seemed a rough norm for the award of the Knight's Cross. With mission counts being taken as a yardstick for its award, clearly the other crew members as well as the pilot would qualify, and although the pilot was considered the most important crew member, some radio-operators were also decorated. Hans Ulrich Rudel's radio operator, Erwin Henschel, had flown nearly 1,500 missions, and was decorated with the Knight's Cross on Rudel's recommendation.

Oakleaves and Swords and Oakleaves clasps were only rarely awarded to these individual pilots, being normally approved for unit commanders. An example of this being Major Friedrich Lang of Schlachtgeschwader 1 who was awarded the Swords on 2 July after having flown 1,000 missions, and Major Theodor Nordmann of Schlachtgeschwader 3, receiving the Swords in September 1944 after flying 1,140 missions.

Losses in the bomber and assault forces were considerable and many fine pilots were killed before they could complete sufficient missions to qualify for the Knight's Cross. Those who did survive to complete large numbers of missions and gain the Knight's Cross were invariably pilots of the very highest calibre, richly deserving their award and the status of ace.

OBERFELDWEBEL GÜNTHER BAHR

Night fighter ace Günther Bahr was born in Königsberg in East Prussia on 18 July 1921. As a boy he had always had an interest in flight and was a keen aircraft and glider modeller. At the age of 14 he attended glider flying lessons and qualified for his glider pilot's licence, grade C, this being the top grade. He joined the Luftwaffe in October 1938 and after completing his basic training and qualifying for his pilot's licence, he served with Ausbildungsgruppe II of the Zerstörer School at Schleissheim as a flying instructor.

From the end of 1941 until May 1942 Bahr served as a pilot with Schlachtkampfgruppe 210 on the Eastern Front where he scored his first combat victory, shooting down a Soviet R5. Like so many of his contemporaries who had began their careers as Zerstörer pilots, he went on to train as a night fighter pilot. Initially he joined Nachtjagdgeschwader 4 and in August 1943 transferred to 1/Nachtjagdgeschwader 6. He was decorated with the German Cross in Gold in October 1944.

On one occasion, during the night of 28 January 1945, Bahr shot down three American B-17 and 1 B-24 Liberator bombers from a massive bomber raid over Munich. This was only one of several multiple kills made by Bahr. On the night of 21/22 February 1945, he destroyed seven bombers within just 29 minutes of savage combat. Flying Fortresses, Liberators, Lancasters and Halifaxes all fell victim to Bahr's guns. On 28 March 1945, he was decorated with the Knight's Cross of the Iron Cross. He was also a recipient of the Honour Roll Clasp of the Luftwaffe.

Bahr modestly rejects any suggestion of heroism and puts his success down to good training and fast reactions. After the war, he went into the motor trade and worked for Ford in Germany. In 1960 he attended officer school and was taken into the Luftwaffe as a Leutnant. In 1962 he was promoted to Oberleutnant and assigned to the Heeresfliegertruppe of the Bundeswehr, serving variously as Einsatzoffizier, Staffelkapitän, Flieger Technisches Stabsoffizier and Flugplatzkommandant. After two years as a staff officer with a Divisional Staff, he was granted an extension to his service and went on to become Commander of Heeresflugplatz Kommandantur 103, Rhein-Bentlage, before retiring in 1975 with the rank of Major.

After his retirement from military service, Bahr worked in Iran for several years. From 1981 to 1984 he fulfilled a long-held ambition and constructed his own 60-foot yacht in steel and has successfully covered nearly 20,000 sea miles in his own vessel. Bahr emigrated to Canada in 1984, where he now lives near Alberta.

OBERSTLEUTNANT HEINZ BÄR

One of Germany's most experienced fighter aces, 'Pritzl' Bär was born in Sommerfeld near Leipzig in March 1913. A farmer's son, Bär had a youthful interest in gliding, like so many of his contemporaries. Qualifying as a pilot of powered aircraft in 1930, his initial aspirations were towards becoming a civil pilot with the state airline Lufthansa, but his lack of a commerical pilot's licence prevented this. Instead, in 1937, he joined the Luftwaffe, intending to use his military training as a stepping-stone towards obtaining his civil licence.

The outbreak of war in 1939 put paid to such prospects and found Bär as a Sergeant Pilot. On 25 September 1939, he scored his first victory, the first of many. His considerable experience in combat against RAF pilots, gained in serving throughout the Battle of Britain with Jagdgeschwader 51, was to stand him in good stead in later years. Bär often staggered home with his Me 109 severely battered after fierce dogfights. His service during this period earned him a commission to the rank of Leutnant. He was decorated with the Knight's Cross on 2 July 1941 after his score reached 27 aircraft destroyed.

Jagdgeschwader 51 was posted to the Eastern Front for Operation 'Barbarossa' and during the early part of the war in the east Bär found the Russians easier prey than the RAF pilots and his tally of kills grew steadily. By 14 August 1941, Bär, now an Oberleutnant, had reached his 60th victory, bringing him the Oakleaves to his Knight's Cross. On 30 August he shot down six Soviet aircraft in a single day. His daredevil attitude often put him in positions of great danger. On one occasion, shortly after the award of the Oakleaves, he pursued an enemy aircraft well behind Soviet lines and was himself shot down. Bailing out he landed heavily and suffered a double fracture of the spine. In agony he stealthily made his way through enemy-held territory back to his own lines, a distance of more than 50 kilometres. On reaching the German lines he was hospitalized for several months to recover from his spinal injuries.

Returning to the front after his recovery, Bär once again began to run up his score. On 16 February 1942, he added the Swords to his Oakleaves after scoring his 90th victory while serving as a Hauptmann, still with Jagdgeschwader 51. Shortly thereafter, in the spring of 1942, he was promoted to Major and Kommodore of Jagdgeschwader 77 which was serving in Sicily. With his new Geschwader, he saw much action on the North African Front and the Mediterranean, and was involved in the furious German air assault on Malta. A further 45 victories were added to his score during this period, all achieved against the Western Allies. Bär commanded Jagdgeschwader 1 and Jagdgeschwader 3 during the air defence of Germany, and achieved his 200th kill in April 1944.

Bär became a jet fighter pilot in January 1945 when he took command of Lechfeld Jet Fighter School. After a period training other pilots, he returned to combat flying with Galland's Jagdverbande 44, the 'Squadron of Experts'. He became the most successful of the jet aces, scoring sixteen victories with the excellent Me 262. He became Commander of Jagdverband 44 in the closing days of the war.

Bär was undoubtedly one of Germany's finest pilots. Beginning his combat career as a Feldwebel, he ended the war as an Oberstleutnant with a total score of 220 aircraft destroyed in the course of well over 1,000 missions. Most of his victories were against the Western Allies. No stranger to danger, he was himself shot down eighteen times.

After the war, Bär became involved with civil sports flying. On 28 April 1957, while demonstrating a light aircraft near Brunswick, he crashed to his death.

MAJOR GERHARD BARKHORN

One of the fighter arm's most charismatic figures, Gerd Barkhorn was born on 20 March 1919 in Königsberg, East Prussia. When war broke out in 1939 Barkhorn was already a qualified pilot. Like several of his contemporaries, he took some time before achieving his first combat victory. During the early stages he flew with Jagdgeschwader Richthofen before transferring to Jagdgeschwader 52 in August 1940. Barkhorn flew throughout the Battle of Britain without scoring a single kill.

Barkhorn had more than 100 missions to his credit when Jagdgeschwader 52 was transferred to the Eastern Front in July 1941, and on 2 July scored his first victory. His score rose steadily thereafter. His highest score in a single sortie was four kills, in July 1942. On 23 August 1942 Barkhorn was decorated with the Knight's Cross of the Iron Cross after scoring his 59th victory. The award of the German Cross in Gold followed on 7 September 1941.

Favouring the Messerschmitt Me 109F over all other German fighters, including the excellent Focke-Wulf Fw 190 and the Me 262 jet, Barkhorn flew his favourite fighter against all the major Allied types, He had a healthy respect for the pilots of the Red Airforce, and some of their better aircraft, such as the Yak-9, certainly gave him trouble. Barkhorn himself was shot down nine times.

Oberleutnant Barkhorn was decorated with the Oakleaves on 12 January 1943 after scoring his 175th victory. The requirement of such a high score for the Oakleaves is some indication of the variation in the scoring required for the higher decorations. Galland was awarded the Diamonds after 94 victories, Marseille after 126 and Gollob after 150. On 2 March 1944, while still serving with Jagdgeschwader 52 as a Hauptmann, Barkhorn received the Swords following his 250th victory. He was the 52nd recipient of this coveted decoration. In January 1945 Barkhorn reached two milestones in his career, his 300th victory and his departure from his beloved Jagdgeschwader 52. After a short spell with Jagdgeschwader 6 on the Western Front and conversion training for jets, Barkhorn joined Galland's Jagdverbande 44, flying the Messerschmitt Me 262.

On only his second mission, one of his engines failed during an attack on an American bomber force. Returning his crippled fighter to his base he was attacked by P-51D Mustang fighters and forced down. He spent the rest of the war in hospital recovering from his injuries. Ending the war with the rank of Major, Barkhorn had flown 1,100 missions and scored a total of 301 kills, making him the second highest-scoring ace in history. He rejoined the Bundesluftwaffe in 1955 and was retrained in jet flying by the RAF. He ultimately reached the rank of Generalmajor before finally retiring.

An immensely popular figure and one of the most chivalrous of men, the esteem in which he was held by his peers can be judged by the opinion expressed by the greatest ace of them all, Erich Hartmann, who described Barkhorn as the commander of whom every fighter pilot dreamed: 'Leader, friend, comrade, father – the best I ever met.'

MAJOR WILHELM BATZ

Wilhelm Batz was born in Bamberg on 21 May 1916. He joined the fledgling Luftwaffe in 1935. Despite his obvious desire to become a fighter pilot, his superiors had decided that he should be an instructor, and he took up these duties in 1937. The outbreak of war in 1939 brought no respite. The Luftwaffe at its peak strength did not feel that it required the transfer of key instructional personnel to combat duty. It was only in 1942 that Batz's continual pleas for a combat posting, coupled with manpower shortages due to combat losses, allowed his ambition to be achieved.

In December 1942, Batz joined II/Jagdgeschwader 52 on the Eastern Front. Although this was his first posting, Batz was already a superb pilot, with more than 5,000 flying hours to his credit. He was appointed Adjutant to Johannes Steinhoff. Despite his undoubted flying skills, he was unable to score any combat victories due to his terrible marksmanship. His frustration at his lack of success almost drove him to distraction and at one point, having decided that he would never make the grade as a fighter pilot, he applied for a transfer to bombers. Fortunately for the Luftwaffe, his request was denied and eventually, on 11 March 1943, he made his first kill.

When he was promoted to Oberleutnant in May 1943, he still had only that single kill, and his second did not come until June of that year. With several years of flying experience and six months' front-line combat duty on the Eastern Front, Batz was still not an official ace. Perseverance and determination paid off, however, and by the start of 1944, his score had reached fifteen. A modest score perhaps, but he was now an ace and there was to be no looking back, although nagging feelings of inadequacy persisted, as his comrades notched up victory after victory in rapid succession.

Suddenly, however, after spending a couple of weeks on sick leave, he returned to duty and found that, remarkably, everything clicked into place and victories started coming thick and fast. On 26 March 1944, Batz received the Knight's Cross of the Iron Cross having increased his score to a very respectable 75. On 3 April he added the German Cross in Gold to his decorations.

Batz was now shooting down considerable numbers of enemy aircraft. Outstanding in view of his previous lack of success, on one single day, 30 May 1944, he managed to shoot down fifteen aircraft. By 20 July 1944, Batz had increased his score to an amazing 175 victories. Considering that it took him sixteen months to reach the score of 75 for his Knight's Cross, the additional 100 scored in a period of just four months was little short of miraculous. This achievement brought him the Oakleaves to his Knight's Cross. He was the 526th recipient of this award. In August 1944, Batz achieved his best single day's shooting when he brought down sixteen aircraft in a single day's combat.

In June 1944, Batz became Kommandeur of III/Jagdgeschwader 52, taking over from fellow ace, Günther Rall. In January 1945, he was transferred to take command of II/Jagdgeschwader 52, based in Hungary. Though now a highly successful ace, his victories were not always easily come by. He himself was badly enough shot up to have to make forced landings on at least four occasions. On 21 April 1945, Batz was decorated with the Swords to his Oakleaves, the 145th recipient of this award. At the time he held the rank of Major and was still in command of II/Jagdgeschwader 52. His award was made in recognition of his score having exceeded 200.

Wilhelm Batz flew a total of 445 missions. He ended the war operating from a base in Austria. A final score of 237 victories included 2 4-engined bombers. From March 1944 until the end of the war, a period of just fourteen months, he had achieved 222 of his victories. He is the seventh highest-scoring ace in history, overcoming his initial difficulties to combine flying skill and marksmanship in spectacular fashion.

Batz returned to his military career when the West German Bundesluftwaffe was formed, and reached the rank of Oberst before retiring.

OBERST WERNER BAUMBACH

Bomber ace Werner Baumbach was born in the small town of Cloppenburg on 27 December 1916. An interest in flying from an early age led to his taking up gliding and qualifying for his glider pilot's licence. He joined the Luftwaffe at the age of 19 and in April 1936 began his training at the Luftwaffe Kriegsschule at Gatow, Berlin.

As a 22-year-old bomber pilot at the outbreak of war, Baumbach first saw combat during the attack on France and the Low Countries and during the Battle of Britain. His greatest successes were in attacks against enemy shipping in which he eventually scored a total of 300,000 tons sunk, bypassing even the scores of the great U-boat aces.

On 8 May 1940, Baumbach was decorated with the Knight's Cross of the Iron Cross as a Leutnant pilot with Kampfgeschwader 30. After the failure of the Battle of Britain, the Geschwader was transferred to Norway where it was used in attacks on Allied convoys to the Soviet Union, inflicting serious losses. With the rank of Oberleutnant, Baumbach was decorated with the Oakleaves on 14 July 1941. He was the twentieth recipient of this award and received the honour while an Oberleutnant with Kampfgeschwader 30. Success and promotion came quickly to this young bomber virtuoso. Just over a year after the award of the Oakleaves, he became the sixteenth recipient of the Swords, as Hauptmann and Commander of the Geschwader.

During late 1942, Baumbach saw active service in the Mediterranean theatre. This efficient and highly successful commander was appalled by the lack of organization he found. His Wing arrived at its base to find that no one knew it was coming and nothing had been prepared for them. He was constantly tasked with pointless missions, obviously ordered by someone with no knowledge of bomber tactics. Always an outspoken critic of bureaucratic bungling, Major Baumbach bypassed the usual channels and complained direct to the Chief of Staff of the Luftwaffe. His complaint had the desired effect, but unfortunately Göring did not like the idea of a young upstart Major trying to tell the High Command their job. He was removed from his command and Göring used one of his favourite ploys in promoting officers who had incurred his displeasure into backwater jobs where they would be less troublesome. Baumbach was posted to a research establishment testing new guided bombs.

Towards the end of the war, Baumbach was horrified at some of the desperate defensive measures proposed by the Nazi hierarchy. Together with Albert Speer he conspired to block attempts to organize a German version of Japan's *Kamikaze* pilots flying, among other things, a manned version of the V-1 flying bomb. Luckily, Baumbach managed to get access to Hitler who agreed that no German pilot should be sacrificed in missions with no hope of return.

Once again, in January 1945, Baumbach put his career, and indeed his life, on the line when he sent a personal memorandum to Reichsmarschall Göring in which, with no holds barred, he set out his frank opinions and complaints about the management of the war. It was all to no avail. Although no action was taken against Baumbach, his comments were simply ignored by Göring. Baumbach had several times rebuffed attempts to coerce him into making propaganda speeches and had been warned by the Gestapo about his unco-operative attitude. In view of the paranoia which raged throughout the leadership of the Third Reich during the closing months of the war, where any hint of defeatism could cost a man his life, Baumbach's strength of character was admirable. He later learned that there were indeed moves afoot to have him severely dealt with and he was very lucky to have escaped.

Baumbach was taken prisoner along with Dönitz and other senior officers. British soldiers stole all his decorations, including his Pilot-Observers' Badge with Diamonds. Fortunately the perpetrators were apprehended and in 1949 some of his decorations were returned.

In August 1945, Baumbach was charged as a war criminal in that his aircraft had allegedly machine-gunned survivors from attacks on shipping.

After long and exhaustive investigations it was established that the accusations were groundless. No proof was ever produced of any crimes committed by Baumbach or his men and he was released without a stain on his character.

In 1948 Baumbach emigrated to Argentina, where he worked in aircraft development. During a test flight in October 1953, his aircraft crashed in the mouth of the River Plate and he was drowned. Although his wartime experiences had rid him of any interests in militarism, his love of flying had endured to the end.

MAJOR ERNST BÖRNGEN

Born on 7 February 1916 in Meuselwitz, Thuringia, Ernst Börngen began his combat career in 1940 flying with III/Jagdgeschwader 27 on the Western Front and during the Battle of Britain.

When Jagdgeschwader 27 was transferred to North Africa, Börngen became Staffelkapitän of 5/Jagdgeschwader 27. He was decorated with the Knight's Cross of the Iron Cross on 7 March 1941 following his nineteenth victory. At this point in the war, as a general rule, approximately twenty victories were required for the award of the Knight's Cross. Later it would become, 50, 100 or even more. Börngen's nineteen victories were hard-won successes, scored against well-trained RAF pilots flying high-quality aircraft.

In Africa he was again successful against the RAF and during the latter half of the war, he became Gruppenkommandeur of I/Jagdgeschwader 27 in the defence of the Reich. He was himself shot down four times and three times severely wounded. On 19 May 1944 while flying his Messerschmitt Me 109 against an attacking bomber formation over Helmstedt, he rammed a 4-engined bomber. As his stricken fighter plummetted out of control from some 20,000 feet Börngen attempted to bale out but was struck by the aircraft's tailplane. His right arm was so damaged that it had to be amputated.

Börngen achieved a total of 45 victories of which 24 were 4-engined bombers, making him one of the most successful of the pilots involved in the defence of the Reich. He flew a total of 450 missions, and ended the war with the rank of Major and Gruppenkommandeur of Jagdgeschwader 27. After the war he attended the University of Munich, studying business management, graduating in 1953. Despite his handicap he had a long and successful career, as a manager, then as a director of a brewing company. Börngen retired and now lives in Augsburg.

LEUTNANT ARNOLD DÖRING

Arnold Döring was born on 29 January 1918, the son of School Inspector Anton Döring in Heilsberg, East Prussia. His family had a firm connection with aviation, with a grand-uncle involved in airship construction, and an uncle, Otto Porschau, who was one of the few East Prussian pilots to achieve ace status during the First World War, winning the coveted Pour le Mérite. Small wonder then that the young Arnold Döring was fascinated by flying and was a keen aeromodeller and later, a qualified glider pilot.

Döring completed his obligatory training with the Reichsarbeitsdienst in 1938 and on 1 October of that year volunteered for service with the Luftwaffe. After basic training with Flieger Ersatz Abteilung 10 in East Prussia, he joined 3/Jagdgeschwader 1 in Jesau, Königsberg, and there commenced his flight training. Further training was carried out at the Pilots' School in Neukuhren and Wiener-Neustadt and blind flying at Blindflug-schule 4 at Wien-Aspern. On completion of his training in 1940, Döring was posted as a Gefreiter to 9/Kampfgeschwader 53 Legion Condor in France. Thrown into action during the Battle of Britain, KG53 saw heavy combat and suffered considerable losses.

Subsequently posted to Poland in time for the opening phase of Operation 'Barbarossa', the attack on the Soviet Union, KG53 was located in the central sector of the front and saw action around Bialystock, Minsk, Orscha, Smolensk, Kiev, Orel, Moscow, and Byelgorod-Kursk during the winter battles of 1941–42. Gaining both the Second and First Class Iron Crosses during this period on the Eastern Front, Döring also received the Flight Clasp for Bomber Crews in Gold and the Luftwaffe Goblet of Honour for completing 115 missions against the enemy. At this point he was promoted to Unteroffizier.

Following further training and familiarization with newer variants of the Heinkel He 111 bomber, and testing of new bomb-sight apparatus, Döring was transferred to 8/KG55 in June 1942. With this unit, on the southern sector of the Eastern Front, Döring saw further action around Charkow, Isjum, Rostov, the Black Sea ports, the Kuban bridgehead, the Caucasus and the defensive actions around Stalingrad during the winter of 1942–43. During this period Döring was promoted to the rank of Oberfeldwebel and was eventually sent for officer training at Luftkriegsschule 4 in Fürstenfeld-bruck.

Following three night victories against Soviet 4-engined bombers with the He 111 in the vicinity of Stalingrad, Döring was posted on 18 August 1943 to the 'Wilde Sau' night fighter programme with 2/Jagdgeschwader 300 at Bonn-Hangelar where the Luftwaffe's early experimentation using the Me 109 as a night fighter in the defence of the Reich was progressing. On 1 October 1943 Döring was commissioned as a Leutnant. After the formation of 3/Jagdgeschwader 300 in Wiesbaden-Erbenheim in February 1944, Döring served for a short period as Squadron Leader of 7 Staffel and in

May 1944 was transferred at his own request to heavy night fighters with III/Nachtjagdgeschwader 2, flying the Junkers Ju 88. From November 1944 to April 1945 he served with IV/NJG 3 and in the closing days of the war with 10/NJG 3 operating from bases in Holland and Germany. After scoring two victories (his 19th and 20th respectively) against a British 1000-bomber raid, Leutnant Döring was awarded the Knight's Cross of the Iron Cross in 1945. By the war's end he had flown a total of 392 missions (348 in bombers) and had scored 23 victories. In addition he had destroyed in bombing missions, large numbers of tanks, vehicles, trains, guns, ammunition dumps, and sunk approximately 19,000 tons of shipping.

At the surrender Döring was taken into British captivity until his release in October 1945. In 1956, he rejoined the Luftwaffe of the West German Federal Republic and served with the Luftwaffe Training Regiment in Uetersen. From May 1958 to September 1963 he was a squadron leader with 4/Flying Training Regiment, where his combat experience was put to good use, training new pilots for the Bundeswehr. Arnold Döring retired in 1972 with the rank of Hauptmann.

MAJOR MARTIN DREWES

Night fighter ace Martin Drewes was born on 20 October 1918 near Braunschweig. His early military career was with the Army, having joined Panzer Regiment 6 in Neuruppen in November 1937. Drewes entered the Army as a Fahnenjunker or officer candidate and in October 1938 was sent to the Kriegsschule in Munich for his commissioning course. On 1 August 1939 he became a Leutnant. He transferred to the Luftwaffe in September 1939 and after basic flying training at Werder he attended blind flying school at Königsberg and training for destroyer pilots at Schleissheim.

As a Zerstörer (destroyer) pilot, flying the Messerschmitt Me 110, Drewes joined II/Zerstörergeschwader 76 in February 1941. This was the famous Haifischgruppe (Shark Group) whose insignia was the ferocious shark's mouth painted on the nose of its aircraft. This design was also adopted by the pilots of many US squadrons. At this time Zerstörergeschwader 76 was flying operations over the North Sea. In May 1941 Drewes was posted to the Middle East, and, from bases in Greece, flew operations over Iraq and Syria, and shot down his first enemy aircraft, a Gloster Gladiator biplane fighter. By July 1941, Drewes was back in Europe, once again flying operations over the North Sea. II/Zerstörergeschwader 76 was operating out of Leeuwarden in Holland at this time. On 1 November 1941, Drewes was promoted to Oberleutnant and posted to night fighter operations, training with III/Nachtjagdgeschwader 3 at Echterdingen. In January 1942, he joined 9/Nachtjagdgeschwader 3 which was involved in the night defence of the Hamburg area. From then on his score of night victories, the majority of which were 4-engined heavy bombers – notoriously difficult kills – grew steadily.

In February 1943, Drewes was promoted to Staffelkapitän of 7/
Nachtjagdgeschwader 3 which was operating from Copenhagen. He served
in this post until June 1943 when he transferred to IV/Nachtjagdeschwader
1 at Leeuwarden. Two months later he became Staffelkapitän of II/
Nachtjagdgeschwader 1. This was the most successful Nachtjagdgeschwader staffel of them all. February 1944 found Oberleutnant Drewes as
Commander of III/Nachtjagdgeschwader 1 whose principal areas of responsibility were Leeuwarden and Stoermede. Promoted to Hauptmann on 1
April 1944, he continued to build up his score and on 27 July 1944 was
awarded the Kight's Cross of the Iron Cross when his overall score reached
48.

Drewes remained with this top night fighter Geschwader until the end of
the war. On 1 December 1944 he was promoted to the rank of Major and
on 17 April 1945 received a telegram from Berlin which read: 'In grateful
appreciation of your heroic actions in the battle for the future of our people,
I award you, as the 839th soldier of the German Wehrmacht, the Oakleaves
to the Knight's Cross of the Iron Cross. Adolf Hitler.' Despite the valiant
efforts of Drewes and his pilots, however, the fate of Germany was sealed.
The Allies were suffering heavy losses, but the attrition rate among the
Luftwaffe's men and machines was crippling her defensive abilities, and
fuel supplies were rapidly running out. At the surrender in May 1945,
Drewes was still serving with Nachtjagdgeschwader 1, this time from the
airfield at Husum. He went into captivity and was held until February 1947.

Martin Drewes flew a total of 235 missions, scoring 50 victories against
4-engined bombers, 43 of which were night victories, and two victories
against fighters. He was the Luftwaffe's twentieth highest-scoring night
fighter ace. He is still alive, and lives in Brazil.

OBERST ALFRED DRUSCHEL

Born on 4 February 1917 in Bindsachsen, Alfred Druschel joined the
Luftwaffe in April 1936 as an officer cadet at the Air Warfare School in
Berlin. Commissioned Leutnant in 1938, he trained as an Observer at the
Kampffliegerschule in Tutow. On completion of his training he became a
staff officer for a short period before joining II (S)/Lehrgeschwader 2 in
November 1938. This unit flew the obsolescent but effective Henschel Hs
123 biplane during the Polish Campaign and the attack on France, achieving
considerable success in low-level ground-attack and strafing missions.
Druschel was awarded the Iron Cross Second Class in September 1939
during the Polish Campaign, and the First Class in May 1940 during the
French Campaign.

After the fall of France, Druschel flew attack missions on British shipping
in the Channel, and against targets in the United Kingdom. In the spring
of 1941 his unit was posted to the Balkans and in the summer of that year,
to the Russian Front where once again he achieved considerable success as

the Soviets fell back in disarray from the massive initial assault.

On 21 August 1941, Oberleutnant Druschel was decorated with the Knight's Cross of the Iron Cross, having flown more than 200 missions and having achieved ace status by shooting down seven aircraft. In the autumn of that year he became Staffelkapitän of 2/Schlachtgeschwader 1. In early 1942 he joined 1/Schlachtgeschwader 1. This unit was heavily involved in action in almost all of the major operations in the central and southern sectors of the Eastern Front. So much so that by September 1942, Druschel, now a Hauptmann, had flown more than 600 missions. This brought him, on 3 September 1942, the Oakleaves to his Knight's Cross. Just one month later, his mission count had risen to 700.

On 19 February 1943, the Swords were added to Druschel's Oakleaves. In the following month, Druschel was promoted to Major and appointed Kommodore of Schlachtgeschwader 1. His personal and unit success continued and was rewarded by his promotion to the post of Inspector of Day Assault Units, on the staff of the General of Assault Forces. He was promoted to Oberstleutnant in April 1944.

From Christmas Day 1944 the remaining Schlachtgeschwader in the west were thrown into a massed attack on Allied airfields, Operation 'Bodenplatz'. This operation, intended to support Hitler's offensive in the Ardennes by neutralizing Allied air support, was able to achieve considerable success. However, the Allies were able to make good their losses quite quickly whereas the irreplaceable losses suffered by the Luftwaffe sounded its death-knell.

On 1 January 1945, Druschel, in his Focke-Wulf Fw 190 was involved in an attack on an Allied airfield when his aircraft was reported as being hit by Flak. He is thought to have crashed somewhere south of Aachen, but his remains were never discovered. Druschel had flown approximately 800 missions and was posthumously promoted to Oberst.

MAJOR GEORG-PETER EDER

This chivalrous Knight of the Air was born on 8 March 1921 in Frankfurt. In 1938 he jointed the Luftwaffe at the age of 17 as an officer candidate. On the outbreak of war he was halfway through his pilot training. Obtaining his pilot's wings in April 1940, Eder was posted to fighters. One year after the start of the war, Eder joined Jagdgeschwader 51, his first combat posting.

Although he flew during the Battle of Britain, he failed to score any victories. Transferring to the Eastern Front with Jagdgeschwader 51 in the summer of 1941, he scored his first two victories on the first day of hostilities against the Soviet Union. During the next four weeks Eder began to run up a number of kills before being shot down himself on 24 July. Seriously wounded, he was hospitalized for three months before being posted to the Jagdfliegerschule at Zerbst where he served as a Squadron Leader until being posted to Jagdgeschwader 2 in February 1942.

Eder earned a considerable reputation as an experienced *Viermot* killer. It took a tremendous degree of courage to attack a concentrated bomber formation, where the combined defensive firepower was a daunting thought even to the bravest. Eder was responsible for pioneering a head-on method of attack, tearing into the enemy formation at tremendous speed. This was a dangerous ploy, as evidenced by the fact that Eder himself was shot down seventeen times and wounded fourteen times. Spurning superstition, Eder flew an aircraft with the number 13 and soon became well known for this idiosyncrasy. Eder also began to earn an admirable reputation as a chivalrous adversary. On numerous occasions having disabled enemy bombers he refused to make the kill when his enemy was defenceless, or until the crew had baled out. Soon, Allied pilots began to refer to Eder as lucky 13, knowing that even if their aircraft was struck a mortal blow by the German, they would be given every chance to bale out to safety before the final kill was made.

Eder joined Jagdgeschwader 1 Oesau in March 1943. While serving with this élite unit, he scored his 49th victory, bringing the award of the Knight's Cross on 24 June 1944. In October 1944 he was picked by Adolf Galland to join his select band of aces flying the Messerschmitt Me 262 jet. Eder scored at least twelve kills with this formidable fighter. On 25 November he added the Oakleaves to his Knight's Cross. His total score was 78 aircraft and three tanks. As well as shooting down aircraft in combat, Eder was also responsible for the destruction of many aircraft on the ground. In one attack on an Allied airfield during the Ardennes Offensive, Eder, flying the Me 262, destroyed 40 American Thunderbolt fighters.

The end of the war found Eder in hospital recovering from wounds. In view of his own chivalrous conduct during the war, his treatment by his British captors was very unfortunate. His ill-treatment reduced this fit young fighter ace to an emaciated shadow of his former self. Their interrogation of him in their quest for information on the superb jet fighter was excessive by any terms. He was released in 1946, and became a successful businessman in Frankfurt. He died in March 1986.

Although his total score may seem modest in comparison with some other aces, it is none the less impressive in the number of 4-engined bombers destroyed. Eder also achieved the status of fourth highest-scoring jet fighter ace. Ironically it was his chivalrous attitude to combat which probably contributed to his score being kept at a modest level, as compared to his peers. Nevertheless, Georg-Peter Eder was indeed one of the Luftwaffe's greatest aces.

MAJOR HEINRICH EHRLER

Born in Oberbalbach on 14 September 1917, Heinrich Ehrler was one of Germany's most successful fighter aces before tragedy struck his career in September 1944 when he was held to be responsible for the loss of the Kriegsmarine's last remaining capital ship, *Tirpitz*.

Initially Ehrler served with the anti-aircraft arm and only transferred to flying duties in 1940. Ehrler served principally on the far north front with Jagdgeschwader 5, the Eismeer Geschwader. By 1942 he had command of 6/Jagdgeschwader 5 and on 21 October 1942 he was decorated with the Knight's Cross of the Iron Cross following his 41st victory. On 12 April 1943 Ehrler was promoted to command III/Jagdgeschwader 5. His personal score continued to grow steadily and by 2 August had reached 112 victories. This achievement brought him the award of the Oakleaves to his Knight's Cross. At this point he held the rank of Hauptmann and was the 265th recipient of the Oakleaves.

His proficiency as a fighter pilot brought Ehrler an ever-increasing score and in 1944 he was nominated for the Swords. Fate intervened, however, and brought disaster to Germany and to Ehrler personally. The battleship *Tirpitz*, sister to the ill-fated *Bismarck* had been moored in Tromso Fiord after sustaining such damage in an RAF raid that she could not be made seaworthy again. For some reason the ship was moored in fairly deep water rather than in the shallows. This was to be a fatal error. The RAF's famous 'Dam Busters' of 617 Squadron launched an attack on *Tirpitz* with massive 6-ton 'Tallboy' bombs on 12 November 1944. The attack was deadly accurate and *Tirpitz*, fatally damaged, capsized. Although her status as a floating fortress meant a smaller than normal complement, more than 1,000 seamen died.

At nearby Bardufoss was a fighter element from Jagdgeschwader 5 tasked with the defence of *Tirpitz*. Although given plenty of warning of the impending attack, no fighters responded to *Tirpitz*'s calls for assistance. As Major Ehrler was Wing Commander of Jagdgeschwader 5 he was held personally responsible for the disaster. At the time of the attack Ehrler was said to have been on unofficial leave, visiting a lady friend in Oslo and could not be contacted. Charged with dereliction of duty he was court-martialled and found guilty. Sentenced to death, Ehrler was reprieved because of his exemplary war record and his undoubted personal bravery. From that day on however, Erhler was a broken man. With more than 1,000 German lives on his conscience, he became little more than an automaton, a shadow of his former self.

Deprived of his command, he was posted to Jagdgeschwader 7 which at this time was flying the Messerschmitt Me 262 jet fighter. Ehrler scored at least five kills with the Me 262, becoming one of only 23 pilots to achieve ace status on jet fighters. His heart was no longer in his flying, however, and on 4 April 1945 his jet was attacked by five American P-51 Mustang fighters and shot down. Under normal circumstances, an ace of Ehrler's stature, flying the Me 262 would have had no real problem either disposing of, or avoiding the Americans. Notwithstanding the *Tirpitz* fiasco, Ehrler was an accomplished ace with a total of 209 victories to his credit, making him the tenth most successful ace in history. The award of the Swords for which he was recommended would surely have been approved had it not been for the *Tirpitz* incident for which he was made a convenient scapegoat. NOTE. Some dispute exists over Ehrler's total score. Certainly at least 204, some sources credit him with as many as 220, making him the eighth ranking Luftwaffe ace.

OBERST WOLFGANG FALCK

At first glance Falck may seem an odd choice for inclusion in a book about aces. Certainly there are hundreds of Luftwaffe pilots who achieved far greater scores than his. Indeed with only seven confirmed kills, Falck only just qualifies for ace status. However, such was his influence in pioneering the art of night fighting and such were his own personal qualities of gallantry and chivalry that his name is still held in the same high regard as the greatest of the Luftwaffe's high-scoring aces.

A Berliner, born on 19 August 1910, Falck was one of the few soldiers to have been taught to fly with the Reichswehr, the Armed Forces of the Weimar Republic. By the time Hitler came to power, Falck was already a trained fighter pilot, thanks to secret agreements between Germany and the Soviet Union by which German pilots were trained in Russia by the Red Airforce.

Initially with the famous Richthofen Fighter Wing, Falck was posted to Me 110s shortly before the outbreak of war. He served in the Polish Campaign and was involved in the first real clash with the RAF in December 1939 when his unit attacked a force of Wellington bombers raiding Wilhelmshaven. The Me 110s easily drove off the British and the resultant publicity given to this affair by the German propaganda machine made Falck famous overnight. This publicity did his career no harm whatsoever and shortly afterwards he was appointed to command I/Zerstörergeschwader 1.

At this point Falck joined the pioneers of night fighting. Angry at their inability to hit back at British bombers during night raids, Falck and his men took off after the departing bombers. Although none of the bombers was shot down in the action, all the German pilots landed safely, with no radar or radio communications, thus proving at least that the Me 110 had good potential as a night fighter.

Although he was subsequently posted to the Western Front to take part in the attack on France, his report on the night action resulted in his appointment to join a night fighter force, on the conclusion of the French Campaign. Personally appointed Kommodore of Nachtjagdgeschwader 1 by Göring while still only a Hauptmann, Falck became the first ever Kommodore of such low rank. During these early days Falck found little co-operation from those who disagreed with his ideas. When one particularly obstinate Flak Oberst began to insult his pilots, Falck recommended that he be taken up in an Me 110 to experience night fighting for himself. The Oberst declined, but thereafter ceased his criticism and became much more co-operative.

As Falck's night fighter tactics developed and successes mounted, General Kammhuber (then an Oberst) was posted to take command of the coordination of Radar, Searchlight and Flight Operations. This team did sterling work over the next three years, but growing differences of opinion eventually led to the parting of the ways for the two night fighter experts.

From 1943 until July 1944 Falck was given command of the Fighter Defence of the Reich, but he yearned for a posting to flying duties again, and his old friend General der Jagdflieger Adolf Galland organized a posting for him as commander of fighter units in the Balkans. This was the perfect answer for Falck, but the fates were against him. On the very day that he arrived at his new Belgrade HQ, Roumania changed sides and went over to the Russians. With the enemy rapidly closing in, Falck evacuated his command to Austria.

Subsequently, Falck was appointed to command all flight training. At this stage of the war there was little enough fuel for combat operations, let alone flying training, so this new posting was not a happy one for Falck. During the closing weeks of the war, Falck was made Commander of Fighter Units in the Rhineland. In the chaos of the closing days, Falck was touring around trying to establish accurate locations of his staff and HQ when he was captured by US troops. His endearing personality and charisma made an immediate impact on his captors and within a few weeks he was a free man thanks to the connivance of friendly US Military Police and Intelligence Officers. Soon afterwards, Falck became an employee of the British, supervising German civilians employed by the Royal Engineers on demolition and reconstruction work. He was eventually employed by McDonell Douglas Aircraft as their German representative and became a highly successful businessman.

Falck had been decorated with the Knight's Cross of the Iron Cross on 1 October 1940, despite his lowly score. Technically speaking, he was ace, but more importantly he was an ace maker, his development of Nachtjagd-geschwader 1 being responsible for the successful careers of many of the great night fighter aces. Falck was one of the war's true gentlemen. On many occasions he entertained shot-down RAF bomber crews in his unit Mess, and made many friends of former enemies.

OBERFELDWEBEL JOSEF FLÖGEL

Josef Flögel was born on 19 October 1919 in Weigelsdorf, the son of a Gasthof owner. An early interest in flying led to his becoming a member of the NSFK, the National Socialist Flying Corps. It was in this organization, together with the Flieger Hitlerjugend, that many of Germany's future aces were initially trained. Under the guise of glider and sport flying, these pilots gained the flying skills and experience which would help make them formidable fighter pilots in later years.

Flögel served with 3/Nachtschlachtgruppe 5 on the Eastern Front, having seen previous service with fighter units, and also having been a flying instructor for a short time. 3/Nachtschlachtgruppe 5 was created in 1943 and its principal task was to fly night attacks to harass Soviet-held positions and supply routes. The unit's aircraft were generally obsolete or obsolescent types such as the two-seater Arado Ar 66, an unarmed training plane, or the Gotha Go 145, a two-seater biplane trainer not unlike the RAF's old Tiger Moth in appearance. Interestingly, an entire Staffel of these biplanes were flown by former Soviet POWs who had volunteered to serve with the Luftwaffe.

After 1944, when the Luftwaffe's Ju 87 Stuka units were gradually being re-equipped with the excellent Focke-Wulf Fw 190, the Stukas were used to upgrade the Nachtschlachtgruppen and the effectiveness of these units improved dramatically. Until then their effect had been one of lowering enemy morale by constant night attacks, rather than by the amount of physical damage they caused.

Flögel was a much admired pilot within his Gruppe, having gained a considerable reputation as a cool and dependable pilot. On occasion he had flown as many as eighteen sorties in a single night. Josef Flögel was decorated with the German Cross in Gold on 5 February 1944. He was also a holder of the Flight Clasp for Schlachtflieger in Gold. Nachtschlacht-gruppe 5 also possessed a number of Fieseler Storch communications aircraft. In the early part of February 1945, when the Red Army offensive into Hungary had cut off the Germans garrisoned there, Nachtschlacht-gruppe 5's Fieseler Storch were used to fly communication and supply missions into the Budapest pocket. Given the strength of Soviet air power at this point in the war, these slow-flying aircraft had little chance if intercepted by Soviet fighters, yet achieved considerable success. For his part in these missions, Josef Flögel was decorated with the Knight's Cross of the Iron Cross on 19 February 1945. The official communiqué read:

> 'The Führer has awarded the Knight's Cross of the Iron Cross to Oberfeld-webel Josef Flögel, from Weigelsdorf, Kreis Trautenau, pilot in a Nachtsch-lachtgruppe. Oberfeldwebel Flögel has personally flown 625 missions as a Nachtschlachtflieger and has distinguished himself among others in the Kuban bridgehead, in the Crimea, in fortress Sevastopol and latterly in the battle for Budapest.'

The award was approved four days after Flögel had actually been captured by the Soviets in Budapest. Flögel was also decorated with the Luftwaffe Goblet of Honour for special achievement in the air war.

GENERALLEUTNANT ADOLF GALLAND

Adolf Galland was born on 19 March 1912 in Westerholt in Westphalia, Like many of his contemporaries, he had an early interest in flying and began his career through gliding, which was an immensely popular sport in Germany in the 1930s. His career in military flying commenced with 'civil' training in Germany, and also in Italy and the Soviet Union, both of which were training German military airmen in secret.

By April 1935, Galland, now a qualified pilot, was posted to Jagdgeschwader 2 Richthofen. The outbreak of the Spanish Civil War found him volunteering for action with the Condor Legion. Flying the obsolete Heinkel He 51 biplane against the Loyalist forces armed with up-to-date Soviet and American aircraft, Galland and his squadron were used primarily in a ground support role. When he was posted back to Germany, his replacement was none other than Werner Mölders.

Galland's study of tactics and operations in Spain, and the reports he submitted thereon, led to a staff posting at the Air Ministry. Desk work, however, was anathema to him and he was greatly relieved to be released for flying duties once again in late 1938. Once again, however, his duties were in the ground support role, flying Henschel Hs 123 biplanes.

On the outbreak of war, Galland's unit performed well during the invasion of Poland, Galland winning the Iron Cross Second Class. Despite his success in the ground attack role, he was determined to be a fighter pilot and with the help of a friendly doctor feigned rheumatism which resulted in his being restricted to closed cockpit flying (the Henschel Hs 123 had an open cockpit). In effect, this meant a transfer to fighters for Galland.

On 12 May 1940, Hauptmann Galland, now flying on the Western Front with Jagdgeschwader 27, scored his first victory, an RAF Hurricane. From then on his score rose steadily. From 12 May to 9 June 1940, he shot down twelve enemy aircraft. In June 1940, he was posted to Jagdgeschwader 26 Schlageter whose notorious yellow-nosed Messerschmitt fighters were well known to the RAF. Promoted to Major on 1 August 1940, he was decorated with the Knight's Cross of the Iron Cross on the 8th, having achieved a total of seventeen victories. Appointed Kommodore of Jagdgeschwader 26 on 22 August, he served with this famous unit throughout the Battle of Britain. By September 1940, his score had reached 40, and on the 25th of that month he was summoned to the Reichskanzlei where Hitler personally awarded him the Oakleaves to his Knight's Cross. He was only the third recipient of this award. On 1 November 1940, after achieving kill number 50, Galland was promoted to the rank of Oberstleutnant. On 21 June 1941, he received the Swords after his 69th victory, having narrowly escaped death himself when his Me 109 was bounced by a Spitfire and shot down.

On 9 August 1941, a pilot from Jagdgeschwader 26 shot down the legless British ace Douglas Bader. The chivalrous pilots of Schlageter invited Bader to their airfield where he was the guest of the unit Mess. Afterwards he was allowed to sit at the controls of an Me 109. Galland presented him with a box of his own cigars before he was taken to a POW camp, and also arranged with Göring that safe passage be granted to an RAF aircraft to drop a replacement set of artificial legs for Bader, who had lost his when bailing out of his stricken aircraft. Indeed the British sent over a plane to drop the legs, but somewhat unchivalrously in the circumstances, dropped bombs on the same mission. After the war, Galland and Bader became good friends.

On 4 December 1941, Galland was promoted to Oberst. His victory tally continued to grow and on 28 January 1942, his score reached 94, bringing him the Diamonds as only the second recipient of this rare award. Some of these initial awards of the Diamonds were in fact standard sets of solid silver Swords and Oakleaves in which had been set numerous small diamonds. It is interesting to note that Göring, on seeing the Diamonds which Galland had received, was furious, insisting that the piece was sub-standard. Göring told Hitler of this, being annoyed that Germany's highest award should be anything other than perfect. He then arranged for a replacement set to be made, as did Hitler, each unaware that the other had done the same. Galland therefore ended up with several sets. Then when his Diamonds were lost during an air raid, Göring had yet another set made.

After the death of his good friend, Werner Mölders, Galland was nominated General der Jagdflieger and in November 1942 he was promoted to the rank of Generalmajor, at the age of just 29. Once again he found himself with a hated desk job. His enemies were not now the pilots of the RAF, but the bureaucrats on his own side, and the in-fighting and back-stabbing with which he had to contend.

As Germany's fortunes began to wane, the Fighter Arm was often used as a convenient scapegoat on which almost anything could be blamed. Unbelievably, Hitler insisted that bombers be given priority, so that revenge could be extracted for the Allied bombing offensive on Germany. As Göring succumbed more and more to his drug addiction, he became little more than a yes-man in Hitler's entourage. He gave Galland little or no moral support, and on more than one occasion had the audacity to accuse the Fighter Arm of cowardice. Considering the heavy losses sustained by the Fighters in the face of overwhelming odds, it is not surprising that Galland had numerous vehement confrontations with his Commander-in-Chief.

On 22 May 1943, Galland had witnessed the test flight of the Messerschmitt Me 262 jet and was greatly impressed. Having test-flown the aircraft himself, Galland felt that even at this stage of the war, Germany might just be able to regain the initiative if the new fighter were put into volume production. Hitler, however, irrationally insisted that the new jet be used as a bomber, slowing it down so much that its speed advantage over Allied fighters would be totally lost. Galland argued forcefully against this and many other of Hitler's decisions, making himself very unpopular with the Nazi hierarchy. Galland would be nobody's yes-man. Galland took the side of his fighter pilot comrades to the last. He eventually fell from favour and was dismissed as General der Jagdflieger in January 1945.

Hitler then insisted that Galland form a new jet fighter unit and prove his contentions about its use as a fighter rather than a bomber, or die in the attempt. Far from being upset by the intended slight, Galland was delighted to return to combat flying again. Generalleutnant Galland joined Jagdverbande 44 flying the Me 262. This so-called squadron of experts, most of whom were highly experienced aces and holders of the Knight's Cross, included such men as Günther Lützow, Johannes Steinhoff, Gerd Barkhorn and Walter Krupinski. These were fitting comrades for Galland as he and his squadron fought through the closing stages of the war.

Adolf Galland achieved a total score of 104 enemy aircraft destroyed, in more than 700 missions flown. Considering that for more than two years Galland was in a staff posting and that all his victories were achieved against pilots of the Western Allies, his achievements were outstanding. He scored seven victories flying the Me 262 and will probably never be bested as the highest scoring jet ace with the rank of General. He was held as a POW for two years and on his release in 1947, accepted a contract to help build the Argentinian Air Force. He returned to Germany eight years later and became a successful businessman.

Few aces from any country have earned so much international respect and esteem as has Adolf Galland. Wherever former fighter pilots gather, he is welcomed as a friend. After the war he struck up a close personal friendship with British ace, Bob Stanford-Tuck. While his personal score has been surpassed by several other aces, his total achievements during his military career were unequalled.

OBERST HERMANN GRAF

Born in 1912 in the town of Engen to a blacksmith's family, Hermann Graf was to become one of the Luftwaffe's greatest aces. Lack of money meant that his schooling was rather modest. Because of his lack of academic qualifications he had no opportunity to take up a formal career in military flying, but he became an accomplished glider pilot in his early twenties and by 1936 had acquired his civil pilot's licence for powered aircraft.

On completing his training he worked as a local government clerk until the outbreak of war. As a qualified pilot he was a natural choice for induction into the Luftwaffe which he joined in 1938 at the age of 26. Initially given the rank of Oberfeldwebel, on completion of his training he was commissioned Leutnant. Although still a young man, Graf was old compared to many of his comrades, and his early career was singularly unspectacular.

Despite serving in the western campaign and in the Mediterranean, he did not achieve his first victory until August 1941 when serving on the Eastern Front with 9/Jagdgeschwader 52. From then on his career was little short of meteoric. A mere thirteen months later he was one of Germany's top aces and a holder of the coveted Diamonds.

Only five months after his first victory, on 24 January 1942, Graf was awarded the Knight's Cross of the Iron Cross on achieving his 42nd victory. Just four months after this, in May 1942, he had raised his score to 104, bringing the award of the Oakleaves, and just two days after the Oakleaves were awarded, the Swords followed on 19 May 1942. He was the 11th recipient of this decoration, and at that time his score stood at 106. Graf was only the seventh Luftwaffe pilot to exceed the score of 100.

He showed great skill, and his cool-headed attitude in combat brought him many superb achievements. Shooting down 47 enemy aircraft within a 17-day period was only one of these. On 16 September 1942, he became the fifth recipient of his country's highest award, the Diamonds. From the beginning of September to the beginning of October, Graf destroyed 75 aircraft and on 2 October became the first ace in history to reach a score of 200 aircraft destroyed. From November 1943 to April 1944, Graf served with Jagdgeschwader 11 in the defence of the Reich before returning to Jagdgeschwader 52 as Kommodore. He shot down ten 4-engined bombers, bringing his personal score to 212. By the end of the war, Graf held the rank of Oberst. He surrendered to the Americans, but was handed over to the Russians and spent five years in captivity. A considerate and helpful leader, Graf was well liked by his men and admired by his peers. In captivity, however, his attitude towards the Soviets, to some seeming no more than healthy realism now that the war was over, to others seemed close to collaboration and he lost the friendship of many of the fighter pilot fraternity. His true comrades were understanding, however, and Graf is still considered to be one of the true greats by many of the Luftwaffe's top aces. After a long illness Hermann Graf died in 1988.

MAJOR HARTMANN GRASSER

An Austrian, Hartmann Grasser was born in Graz on 23 August 1914, and began his flying career at the age of 20. He qualified as a pilot at the Neustadt pilot's school. Grasser became a Fahnenjunker in 1936 at the aerial warfare school and was commissioned Leutnant in 1938. Inducted into the German Luftwaffe in that same year after the Anschluss, Grasser was serving as a pilot with II/Zerstörergeschwader 52 at the outbreak of war. During the French Campaign he served with II/Zerstörergeschwader 2 and with this unit became an ace during the Battle of Britain. Although the Messerschmitt Me 110, which equipped the Zerstörergeschwader, was to become an excellent night fighter, it was totally outclassed during the Battle of Britain by the Spitfires and Hurricanes of the RAF. At one stage this twin-engined fighter had to be given a fighter escort itself. For a pilot to achieve ace status with the Me 110 during the Battle of Britain was quite a considerable success.

In February 1941, Grasser was transferred to the staff of Jagdgeschwader 51, and served as adjutant to Werner Mölders. When Jagdgeschwader 51 was transferred to the Eastern Front, Grasser was given command of II/Jagdgeschwader 51. At the start of the campaign in June, Grasser had scored seven victories. Just three months later his score had risen to 29, bringing him the Knight's Cross of the Iron Cross.

Grasser commanded II/Jagdgeschwader 51 when it was detached from the Geschwader and sent to North Africa. Although the combat in this theatre against British and American pilots was a different and much more difficult affair than that against the Red Airforce, at least during the early part of the war, Grasser had managed to increase his score to 103 by 31 August 1943, thus earning the Oakleaves to his Knight's Cross.

Following the award of the Oakleaves, Grasser was posted to France where he served as Jagdfliegerkommandant, Paris. Subsequently, he served with Jagdgeschwader 1 Oesau before being posted to Galland's staff where his efforts were instrumental in helping to rebuild Germany's depleted fighter reserves. His efforts were to be in vain, however, as Hitler squandered the reserves as soon as he discovered them.

Posted as Kommodore to Jagdgeschwader 210, Grasser ended the war with the rank of Major. He had flown 700 missions and scored 103 victories, seventeen in the west and 86 on the Eastern Front. Despite having surrendered to the Western Allies, he was handed over to the Russians and spent four years in prison camps under the harshest conditions.

On his release in 1949, a disillusioned Grasser determined never to wear uniform again. His interest in flying continued unabated, however, and in 1949 he moved to India where he became an instructor for civil pilots. Later he was an adviser to the Syrian Air Force before returning to Germany and a career in industry. Unlike many of his comrades who rejoined the new Bundesluftwaffe of the German Federal Republic, Grasser refused when offered the command of a fighter wing.

A gallant and chivalrous officer, Hartmann Grasser earned the respect and admiration of his peers and richly deserved his status as one of Germany's great aces.

MAJOR ERICH HARTMANN

Erich Hartmann was born in Weissach on 19 April 1922, and saw his first combat posting in October 1942, at the age of just 20. This is particularly significant when considering his score, as it means that he did not take part in the opening stages of Operation 'Barbarossa' when many Luftwaffe aces ran up huge scores against their inadequately trained and equipped Soviet adversaries.

Hartmann's performance with his squadron, the renowned Jagdgeschwader 52, was initially less than impressive. His commander, however, top ace Walter Krupinski, coached him with consideration and patience and Hartmann's confidence and ability grew. By April 1943, after seven months with Jagdgeschwader 52 Hartmann had shot down seven aircraft making him an official ace. This score was only achieved after 100 missions, hardly the stuff of which great aces are made. With growing experience, his natural skills as a marksman and his daring method of closing right up to the enemy before firing, began to pay off. By July 1943 his score had risen to 34 and by the end of his first year on the Eastern Front his score was approaching 100 victories.

In one single month, August 1943, Hartmann shot down 49 enemy aircraft and in September of that same year, 25. On 29 October 1943, Leutnant Erich Hartmann was decorated with the Knight's Cross of the Iron Cross after scoring his 148th victory. His score rose rapidly and by 2

March 1944, just over four months later, his tally stood at 200, bringing him the award of the coveted Oakleaves to his Knight's Cross. In July 1944, Hartmann joined the exalted ranks of the *Schwerntträger* as the Swords were added to his Oakleaves after his 239th victory, Hartmann was the 75th recipient of this high honour. His success, however, was to work against him in some ways. His fearsome reputation among Soviet pilots, who dubbed him 'The Black Devil of the Ukraine', resulted in their avoiding combat with him. His distinctively painted Messerschmitt Me 109 with its large tulip design on the nose, was easily recognizable. Hartmann had to paint out his distinctive insignia in order to get a chance to increase his score.

That score now rose appreciably until on 25 August 1944 his 301st victory brought him the award of his country's highest decoration, the Diamonds to his Knight's Cross. He was the 17th of only 28 recipients of this ultimate decoration.

Erich Hartmann's score finally rose to an incredible 352 victories. This achievement was not obtained without a few scares along the way however. He suffered a total of fourteen crash-landings and was shot down twice. On one occasion, having crashed behind enemy lines, he was captured by the Russians. Feigning injury to put his captors off guard, he lept from the truck taking him to the POW cage. Travelling by night and resting by day, he eventually reached the safety of his own lines.

Like most German pilots, he flew almost constantly. Unlike Allied pilots, who were rotated after so many missions, the Germans got no such rest. Hartmann flew more than 1,400 missions in just over two and a half years and took part in more than 800 aerial combats. He continued to fly missions until the very last day of the war. Like most Diamonds winners, he could quite easily have opted for a safe staff posting, but chose to stay with his comrades. This decision was to cost him dear as he was taken into Soviet rather than Western captivity.

His bravery continued throughout his captivity. The Russians tried to bribe him to join the East German airforce, with promises of high rank, status and an early release from captivity. He refused to collaborate and was promptly sentenced to 25 years hard labour as a war criminal. The Soviet reasoning was that of the massive amount of ammunition expended in shooting down 352 aircraft, some of the shots must have missed, fallen to earth and killed helpless Soviet citizens, therefore he was a war criminal. Eventually released in 1955, Hartmann returned to his family pale and emaciated, weighing a mere 100 pounds. His spirit however, was unbroken.

Soon after his return, Hartmann's comrades, themselves great aces such as Krupinski, Barkhorn, Rall and Steinhoff, all encouraged him to return to flying. At first he refused, but was eventually persuaded and re-joined the Luftwaffe in late 1956 with his former rank of Major. Hartmann was the only Diamonds winner to rejoin the armed forces. Major Hauptmann was trained by the US Air Force in jet flying, qualifying in the T-33 trainer and later completing his advanced training at Luke Air Force Base in Arizona, flying the T-33 and F-84 jets. When the new Luftwaffe received its first jet fighter unit, bearing the name of the great ace, Richthofen, it was apt that its commander was the greatest ace of all time, Erich Hartmann.

Despite encountering much petty jealousy and political interference, Hartmann built his Jagdgeschwader into an élite unit. Fiercely proud of his boys, his affection for his pilots was rewarded by the admiration and devotion of the men of Jagdgeschwader Richthofen for their famous commander. Hartmann finally retired from the Bundesluftwaffe with the rank of Oberst. But for the political enmity his forthright manner and frankness had incurred, he would almost certainly have been made a General. It is unlikely, modern warfare being what it is, that any other pilot will ever match the scores of the great Luftwaffe aces, Erich Hartmann, a gentle, polite and modest man will probably remain the greatest fighter ace ever.

OBERST JOACHIM HELBIG

Born on 10 September 1915 in Börln, Hellbig had no strong family military ties or traditions, yet he was to become one of Germany's most highly decorated soldiers. He first joined the Army and served as an Oberfähnrich with the Artillerie. In 1936 he joined the Luftwaffe and served as an observer with the rank of Leutnant before obtaining his pilot's qualification shortly after his promotion to Oberleutnant.

Helbig served with the bomber unit Lehrgeschwader 1 during the Polish Campaign, earning the Iron Cross Second Class. Subsequently he saw much action in the Norwegian and western Campaigns winning the Narvikschild and Iron Cross First Class. On 24 November 1940, Helbig, now holding the rank of Hauptmann, was decorated with the Knight's Cross of the Iron Cross in recognition of his successes and his having flown 122 missions.

In 1941 Helbig and his Geschwader were posted to the Mediterranean where he saw constant heavy action in the air assault on Malta and against Allied supply convoys. On many occasions Helbig's men would fly two or three missions each day. Helbig was to become one of the great aces with the formidable Junkers Ju 88 medium bomber. In January 1942 he was decorated with the Oakleaves to his Knight's Cross after having flown 300 missions. During this period Helbig's Ju 88s became well known to the Allies as the 'Helbig Flyers', and achieved considerable success in actions against Allied shipping in the spring and early summer of 1942, sinking three British destroyers. In July 1942, a British commando raid succeeded in destroying sixteen of his Ju 88s on the ground. the Helbig Flyers were only temporarily halted, however, and were soon to strike back with a vengeance.

By the end of September, Helbig had flown more than 500 missions. His Geschwader had sunk more than 200,000 tons of shipping. In reward for his leadership of the Geschwader during this period, he became the twentieth recipient of the coveted Swords on 28 September 1942, and was promoted to Major at the same time. In November 1942, during an attack on an Allied supply convoy off the Algerian coast, Helbig scored a direct hit on, and sank, a 10,000-ton ammunition ship. Shortly after this came the almost inevitable order restricting Helbig from further combat flying. At this point his tally of ships sunk was in the region of 180,000 tons, including two destroyers and an auxiliary cruiser.

Fortunately, from Helbig's point of view, wartime losses meant that men such as he were too badly needed to be taken off flying duty for long and he was soon back in the thick of the fighting. He saw action in the defence of the Anzio-Nettuno bridgehead and on the Normandy invasion front in the summer of 1944. At the surrender Helbig, holding the rank of Oberst, was taken into American captivity.

Helbig's success also rubbed off on some of his crew. His radio-operator/gunner Oberfeldwebel Franz Schlund became the first radio-operator to win the Knight's Cross of the Iron Cross for his contribution to Helbig's successes. Schlund later went on to serve in Fallschirmpanzerdivision Hermann Göring and also survived the war.

OBERST DIETER HRABAK

Fighter ace Dieter Hrabak was born in Gross Deuben near Leipzig on 19 December 1914. After graduation from grammar school in 1934, he joined the Reichsmarine as an officer cadet and completed his naval training before transferring to the Luftwaffe in November 1935. After an inauspicious start, damaging several aircraft during training, he qualified as a pilot in 1936.

In January 1939, Hrabak was given command of a squadron in Vienna. With this unit, Fighter Gruppe 76, he served in the Polish Campaign and suffered the indignity of being one of the very first German pilots to be shot down when he was attacked by a Polish fighter on his very first combat flight. He scored his first kill on 13 May 1940 during the Battle of France, shooting down a French Potez recce aircraft. Serving throughout the Battle of Britain, he scored a total of sixteen kills which brought him the award of the Knight's Cross of the Iron Cross on 21 October 1940. At this time he held the rank of Hauptmann.

After flying support missions during the German invasion of Greece, Hrabak then served with the newly formed Jagdgeschwader 54 on the Eastern Front. This famous unit, known as the Grünherz (Green Hearts) was formed from Jagdgruppe 76. On 1 November 1942, Hrabak was promoted to Kommodore of Jagdgeschwader 52, a unit which had numbered such aces as Barkhorn, Steinhoff and Hartmann among its personnel.

A popular Kommodore, Hrabak enjoyed the total respect of all his pilots. On 25 November 1943 he was decorated with Oakleaves after achieving his 118th victory. He held the rank of Oberstleutnant at this time. On 1 October

1944, he returned to his old unit, Jagdgeschwader 54, as its Kommodore, remaining in this post until the end of the war, achieving the rank of Oberst. On 1 January 1945 he had been decorated with the German Cross in Gold. He achieved a score of 125 victories in a total of 820 missions flown.

Surviving the war, Hrabak became a sales manager in an engineering company until reformation of the Luftwaffe. He continued to serve his country until 1976 when he retired with the rank of Generalmajor.

OBERST HERBERT IHLEFELD

Born on 1 June 1914 in Pinnow, Pomerania, Herbert Ihlefeld was an early entrant into the Luftwaffe. He served with the Legion Condor in Spain as a Sergeant Pilot in Jagdgeschwader 88 and by the end of the Spanish Civil War was already an ace with seven kills to his credit and a holder of the Spanish Cross in Gold with Swords. In 1938 he joined 1/Lehrgeschwader 2 with which he served until May 1942. On 13 September 1940 during the height of the Battle of Britain, Ihlefeld was decorated with the Knight's Cross of the Iron Cross following his 21st victory. By the end of the Battle of Britain his score stood at 25. On 27 June 1941 Ihlefeld added the Oakleaves to his Knight's Cross following his 40th victory. He was the sixteenth recipient of this rare award which he received while serving as a Hauptmann with Jagdgeschwader 77. Ihlefeld became a popular leader and earned a great reputation as a tutor whose expert knowledge helped to make aces of many other young pilots.

On 20 April 1942 he was decorated with the German Cross in Gold while still serving with Jagdgeschwader 77. Four days later the Swords to his Oakleaves were awarded, making him only the ninth recipient of this decoration. This followed his 101st victory and Ihlefeld was the first of the Luftwaffe's great aces to reach this score. In May 1942 Ihlefeld left Jagdgeschwader 77 and served as Kommodore with numerous Jagdgeschwader including JG1 Oesau, JG11, JG52 and JG103.

Ihlefeld was one of the great personalities of the German fighter fraternity. He ended the war with the rank of Oberst, having scored a total of 103 victories and having flown more than 1,000 missions. Of his total score, seven were achieved in Spain and 56 on the Western Front, approximately fifteen of his victories being 4-engined bombers. He survived the war and now lives in retirement.

OBERSTLEUTNANT HANS-JOACHIM JABS

One of the best known and most popular personalities of the night fighters, Jabs was born on 14 November 1917 in Lübeck. An early entry into the Luftwaffe in 1936 meant that by the outbreak of war in 1939 he was already a fully qualified and experienced pilot. Although he was initially trained as an Me 109 pilot, he transferred to Me 110s in early 1940, serving with II/Zerstörergeschwader 76 against France and during the Battle of Britain.

Jabs was such a superb pilot that even in an outclassed aircraft such as the Me 110, he could get the better of the RAF's Spitfire, which earned him the respect and admiration of his fellow pilots. On 1 October 1940, Oberleutnant Jabs was decorated with the Knight's Cross of the Iron Cross after his score had reached nineteen.

In September 1941 he underwent conversion training for night fighters and was posted to Nachtjagdgeschwader 3, which was involved in the defence of Hamburg against the mounting Allied bomber offensive. Apart from a brief return to a Zerstörergeschwader during the 'Channel Dash', when the Luftwaffe provided an escort for the battleships *Scharnhorst* and *Gneisenau*, this was a rather uneventful phase in his career, and after nine months' service in night fighters he had only achieved one more victory.

In November 1942 Jabs joined IV/Nachtjagdgeschwader 1 as Staffel-kapitän. In this élite Geschwader, his score again began to grow steadily until on 24 March 1944 he became the 430th recipient of the Oakleaves on achieving his 45th victory. Promoted to Kommodore of Nachtjadgeschwader 1, Jabs, now with the rank of Major, continued to fly combat missions. On 29 April 1944 when returning from one such mission Jabs was attacked by eight of the latest mark of Spitfire. Amazingly, Jabs not only survived the encounter, but managed to blast two of the Spitfires from the sky before safely landing at his home base. He had just enough time to land and take cover before the remaining Spitfires blasted his Me 110 to pieces. Jabs remained Kommodore of Nachtjagdgeschwader 1 until the end of the war, ending his career as an Oberstleutnant with 50 kills to his credit, an amazing 22 of these being day victories against Allied fighters technically far superior to his Me 110. Jabs flew a total of 710 missions. He is still alive and is a vice-president of the Gemeinschaft der Jagdflieger.

MAJOR ERHARD JÄHNERT

Erhard Jähnert was born on 17 August 1917 in Panitzsch near Leipzig in Saxony. A keen gliding enthusiast, he was already a qualified glider pilot when he joined the Luftwaffe in 1936. Completing his military pilot training at Kaufbeuren in 1938, he went on to be trained in dive-bombing and during the Polish and French Campaigns served as a Stuka Pilot with Sturzkampf-geschwader 76 and Sturzkampfgeschwader 3.

After service in the Mediterranean theatre, he served in North Africa with Sturzkampfgeschwader 3. This Geschwader saw action throughout the North African Campaign, taking part in every major battle and suffering considerable losses. On conclusion of the campaign, Jähnert saw further action in Sicily and in the attacks on Malta.

This experienced Stuka pilot was decorated with the German Cross in

Gold on 29 June 1942 while serving on the Eastern Front. On 18 May 1943 he added the Knight's Cross of the Iron Cross to his decorations after having completed 300 missions. This was no mean feat in view of the fact that these units were equipped with the long-obsolete Junkers Ju 87. Although an excellent dive-bomber, it had poor speed and manoeuvrability and was easy prey to enemy fighters. Later the Stuka Ju 87 was gradually replaced by the excellent Focke-Wulf Fw 190. Jähnert served in the Crimea and took part in the sinking of three Soviet destroyers in October 1943, during his 500th mission.

In January 1944, he was withdrawn from combat duty and posted as an instructor to the Stuka School at Deutsche Brod in Czechoslovakia where his considerable combat experience was shared with the new pilots undergoing training. He returned to the front in June 1944 in Command of III/Schlachtgeschwader 3, serving on the Kurland front during the closing stages of the war. In February 1945, Jähnert flew his 600th mission and in the last three months of the war alone, flew approximately 100 more missions as the Luftwaffe's ground support arm struggled desperately against the advancing Soviets.

In the last few days of the war, Major Jähnert and his Geschwader escaped to the west and were taken into British captivity. On 30 April 1945, Jähnert had become one of the last soldiers of the Wehrmacht to be awarded the Oakleaves to the Knight's Cross of the Iron Cross. Beginning the war as a Feldwebel, Jähnert's career ended as an Oakleaves winner with the rank of Major and 700 missions to his credit. He is still alive.

OBERSTLEUTNANT BERNHARD JOPE

Born on 10 May 1914 in Leipzig, Bernhard Jope joined the Luftwaffe in 1935 after studying aircraft construction at the Technical High School in Danzig. From 1938 to 1939 he saw action with the Condor Legion in the Spanish Civil War. During the early part of the Second World War, he served in the Polish Campaign, and the campaign against France and the Low Countries.

As a pilot with Kampfgeschwader 40, he flew the huge Focke-Wulf Fw 200 Condor. A pre-war civil airliner, the Condor adapted perfectly to military use and became a highly successful long-range maritime reconnaissance and anti-shipping bomber. On 24 October 1940, Jope detected and attacked the 42,000-ton British steamer *Empress of Britain*, the largest ship in Britain's merchant fleet. Jope's bombs scored direct hits on this large vessel, crippling her. Two days later the *coup de grâce* was given by *U 32* which sank her with torpedoes. For his part in the sinking of this major vessel, one of Britain's most important troopships, Jope was decorated with the Knight's Cross of the Iron Cross on 30 September 1940.

By spring of 1943, Jope had reached the rank of Major and was serving as Kommandeur of 3/Kampfgeschwader 100, becoming Kommodore in August of the same year. His unit subsequently served in the Mediterranean and was one of the first to use the Fritz X FX1400 stand-off missiles. These weapons were used for the first time by III/Kampfgesch-wader 100 in August 1943, launched from Dornier Do 217K twin-engined bombers and scored considerable success against the Anglo-American forces in the Mediterranean.

On 24 March 1944, Major Jope became the 43rd recipient of the Oakleaves to the Knight's Cross for his successful command of Kampfge-schwader 100. In 1945, he became Kommodore of Kampfgeschwader 30. He survived the war and is still alive.

HAUPTMANN HANS-JOACHIM MARSEILLE

The archteypal daredevil fighter ace, Hans-Joachim Marseille had a tragically brief, but phenomenally successful combat career. His skills were awesome. Marseille was young, handsome and chivalrous. He was also deadly.

Born in Berlin in 1919, he was brought up in a family steeped in military tradition. Joining the Luftwaffe in October 1938, Marseille loved flying but hated the discipline of military life, his early career being liberally endorsed with disciplinary offenses. His combat career commenced during the fall of France where he served under Johannes Steinhoff in Jagdgeschwader 52. Although he managed to shoot down seven aircraft, he himself was shot down six times. Despite continually being in trouble for indiscipline, he proved himself in combat and was awarded the Iron Cross Second Class in September 1940. In the spring of 1941, Marseille was posted to North Africa with Jagdgeschwader 27 where his reputation grew to match that of the Desert Fox, Rommel himself. Marseille was to become a superlative marksman. Research carried out at the time established that on average he used only fifteen rounds of ammunition for each victory. The great Adolf Galland himself described Marseille as an 'unequalled virtuoso'. Multiple kills by Marseille became so commonplace as to be unremarkable. On 22 February 1942 Leutnant Marseille was decorated with the Knight's Cross of the Iron Cross after scoring his 50th victory. On 3 June 1942 he shot down six Allied aircraft within only eleven minutes. The Oakleaves to his Knight's Cross followed on 6 June 1942 on achieving 75 victories in total. Oberleutnant Marseille was the 97th recipient of this rare award. On 17 June he again showed his uncanny skill as a marksman by shooting down six aircraft in only seven minutes. By the following day, 18 June 1942, only twelve days after the award of the Oakleaves, his score had passed the 100 mark, bringing him the coveted Swords.

Probably Marseille's greatest achievement occurred on 1 September 1942, when he was flying escort for a Stuka unit. As they approached the target areas, the Germans were intercepted by British fighters. Marseille attacked immediately and within seconds his first victim was crashing to its doom.

Only ten minutes later his second kill was achieved, and a third followed only three minutes afterwards. These Allied fighters had been Curtis Kittyhawks, easily outclassed in his Bf 109. Now, however, a formation of six Spitfires arrived on the scene and hurled themselves into the battle. Marseille and his wingman came under attack. Good though the Allied pilots were, they were no match for Marseille and soon one Spitfire lay shattered and burning on the desert floor. At this point Marseille had to break off the action and return to his base to refuel. His armourers discovered that only twenty rounds of cannon and sixty of machine-gun ammunition had been expended by his Messerschmitt fighter. This to them however was unremarkable. His real triumph was still to come.

Two hours later his squadron was once again in action over Alam El Halfa escorting Stukas once again. Marseille spotted a force of British light bombers with fighter escorts heading towards the German lines. Part of the fighter escort force headed off to intercept the Stukas which Marseille was escorting. These Kittyhawks once again were no match for Marseille as he went hurtling to meet them. The defensive circle they formed was to no avail. Within just two minutes the first Kittyhawk was shot down in flames. As the remainder fled, one more fell to the pursuing ace. Two minutes later yet another fell victim to his guns and only one minute afterwards still another was dispatched by this deadly marksman.

Marseille and his wingman encountered another formation of the Curtis fighters shortly thereafter, and yet another unfortunate Allied pilot was sent to his doom, adding one more to Marseille's ever growing tally of victories. By now, in two engagements in a single day, he had added twelve fighters to his tally, eight of these having been brought down within a space of only ten minutes. He was by no means finished, however, and later that same day took off on a third escort mission. Again attacked by Curtis fighters, he shot down a further five within eight minutes.

His total for the day was seventeen fighters, more than most aces scored in the entire war. This was the greatest success ever achieved against the RAF by one man. Even those accustomed to his usual high scores were astounded by this achievement and on the following day, 2 September 1942, with his score standing at 126, Marseille was awarded his country's highest award, the Swords, Oakleaves and Diamonds to his Knight's Cross. He was the fourth of only twelve Luftwaffe recipients of this award. As circumstances would have it, Marseille never actually received the award. His Diamonds are now on display at the Luftwaffe Museum at Uetersen near Hamburg.

Although Marseille was never to equal this day's achievement, he continued to run up his score and by the end of September 1942 his tally was 158 victories. This total was reached in the course of 382 missions, an outstanding achievement considering that many aces had flown more than 1,000 missions to reach their final scores.

Fate finally caught up with this charismatic figure on 30 September 1942. While returning from a mission on which, ironically, no enemy opposition had been met, his Bf 109 developed engine trouble and his cockpit filled with choking fumes. Determined to nurse his stricken aircraft back over German lines, Marseille waited too long before attempting to bale out. By the time he jettisoned his canopy he must have been almost at the end of his strength. When he finally jumped, his weakened body was slammed into the tailplane of his fighter. His comrades could only watch in horror as his body plummetted to the ground, his parachute having failed to open. The 'Star of Africa' was dead. Always a loner, and an undisciplined daredevil, Marseille however, was much loved by his comrades and greatly admired by all of his fellow aces. His death was a terrible blow to Jagdgeschwader 27 and to the Luftwaffe.

Bearing in mind that all his victories were scored against skilled pilots from the Western Allies, there is every possibility that had he survived he would have joined Erich Hartmann and Gerd Barkhorn in the 300+ Club, and the thought of what a virtuoso like Marseille might have achieved with an Me 262 jet fighter is mind-boggling.

In his short career Marseille certainly became one of the world's greatest aces and his unique achievements are unlikely ever to be equalled. A pilot's pilot, among his greatest admirers are several of the world's other greatest aces.

HAUPTMANN MANFRED MEURER

Born in Hamburg on 8 September 1919, Meurer's military career commenced as a volunteer with the Flakartillerie, after completing his six months' obligatory term with the Reichsarbeitsdienst. Transferring to flying duties in 1939, Meurer served in Me 110 Zerstörer units until, like many of his contemporaries, he joined the Night Fighter arm after the Me 110 was shown to be unable to hold its own against the Allied fighters of the day. It did however, prove to be an excellent night fighter and in the hands of some of the Luftwaffe's aces was responsible for shooting down great numbers of Allied bombers.

Meurer joined Nachtjagdgeschwader 1 in the autumn of 1941, but did not score his first victory until 27 March 1942. In his first complete year as a night fighter pilot, Meurer scored only ten victories. By 16 April 1943, his score had risen to 23, bringing him the award of the Knight's Cross of the Iron Cross. In August 1943, Meurer was given command of II/ Nachtjagdgeschwader 5 for a short period before taking command of I/ Nachtjagdgeschwader 1. On 2 August 1943, he became the 264th recipient of the Oakleaves following his 50th victory. Manfred Meurer and his radio operator, Gerhard Scheibe, made a deadly team, having flown well over 100 missions together. Indeed Scheibe became the first night fighter radio operator to win the Knight's Cross.

Nachtjagdgeschwader 1 was one of the units to receive the excellent Heinkel He 219 Uhu (owl) night fighter. The superb aircraft was truly deadly in the hands of an ace like Meurer. By January 1944 his score stood at 65 night victories making him the fifth highest-scoring night fighter ace. Tragedy struck on 21 January 1944 when, during an Allied bombing raid on Magdeburg, Meurer's He 219 collided with a British 4-engined bomber. Both Meurer's Heinkel and the bomber plunged to their doom. The loss of such a successful team when just reaching the peak of their achievements was a tragic blow to the Luftwaffe's night fighter force. Manfred Meurer is buried in the Ohlsdorfer cemetery in his native Hamburg.

OBERST WERNER MÖLDERS

Born in March 1913 in Gelsenkirchen, Mölders was perhaps the most unlikely of aces. As a young Army Leutnant attempting to transfer to the Luftwaffe, he had failed his medical tests and been told 'you will never make a pilot'. His determination and perseverance prevailed, however, and by the time of his tragic death in 1941 he was one of Germany's greatest war heroes and the holder of his country's highest gallantry awards, having scored more than 100 aerial victories.

Mölders had been born into a military family and had joined the Reichswehr as an officer candidate with Infanterie Regiment 2. His promising career as a Leutnant in the Pioniere was doomed from the day that he took his first ride as a passenger in an aircraft. From that day on he was determined to be a pilot. After his first, unsuccessful attempt to transfer to the Luftwaffe, Mölders persevered through months of arduous training. Sessions in a centrifugal motion tester left him weak and nauseated. He overcame all his problems through sheer determination and willpower and eventually qualified as a pilot.

Combat experience first came for Mölders during the Spanish Civil War when he served with the Legion Condor, scoring a total of fourteen victories and earning himself the Spanish Cross in Gold with Diamonds as the most successful pilot of the campaign. Mölders was, in fact, instrumental in developing many of the fighter tactics which would bring the Luftwaffe such great successes in the early part of the Second World War.

A strict Catholic, Mölders was an outspoken man who often criticised the Nazi regime. Such was his personal charisma, however, that he became one of Göring's personal favourites despite his outspokenness. A mature man who quickly earned the respect and admiration of the pilots he commanded, he soon earned the nickname *Vatti* (Daddy).

On the outbreak of war, Mölders was serving as Hauptmann and Commander of 1/Jagdgeschwader 53. His first victory came on 21 September when he shot down a French Curtiss fighter. For this success he was awarded the Iron Cross Second Class. The First Class followed for his seventh victory. On 29 May 1940, he was decorated with the Knight's Cross of the Iron Cross after scoring his twentieth victory. His promising career was almost terminated on 5 June 1940 when he met an expert French pilot who attacked an unsuspecting Mölders out of the sun. As his blazing Me

109 plumetted to the ground, Mölders parachuted to safety and was captured by French infantrymen. The captivity of Germany's leading ace was to be mercifully short however; the French surrender only two weeks later secured his release. Mölders was rather annoyed that his Knight's Cross was stolen by one of the infantrymen who had taken him prisoner. A rather more chivalrous French officer, however, managed to have it returned to him later.

Promoted to Kommodore of Jagdgeschwader 51, Mölders was soon back in action and on 21 September 1940 he became only the second recipient of the Oakleaves to the Knight's Cross following his 40th victory, the first pilot to reach this score. Jagdgeschwader 51 was one of the most successful of all fighter wings and Mölders personal achievements grew alongside those of his Geschwader. On 22 June 1941, he became the second recipient of the coveted Swords after his 72nd victory. At this point he held the rank of Oberstleutnant at the age of just 28 years.

On the opening of the campaign against the Soviet Union, Jagdgeschwader 51 was moved to the Eastern Front and there his score rose rapidly. Accustomed to extremely hard-earned victories against RAF pilots, he found the ill-trained and ill-equipped Soviet pilots easy prey. On 15 July 1941 he became the first pilot in history to score more than 100 kills. Although several of his contemporaries subsequently passed his score, Mölders assured his place in the history books by being the first man to better the score of the legendary Baron von Richthofen. On the following day he became the first ever airman to win the Diamonds.

Appointed General der Jagdfliefer, as previously mentioned, Mölders was an outspoken man. On the occasion of the investiture with the Diamonds he took the opportunity to complain to Hitler about the persecution of the Bishop of Münster by the Nazi authorities and the Gestapo. Hitler intervened and stopped the harassment. This interference in what was considered a political matter, earned Mölders many enemies among the Nazi hierarchy, as well as a file at Gestapo Headquarters. Hitler, however, had great admiration for this brave man and retorted to Bormann, 'Mölders is a believing Christian, a man without deceit. Do not point your finger at this decent soldier.'

In November 1941, Mölders received a summons to attend the state funeral of Generalluftzeigmeister Ernst Udet who had committed suicide, or in the official version, had died in a test flight. Mölders set off for Berlin on 22 November in a Heinkel He 111 bomber flown by a fellow Legion Condor veteran, Oberleutnant Kalbe. The weather was atrocious. Flying into strong headwinds, the fuel tanks of the Heinkel were emptying rapidly and just outside Breslau first one engine then the other failed. Despite the pilot's best efforts the stricken bomber crashed to the ground and both the pilot and Mölders, who suffered a broken neck, were killed. His death shattered the Luftwaffe and he was mourned by the entire nation. Werner Mölders had flown more than 300 missions and achieved 115 victories. He is remembered, however, as much for his personal attributes as for his combat achievements. His Geschwader was titled Jagdgeschwader Mölders in his honour.

Left: Hauptmann Bodo Spranz. In this well-known postcard photograph, Spranz's field grey Assault Gun uniform jacket is seen to good advantage. On his right sleeve are four badges for the single-handed destruction of enemy tanks and on the right breast the German Cross in Gold. Spranz won the Oakleaves and Knight's Cross together on 3 October 1943, a rare distinction. He commanded Assault Gun 111 in 1 Batterie of Sturmgeschütz Abteilung 237 and the Abteilung number can just be seen on his braid shoulder-straps.

Right: SS-Obersturmbannfuhrer Christian Tyschen. An instantly recognizable figure with his badly scarred jaw, Tychsen was extremely popular with his men. He was decorated with the Oakleaves to his Knight's Cross in December 1943 as commander of SS-Panzer Regiment 2, in the élite 2 SS-Panzer Division Das Reich.

Right: A fine portrait study of Sturmgeschütz ace Wilhelm Wegner. Oberwachtmeister Wegner was Zugführer in Sturmgeschütz Abteilung Grossdeutschland. His divisional cuffband and the 'GD' monogram on his shoulder-straps can be clearly seen. Below his Iron Cross First Class can be seen the General Assault Badge commonly awarded to Sturmgeschütz personnel. On his right breast pocket is the German Cross in Gold and at his neck the Knight's Cross, won on 13 June 1943. (Wilhelm Wegner)

Left: SS-Obersturmbannführer Hans Weiss. This tough Waffen-SS Panzer officer commanded schwere SS-Panzer Abteilung 502, having been awarded the Knight's Cross while serving with SS-Panzeraufklärungsabteilung 2 in the élite Das Reich Division.

Right: Oberleutnant Max Wirsching, prior to the award of his Knight's Cross. He is standing in the turret of his Tiger tank, somewhere on the Eastern Front. On the original print his Honour Roll Clasp is just visible on the Iron Cross ribbon in his buttonhole. On his left breast is the 25/50 pattern Panzer Assault Badge in Silver. (Max Wirsching)

Right: Ace of aces, Hauptsturmführer Michael Wittmann. Believed to have been taken on the Normandy front, before his award of the Swords, this photograph shows Wittmann wearing the black leather U-boat jacket over his standard Panzerjacke. These leather jackets were extremely popular with some SS-Panzer units. The 'LAH' monogram of the élite Leibstandarte can just be made out on Wittmann's shoulder straps.

Above left: Night Fighter ace Günther Bahr served as an Oberfeldwebel with 1./N.J.G.6 and was decorated with the Knight's Cross on 28 March 1945, having shot down 36 four-engined bombers and one fighter. This photograph was taken at the award ceremony. Bahr is wearing the popular Fliegerbluse on which can be seen his Iron Cross First Class and Pilot's Badge. The Night Fighter Flight Clasp is on his left breast. (Günther Bahr)

Above: Major Wilhelm Batz was certainly one of the Luftwaffe's most experienced pilots, having flown more than 5,000 hours as an instructor before coming to combat duties. From his first victory in March 1943 until the end of the war he succeeded in shooting down 237 enemy aircraft in more than 440 missions.

Left: Oberstleutnant Heinz Bär. Photographed here shortly after the award of the Swords, Bär at the time held the rank of Hauptmann and Staffelkapitän of I./J.G. 51 Mölders. The Flight Clasp in Gold for Fighter Pilots can be clearly seen over his left breast pocket. Bär is still the world's top scoring jet fighter ace with sixteen victories in the Messerschmitt Me 262, from a total score of 220.

Left: Oberst Werner Baumbach, seen here as a Hauptmann, was the first bomber pilot to win the Swords. Despite being appointed as General der Kampfflieger, he never achieved General's rank, probably due to his outspoken criticism of Hitler's handling of the Luftwaffe. All of his awards were earned while he served with K.G.30, first as a pilot and ultimately as its Commander.

Right: This fine portrait shows Major Ernst Börngen in August 1944, shortly after the award of his Knight's Cross as Hauptmann and Staffelkapitän of 5./J.G.27. Börngen's Knight's Cross, German Cross and Iron Cross First Class can be clearly seen, as can his Flight Clasp over the left breast pocket. Even at this late stage, the early pre-war type breast eagle with drooped tail is still frequently worn. Börngen went on to become Kommodore of J.G.27 and flew more than 650 missions, shooting down 45 enemy aircraft of which 24 were four-engined bombers. (Ernst Börngen)

Left: Leutnant Arnold Döring was originally a successful bomber pilot with nearly 350 missions to his credit when he transferred to night fighters. His Knight's Cross was awarded in April 1945 for a combination of his bomber successes and his victories as a night fighter pilot. His total mission count was 392 with 23 arial victories. (Arnold Döring)

Left: Night fighter ace Major Martin Drewes. He began as a Me 110 Zerstörer pilot before transferring to night fighters, and flew a total of 235 missions, scoring 52 victories. As well as his other decorations, the photograph shows his Night Fighter Clasp (bearing a downward-pointing winged arrow and wreath in black) in Gold with the pendant for 200 combat missions. (Martin Drewes)

Right: As an Oberleutnant in 2./ Lehrgeschwader 2, Alfred Druschel was awarded the Knight's Cross in August 1941. Eighteen months later he had reached the rank of Hauptmann and earned the Swords. This 1943 photograph of him as a Major and Kommodore of S.G.1, affords a particularly clear view of the Flight Clasps for air to ground support squadrons with pendant for 400 missions, in its pre-1944 design. The later version featured crossed swords in the centre.

Above left: Georg Peter Eder, seen here as a Hauptmann and Staffelkapitän with 6./J.G.1 was to become one of Germany's first jet aces. He scored a total of 78 victories, including 36 four-engined bombers as well as knocking out three tanks. (Georg Peter Eder)

Above: Major Heinrich Ehrler, here shown as a Hauptmann at the time of the award of his Oakleaves, was Kommodore of J.G.5 and scored well over 200 victories.

Left: Major Wolfgang Falck was one of the most important figures in the Luftwaffe's Night Fighter Arm. Although his personal victory score of seven only just qualifies him as an ace, his contribution to the organization of the Night Fighters was unsurpassed. It was for this he was decorated with the Knight's Cross in October 1940. Above the ribbon bar on his left breast can be seen the Flight Clasp for Fighter Pilots earned while flying Me 110 fighters. Falck rose to the rank of Oberst. (Josef Charita)

Right: Oberfeldwebel Josef Flögel. A Night Assault Flyer, or Nachtschlacht-flieger, Flögel was decorated with the Knight's Cross in February 1945. On his Fliegerbluse can be seen the German Cross in Gold and the Iron Cross First Class. Just below the Iron Cross is the Pilots Badge while above it is the Flight Clasp for Bomber Crew in the centre of which is featured a small winged bomb emblem. (Josef Flögel)

Below: Generalleutnant Adolf Galland, probably the best known of all Germany's great fighter aces. In this portrait study Galland is wearing the Swords, Oakleaves and Diamonds as well as the Pilot/Observers Badge with Diamonds. Just visible on his right sleeve is the Jagdgeschwader Schlageter cuffband. Galland was Kommodore of this Geschwader at the time his Diamonds were awarded.

Above left: A fine portrait study of Brillantenträger Major Hermann Graf. He wo the coveted Diamonds when only an Oberleutnant, with 9/J.G. 52 in September 1942. In this photograph the actual award Diamonds are being worn. Graf's German Cross in Gold is being worn on the right breast pocket while above the left pocket is the Flight Clasp for Fighter Pilots with pendant for flying 500 missions. Graf died after a long illness in 1988. (Hermann Graf)

Above: Major Hartmann Grasser began his career flying the Me 110 during the Battle fc France, and the Battle of Britain. Winning the Knight's Cross thereafter as a fighter pilot with J.G.51, he went on to win the Oakleave in August 1943 as Kommandeur of II./J.G. 5 after his 103rd victory. A veteran of both Eas and West Fronts as well as North Africa, he flew a total of 700 missions, and survived the war.

Left: The greatest German Fighter ace, Majo Erich Hartmann. This early photograph was taken when Hartmann held the rank of Leutnant, serving with 9./J.G.52 and before the award of his Oakleaves in March 1944. C interest are the two small enamelled lapel badges. These were unofficial badges depicting squadron emblems and can be seen worn by many aces. Just visible above Hartmann's left breast pocket is the Flight Clasp for Fighter Pilots. (Josef Charita)

Right: Bomber ace Joachim Helbig. He became the twentieth recipient of the coveted Swords in September 1942 while serving as Hauptmann, Kommandeur of 1./ Kampf-Lehr-Geschwader 1 after completing his 500th mission. His Junkers 88 unit was nicknamed the 'Helbig Flyers' by the Allies and were one of the Luftwaffe's most successful bomber units. As in so many photographs of him Helbig is shown here wearing his favourite fleece-lined jacket.

Below: Two of Germany's top aces chat together on the Eastern Front in March 1944, with one of J.G.52's Messerschmitt Me 109 fighters in the background. On the left is Oberstleutnant Dieter Hrabak, Oakleaves winner and Kommodore of J.G.52. On the right is Hauptmann Gerd Barkhorn, Kommandeur of II/J.G.52 and also a Swords winner. Between them, these two aces accounted for 419 enemy aircraft. (Josef Charita)

Left: Oberst Herbert Ihlefeld, here shown as an Oberstleutnant, flew the bulk of his combat career with J.G.77 before becoming Kommodore of various units. Ihlefeld flew more than 1,000 missions, gaining 130 victories. He won his Knight's Cross in hard combat against skilled RAF pilots durin the Battle of Britain in September 1940 (Herbert Ihlefeld)

Right: Oberstleutnant Hans-Joachim Jabs, Kommodore of N.J.G.1. Like many night fighter pilots, Jabs originally served with the Me 110 Zerstörer units. He flew a total of 710 missions, achieving 50 victories of which 28 were scored at night. Jabs wears the officer quality version of the Fliegerbluse with silver collar piping. On his left breast is the Night Fighter Clasp with 500 mission pendant. (Hans-Joachim Jabs)

Right: Stuka ace Hauptmann Erhard
Jähnert was awarded the Knight's Cross in
May 1943 after completing 300 missions.
In the closing stages of the war, he was
nominated for the Oakleaves on completion
of his 700th mission. These were approved
on 30 April. Jähnert ended the war with the
rank of Major. (Erhard Jähnert)

Below: Bernhard Jope, seen here as a
Hauptmann, won the Knight's Cross in
December 1940 as a pilot with K.G.40. As
commander of K.G.100 with the rank of
Major, he also earned the Oakleaves in
March 1944. Compare the details of
his later-pattern breast eagle with that
in the photograph of Walter Storp. (Jope)

Below right: Major Günther Lützow. This
photograph taken in the late summer of
1941, shows Lützow before the award of
his Swords. He is wearing the fur-lined
flying-jacket and officers' version of the
forage cap. Although it bears officers'
silver piping to the flap, it appears to
have basic cotton embroidered other
ranks insignia, a common combination.
Lützow went on to reach the rank of
Oberst.

Left: Legendary Fighter ace, Hans Joachim Marseille. This photograph shows the young Oberleutnant Marseille on home leave in Berlin with his mother, in the summer of 1942. He is wearing the basic Swords and Oakleaves here, and the German Cross in Gold can be seen on his right breast pocket. On the lower left breast pocket is his Pilot's Badge, below the Iron Cross First Class. (Josef Charita)

Left: Hauptmann Manfred Meurer was an accomplished Night Fighter ace with N.J.G.1 and N.J.G.5. He was awarded the Oakleaves in August 1943 after achieving his 50th victory. Meurer ultimately raised his score to 65 before being killed in action when his Heinkel He 219 Uhu night fighter collided with a bomber.

ght: Oberst Werner Mölders. The first
an in the German armed forces to win the
veted Diamonds. Few fighter aces of the
ftwaffe were admired and respected as
uch as this superb pilot, nicknamed Vatti
addy) by his men. Many future aces
atured into fine pilots under his expert
telage.

low: Major Walter Nowotny. One of the
ost popular figures of the Fighter Arm,
owotny is shown here as a Hauptmann
d Kommandeur of I./J.G. 54 just after the
vard of his Swords. Nowotny went on to
in the Diamonds in October 1943 after
hieving his 250th victory. He was the first
lot to reach this score. He was killed when
s Messerschmitt jet fighter crashed after
1 engine failure in combat. He had
hieved 258 victories.

low right: Only the third soldier to win
e Swords, Major Walter Oesau is shown
re wearing his award together with the
re Spanish Cross in Gold with Diamonds.
is black wound badge is also the pattern
varded for those wounded during the
panish Civil War. Oesau went on to reach
e rank of Oberst and Kommodore of
G.1. At the time of his death in combat on
 May 1944, he had achieved a score of
23 victories.

Left: Generalmajor Dietrich Peltz. Origina an Army officer, Peltz joined the Luftwaff in 1935 and had a highly successful caree first as a Stuka pilot, then in bombers. His Swords were awarded in July 1943 after completing his 300th mission. He ended the war as Commanding General of 1 Fliegerkorps. In this photograph Peltz we the Fliegerbluse for Generals with gilt piping to the collar and gilt wire insignia on a white base.

Right: Oberfeldwebel Johann Pichler. A veteran of more than 700 missions, Pichler scored 75 victories of which sixteen were four-engined bombers. He was commissioned Leutnant in the latter part of the war. (Johann Pichler)

Werner Mölders was an exemplary soldier, a brilliant tactician, a superb pilot and a first-class leader of men. He had an unrivalled reputation for being both disciplined and fair. His sense of fairness also extended to his enemies. In combat he was chivalrous in the extreme. On at least one recorded occasion a furious Mölders is known to have given a fellow fighter pilot a severe reprimand for attacking what Mölders considered not to be a legitimate target, in this case a train which could well have been carrying civilians.

Even today, in a Germany where many would wish to forget their country's wartime history, Mölder's name is honoured by the Bundesluftwaffe in which a fighter squadron carries the honour title Geschwader Mölders, and by the Bundesmarine in which a modern destroyer bears his name.

OBERST GÜNTHER LÜTZOW

Born in Kiel on 4 September 1912, Günther Lützow came from one of Germany's greatest military families. Educated in theology, he was nevertheless drawn towards a military career by the exciting events of the military expansion of Germany during the thirties. An early volunteer for the Luftwaffe, Lützow served in the Condor Legion during the Spanish Civil War. By the end of that conflict he had already achieved ace status by shooting down five aircraft. His invaluable experiences in Spain, where he had been decorated with the Spanish Cross in Gold, led to a posting to Jagdfliegerschule 1 where he could pass on the valuable tactical lessons he had learned to the young trainees who could only hope for simulated combat at that time.

Lützow then commanded I/Jagdgeschwader 3 Udet before becoming Kommodore of the Geschwader in August 1940. After scoring his tenth victory, against the RAF, thus bringing his total score to fifteen, Hauptmann Lützow was decorated with the Knight's Cross of the Iron Cross on 18 September 1940. By the time of Germany's invasion of the Soviet Union in the summer of 1941, Lützow had increased his score to more than 40. On 20 July 1941 he became the 27th recipient of the Oakleaves to the Knight's Cross. He held the rank of Major at that time. Just 76 days later, Lützow had more than doubled his score and on 11 October he was awarded the Swords after achieving his 92nd victory. Later than same month he became only the second pilot in the Luftwaffe to score 100 victories.

At this point in his career, Lützow was appointed to the first of a number of staff postings, ultimately becoming Jagdfliegerführer, or fighter leader. Günther Lützow was exactly the type of man this job required. His strong family background and theological training had formed his strong character at an early age. He would be nobody's yes-man. Although rather formal and haughty-looking, Lützow had a great sense of humour and made many firm

friends amongst his peers. It has been said of Lützow that he epitomized
all that was decent, honourable and correct about the German military
character. Certainly he stood up to Reichsmarschall Göring on numerous
occasions. Lützow would never let himself be browbeaten by the pompous
Commander-in-Chief of the Luftwaffe, and invariably took the side of the
men fighting at the front against the chairborne bureaucrats.

At the famous conference called by Göring in Berlin in January 1945,
ostensibly to discuss the problems from which the fighter arm was suffering,
Lützow held nothing back. Incensed by Göring's treatment of Adolf
Galland, sacked as General der Jagdflieger, and his constant attacks on the
integrity of the fighter arm as a whole, Lützow clearly and concisely laid
down all the complaints the fighter pilots had about their mistreatment. The
Reichsmarschall did not enjoy hearing the truth so plainly spoken. The Nazi
leadership was accustomed to being surrounded by fawning sycophants
more concerned with furthering their own career than admitting to
unpleasant truths. Furious at Lützow's audacity, Göring stormed from the
room screaming abuse at Lützow, branding him a traitor and threatening
to have him court-martialled.

Even Göring must have realized that he had gone too far, and this threat
was never carried out. Lützow, however, was sent into virtual exile in a post
in Italy as Jagdfliegerführer, taking over from his friend, Oberst Neumann.
Towards the end of the war, Lützow jumped at the chance to return to
combat duties and joined Adolf Galland in Jagdverband 44, the aptly named
'Squadron of Experts'. The deadly Messerschmitt Me 262 could be a
formidable weapon in the hands of such aces. Lützow scored two kills with
the Me 262 before being reported missing in action on 24 April 1945 near
Donauwörth. It is assumed that he was shot down while attacking a daylight
bombing force of US four-engined heavy bombers.

Lützow's final score was 108 victories, scored during 300 missions. His
last commander, Generalleutnant Galland, described him as an outstanding
leader. The subject of great respect and admiration, both for his personal
gallantry, and for his moral fortitude, Lützow was a true Knight of the Skies
and one of the great aces.

MAJOR WALTER NOWOTNY

One of several Luftwaffe aces of Austrian origin, Walter Nowotny was born
in Gmünd on 7 December 1920. He joined the Luftwaffe in 1939, one
month after the start of the war. At this point, young pilots like Nowotny
were able to experience the relative luxury of the full spectrum of pre-war
quality training as no real manpower shortages had yet forced the
curtailment of the training period, or the rushing of pilots to the front with
inadequate training.

Joining Jagdgeschwader 54, the famous 'Greenhearts', in February 1941,
Leutnant Nowotny scored his first victory on 19 July when he shot down

three Soviet aircraft near the Island of Osel. His own aircraft was also hit, however, and he crashed into the Baltic. He spent three days and nights paddling his dinghy with his hands before reaching land. It took Nowotny just over a year to bring his score up to 54, a score he reached on 4 August 1943 after shooting down seven aircraft in a single day. Exactly one month later, on 4 September 1942, he was decorated with the Knight's Cross of the Iron Cross after scoring his 56th victory. On 25 October 1942 he was given command of 9/Jagdgeschwader 54, a considerable responsibility for a 21-year-old.

During the summer of 1943, Nowotny's score really began to soar. He scored 41 victories in this one month alone, a total which included two kills in a single day, 24 June 1943. On 15 June his score passed the 100 mark. August saw a further 49 victories, including a single day's total of nine kills on 13 August and seven more on the 21st. On 18 August 1943, Nowotny's score had passed the 150 mark. At this point in the war, even this impressive score was not sufficient to bring the award of the Oakleaves, and it was not until 4 September and his 189th victory that this coveted decoration was awarded. September's total score of 45 kills took him well over the 200 mark and still the victories came. On 22 September, Nowotny was awarded the Swords to his Oakleaves following his 218th victory. He was the 37th recipient of this decoration.

Nowotny's success rate peaked in October 1943. During that month in only a 10-day period he brought down 32 Soviet aircraft. On 14 October he became the first pilot ever to reach a score of 250 victories. Nowotny was now the Luftwaffe's most successful ace. For this achievement he became the eighth recipient of the Diamonds. At the age of just 22, Nowotny held his country's highest honour. Only nine fighter pilots ever received this special honour. Nowotny's successes were only ever to be bettered by four of his comrades, Hartmann, Barkhorn, Rall and Kittel. His achievements are all the more impressive in that they were achieved in the space of just 442 missions.

Leaving the Eastern Front in February 1944, Nowotny was posted to command Schulegeschwader 101 in France, where he remained for five months, imparting his considerable knowledge to the new pilots undergoing training. Nowotny not only had a great reputation as a fighter pilot, but was also an excellent teacher. Many of his pupils went on to be successful aces thanks to his tutelage. In July 1944, he formed Kommando Nowotny, an experimental unit testing the new Me 262 jet fighter. With this superb jet, Nowotny added a further three victories to his tally.

On 8 November 1944, Nowotny took off to attack a formation of heavy bombers. The exact circumstances are not known, but either enemy fire or mechanical failure caused him to loose power in one engine. The loss of speed left him vulnerable to the bomber's escorting P51-D Mustang fighters. Witnesses on the ground saw Nowotny's Me 262 plunge vertically through the clouds and hit the ground with a huge explosion. At the time of his death, Nowotny had scored a total of 258 victories, all but the last three of which were scored on the Eastern Front.

OBERST WALTER OESAU

Born on 28 June 1913 in Farnewinkel in Holstein, the son of a bank official, Oesau served the usual six-month term with the Reichsarbeitsdienst before commencing his military career with the Army. He joined III/Artillerie Regiment 2 in Itzehoe before transferring to the transport flying school and later to the Hanover war school.

On completing his training, Leutnant Oesau was posted to Jagdgeschwader Richthofen. In early 1938, he joined the small band of German pilots serving with the Legion Condor in Spain. After a fruitless few months, he succeeded in shooting down an enemy aircraft, this being a Soviet-built I 15 Rata, on 15 July 1938. In February 1939 he was promoted to Oberleutnant and by the time he returned to Germany he was a fully-fledged ace, having shot down a total of eight aircraft. Oberleutnant Oesau was one of the few recipients of the Spanish Cross in Gold with Diamonds. Among the other Luftwaffe flyers who became aces during the Spanish Civil War and received this award were such experts as Galland, Mölders, Lützow and Balthasar, all of whom were also to become great aces during the Second World War.

During the Polish Campaign, Oesau served with Jagdgeschwader 51 under Theo Osterkamp, a popular commander widely known as *Onkel Theo* (Uncle Theo), due to his kind and helpful attitude towards his young pilots. Oesau saw no action during this period and thus did not have the opportunity to add to his score until the western campaign, where he took his total to twelve. He received the Iron Cross Second Class during this period.

At the start of the Luftwaffe's air assault on Britain, Oesau was tasked on one occasion with escorting a photo-recce mission. Attacked by six Spitfires, he shot down one and his comrades drove off the others. On reaching his home base, he was decorated with the Iron Cross First Class, the first pilot in his Gruppe to be so honoured. On the following day, in a single action lasting only twenty minutes, Oesau added three more enemy fighters to his score. Shortly afterwards he was promoted to the rank of Hauptmann. On 20 August 1940, his score having reached twenty kills, Hauptmann Oesau was decorated with the Knight's Cross of the Iron Cross and given a well-earned home leave. On his return to duty, he took command of III/Jagdgeschwader 51.

Oesau was only the fifth fighter pilot to reach a score of twenty kills, and during the next six months his score rose steadily until on 5 February 1941 his 40th victory brought him the Oakleaves to his Knight's Cross. He was only the ninth recipient of the Oakleaves, and only the fourth fighter pilot to be so decorated. In the summer of 1941, Oesau commanded III/Jagdgeschwader 3 on the Eastern Front. After the tough opposition put up by the RAF's Spitfires and Hurricanes, the pilots of the Soviet Air Force in their obsolescent aircraft were to be easy meat for this accomplished ace. During a period of sixteen days he added sixteen kills to his score. Only five months after the award of the Oakleaves, he had doubled his score to 80 and on 15 July 1941 he became the third recipient of the newly instituted Swords to the Oakleaves. This award was personally presented to him by Adolf Hitler. Oesau was then posted back to Jagdgeschwader Richthofen on the Western Front as Kommodore with the rank of Major.

Oesau's 100th victory, a Spitfire, was shot down on 26 October 1941. He was only the third pilot to reach this score. His success rate brought him bad news, however, when he was ordered to stop flying combat missions. This was a cross that many successful pilots were forced to bear. At this point in the war, when Germany's fortunes were still riding high, the Luftwaffe could afford to take such experienced aces off combat duties rather than risk their loss. Later in the war, manpower shortages would not permit such luxuries. On odd occasions, when circumstances were thought to warrant it, Oesau was permitted to fly on combat sorties, such a case being during the Allied landings at Dieppe. Oesau's return to full combat status did not come until 1943 when he was appointed to replace the Kommodore of Jagdgeschwader 1, Oberstleutnant Philipp, who had been killed in action. Oesau went on to increase his score to 123 victories, ten of which were 4-engined bombers. On 11 May 1944, Walter Oesau met his death in action over the Eifel mountains when his Messerschmitt Me 109 was bounced by an American P-38 Lightning. On 15 May an official communiqué announced his death:

'The commander of a fighter squadron, Oberst Walter Oesau, the third officer of the German Wehrmacht to be decorated with the Swords and Oakleaves has found a hero's death in aerial battle. With him, the Luftwaffe has lost one of its outstanding fighter pilots and formation commanders.'

GENERALMAJOR DIETRICH PELTZ

Peltz was born on 9 June 1914 in Gera, Thuringia. An aviation enthusiast, he had qualified as a civil pilot by the time he was 18. On completion of his education he became an employee of Daimler-Benz in Stuttgart until he was drafted into the Army in 1934. Naturally enough, his flying abilities led to a transfer to the Luftwaffe and as a young officer cadet he underwent his military flying training from 1935 to 1936.

Commissioned Leutnant in 1936, he joined the Immelmann Geschwader, flying the Junkers Ju 87 dive-bomber. Just before the outbreak of war Peltz took part in a major training demonstration which almost ended in his death. His unit was to demonstrate the abilities of the Ju 87 to an assembled audience of the military hierarchy. The weather was atrocious, with extremely dense fog. The pilots took off in their Ju 87s but, at the last minute before going into their demonstration flight patterns, they were recalled. Peltz was one of the few who received the message. Many of his comrades did not and, in almost vertical dives, the pilots were unable to judge the distance from the ground correctly and several plunged straight to their doom. Twenty young airmen died in this mishap.

During the Polish Campaign, Peltz flew more than 40 missions, winning himself the Iron Cross Second and First Classes. Transferred to the Western Front after the fall of Poland, Peltz flew missions against British and French forces in support of Rommel's Panzers in their dash to the Channel coast. During the attack on the beleaguered British Expeditionary Force at Dunkirk, Peltz sank a troopship and destroyed a munitions train. By the end of the western campaign, Peltz had flown more than 100 missions.

This battle-hardened young officer now underwent conversion training to the Junkers Ju 88 bomber, joining Kampfgeschwader 77 in August 1940. He flew several missions during the night *Blitz* on England. On 14 October 1940, in recognition of his successes during the Polish and French Campaigns, and the *Blitz* on England, Peltz was decorated with the Knight's Cross of the Iron Cross.

In March 1941, Peltz became Gruppenkommandeur of II/Kampfgeschwader 77. During the late summer of that year, after intensive involvement in the Battle of Britain, the Geschwader was transferred to the Eastern Front. Operating on the northern sector, Peltz was particularly successful in attacking Soviet supply routes. Railway lines, marshalling yards, canals, roads – any route open to the Soviets was a target for Peltz. His continuing success brought him the award of the Oakleaves to his Knight's Cross in October 1941, as only the fourth recipient of this award. At the end of that year Peltz was posted to command the Kampffliegerschule in Foggia, with the rank of Major. In this new post, he was able to give new pilots under training the benefit of his considerable combat experience, and was responsible for introducing many much-needed fresh tactical methods of operation.

In the summer of 1942, Peltz was rewarded with a combat posting and took command of I/Kampfgeschwader 66 in France. He was involved in trials for anti-shipping strikes using rocket projectiles. Initially intended for operation from Norway against Allied convoys bound for Murmansk, the invasion of North Africa in the 'Torch' landings put paid to this and his unit was hurriedly posted to the Mediterranean theatre, where his successful strikes against shipping brought him promotion to Oberstleutnant in December 1942.

In July 1943, Peltz became the 31st recipient of the Swords to his Oakleaves for his continued achievements in the air war. The award was personally presented by Hitler. Promoted to Oberst, Peltz was nominated Angriffsführer England as Göring attempted to repay the British for their devastating bombing raids on Germany. Peltz was to have command of Kampfgeschwader 2 and 66, elements of Kampfgeschwader 40 and Schnellkampfgeschwader 10 as well as subsidiary units. As part of the IX Fliegerkorps, this group was commanded by a young Oberst whose job titles included General der Kampfflieger and Kommandierender General der IX Fliegerkorps. High Command obviously realized the anomaly in his rank, and Peltz was promoted to Generalmajor becoming, at that time, the youngest General in the German armed forces.

Although he applied himself to his new task with all his usual energy and dedication, and with several new aircraft types such as the Ju 188 and He 177, the tide had already long since turned against the Luftwaffe. The overwhelming Allied air superiority could not now be countered by the Luftwaffe's greatly depleted strength.

In March 1945, Peltz was given overall responsibility for all aircraft designated for the defence of the Reich, and ended the war as Kommandie-render General der 1 Fliegerkorps.

LEUTNANT JOHANN PICHLER

Born in Oberschweinbach in Upper Bavaria on 15 December 1912, Johann Pichler joined Jagdgeschwader 77 in August 1940. His first combat victory came in May 1941, during the battle for Crete. His fighter group subsequently fought through the Eastern Campaign in Russia and Roumania, and in North Africa and Italy.

With a score of 75 victories to his credit, Pichler was in a hospital recovering from wounds when the area was overrun by Soviet troops and he was taken prisoner. On 7 September 1944, he was awarded the Knight's Cross but due to his captivity this was never actually presented. He was also promoted from Oberfeldwebel to Leutnant. Pichler flew a total of approximately 700 missions and scored 75 victories, sixteen of which were 4-engined bombers. He was also involved in the sinking of several Allied ships during the battle for Crete.

OBERST JOSEF PRILLER

Josef Priller was born in Ingolstadt, Bavaria on 27 June 1915. One of the Fighter Arm's true characters, 'Pips' Priller was of small physical stature, but was one of the Luftwaffe's most dynamic personalities. His wit and irrepressible good humour made him an exceptionally popular flyer even with the Nazi hierarchy which took every opportunity to blame Germany's misfortunes on the Luftwaffe during the latter stages of the war.

Priller entered combat service in October 1939 with Jagdgeschwader 51 and served with this famous fighter unit during the Battle of Britain. Having served his apprenticeship under Theo Osterkamp, alongside such greats as Werner Mölders, it was as an experienced fighter ace with more than twenty hard-earned victories to his credit, and with the coveted Knight's Cross at his throat that Priller joined Jagdgeschwader 26 Schlageter in November 1940. Priller had joined the ranks of the Ritterkreuzträger on 19 October 1940 after his twentieth victory.

Initially Staffelkapitän of 1/Jagdgeschwader 26, Oberleutnant Priller continued to run up his score of RAF aircraft until on 20 July 1941 he was decorated with the Oakleaves following his 41st victory. He was the 28th recipient of this rare distinction. In December of 1941 he was promoted to command III/Jagdgeschwader 26. December also saw the award of the German Cross in Gold. Remaining with Jagdgeschwader 26, Priller became Kommodore of the Geschwader on 11 June 1943. On 2 July 1944 he became the 73rd recipient of the Swords following his 100th victory. This score, achieved as it was against RAF and USAAF pilots, was no mean feat. While many Luftwaffe aces exceeded this score, few equalled it, entirely on the Western Front, with most of the victories being against fighter aircraft. Priller had the distinction of being one of a handful of pilots who opposed the Allied landings at Normandy on 6 June 1944. He was also relatively unusual in that he served throughout most of the war with the same Geschwader. During this period he had the opportunity to serve alongside such greats as Walter Krupinski, Emil Lang, Anton Hackl and Joachim Müncheberg. On 27 January 1945 Priller became Inspector of Day Fighters (West) and was serving in this role with the rank of Oberst at the surrender.

'Pips' Priller flew more than 300 missions, achieving 101 victories of which eleven were 4-engined heavy bombers. He survived the war and maintained close contacts with his wartime fighter comrades until his death from a heart attack in 1961 at the age of just 45.

MAJOR GÜNTHER RALL

The third highest scoring ace in history, Günther Rall was born in Gaggenau on 10 March 1918. As a boy Rall was a real outdoors type with a love of nature. His were the simple pleasures of a young boy from a poor family during the depressed years which preceded the Third Reich. Rall joined the Army in 1936 as a potential infantry officer. While a cadet at Dresden Kriegsschule in 1937 he made a close friend of a young Luftwaffe officer. Rall was fascinated by his young comrade's tales of his flying training and determined to transfer to the Luftwaffe himself. His application was successful and he eventually qualified as a pilot in 1939.

Having achieved his commission as Leutnant, Rall was posted to II/ Jagdgeschwader 52. His first victory did not come until 12 May 1940. Rall and his comrades were tasked with the escorting of a reconnaissance mission and as they approached the rendezvous point the reconnaissance aircraft was attacked by French fighters. The German pilots launched themselves into the enemy attackers and in the dog-fight which ensued, Rall brought down his first enemy aircraft.

After the fall of France, Rall and his comrades took part in the Battle of Britain. Jagdgeschwader 52 suffered heavy losses, due to valuable fighters being squandered in escort missions for bombing attacks, making them highly vulnerable to attack by fighters. Because of the attrition rate, Rall found himself rapidly promoted to Squadron Leader, as a mere 22-year-old Leutnant. Jagdgeschwader 52 was withdrawn from the Battle of Britain in October 1940. A period of relative inactivity followed when the unit was posted to Roumania, interrupted by ground support missions assisting the German paratroop assault on Crete.

With the German invasion of the Soviet Union, Rall found himself flying defensive missions against enemy bomber attacks on the Roumanian oilfields, a role which he and his unit fulfilled with considerable success. Subsequently, Jagdgeschwader 52 went on to the offensive, in the southern sector of the Eastern Front, taking part in the battle for the Crimea and the capture of Rostov. On 28 November 1941, after achieving his 36th victory, Rall was shot down. He landed heavily, in darkness, and broke his back in three places. He was out of action for nine months, slowly regaining mobility, and despite official pronunciations that he would never fly again, he was again in action by August 1942. Back on the Eastern Front, Rall was determined to catch up with the scores of his luckier comrades.

On 3 September 1942, Oberleutnant Rall was decorated with the Knight's Cross of the Iron Cross following his 65th victory. During the following month, his score increased, past the 100 mark, bringing him the Oakleaves to his Knight's Cross on 26 October. He was the 134th recipient. From April 1943 until March 1944, Rall served as Kommandeur of III/Jagdgeschwader 52. During this period he achieved his 200th victory, on 29 August 1943, a feat for which he was decorated with the Swords on 12 September of that year. His score passed the 250 mark on 28 November 1943. In one particular month, October 1943, Rall scored 40 victories, more than some aces scored in the entire war. Rall came up against many excellent Soviet pilots, however, and was himself shot down eight times.

In April 1944, Rall was posted to the Western Front as Kommandeur of II/Jagdgeschwader 11. This unit was used in interception attacks on high-flying US daylight bombing raids, and Rall was able to score several more victories during this period before again being shot down. An enemy bullet had severed his thumb and he suffered considerable loss of blood. The wound became infected and again Rall had to endure hospitalization for more than six months.

On his release from hospital, Rall joined the staff of Adolf Galland. In March 1945 Major Rall became Kommodore of Jagdgeschwader 300, a unit which flew the excellent Fock-Wulf Fw 190D. It was in this post that Rall's war ended. He had flown 621 missions and achieved 275 victories, becoming the third highest-scoring ace in history. Taken prisoner by the Americans, he was subjected to intense questioning about the Me 262 jet, an aircraft which he had had the opportunity to fly and in which the Americans were deeply interested, in their desire to build an effective jet fighter force before the Soviets could do so. After his release Rall found difficulty in obtaining work because of his military past. Germany had quickly forgotten her heroes and military men were no longer socially acceptable. Eventually he began work with the huge Siemens firm.

In January 1956 he returned to military service with the newly reformed Luftwaffe. He served his country well and progressed to become head of the German Air Force from December 1970 until April 1974 and then became German military representative at NATO, finally retiring in 1976 with the rank of Generalleutnant. Rall is still alive.

MAJOR HUBERT RAUH

Born on 15 November 1913 in Klein Wolkersdorf in Austria, Hubert Rauh attended Technical High School after taking his school certificate. In March 1933 he volunteered for military service in the Austrian armed forces. After two and a half years with the Army, Rauh began flying training with the Austrian Air Force at Graz.

Following the German occupation of Austria in 1938 the Austrian armed forces were merged with the Wehrmacht and on 1 May 1938 Rauh was taken into the German Luftwaffe. From the outbreak of war until 15 July 1941 he served as a flying instructor at the Brandenburg flying school. Subsequently he undertook extensive blind flying and night fighter training before taking up combat duties with Nachtjagdgeschwader 1 in January 1942. His first victory was scored on 28 April 1942 while flying with 4/Nachtjagdgeschwader 1. He then went on to serve with Nachtjagdgeschwader 4 in France, Belgium and Germany in the defence of the Reich against Allied bomber raids. In October 1942 Rauh took command of 3/Nachtjagdgeschwader 4 in which position he served until May 1944.

On 25 May 1944 Rauh was promoted to the position of Kammandeur of II/Nachtjagdgeschwader 4. At this time the Geschwader was commanded by Diamonds winner Major Heinz Wolfgang Schnaufer, the world's most successful night fighter ace. On 1 January 1945 Rauh's growing success as a night fighter pilot brought him the award of the German Cross in Gold. This was followed on 28 April 1945 by the Knight's Cross of the Iron Cross. Rauh's successes, a total of 31 aircraft shot down, did not come easily. Three times he himself was shot down by defensive fire from Allied bombers, on one occasion suffering a fractured collar-bone in a particularly heavy parachute landing. His gunner and radio operator were less fortunate, being killed in action. Of Rauh's total score of 31 victories, 29 were 4-engined bombers (*Viermots*). This was a considerable achievement by any standards.

Ending the war with the rank of Major, Rauh was taken into British captivity from which he was finally released in February 1946. Ten years later he re-entered military service with the Austrian Armed forces, finally retiring from the service in 1974 with the rank of Oberst. He is still alive.

OBERST HANS ULRICH RUDEL

Hans Ulrich Rudel, the most highly decorated flier in history, was born in 1916. Always an active child, Rudel spent more time taking part in sports than in studying. An early fascination with flying lead to his joining the Luftwaffe in 1936. This in itself was no mean achievement in view of his less than impressive academic achievements and the 98 per cent rejection rate for prospective Luftwaffe applicants. An adequate pupil, Rudel volunteered for Stuka training to avoid a rumoured block posting to bombers. This ploy was soon regretted as all his classmates were posted to fighter squadrons.

After only a short spell on Stukas, Rudel was given reconnaissance training and flew with a reconnaissance flight during the Polish Campaign, earning the Iron Cross 2nd Class. Transferred back to his old unit shortly afterwards, Rudel returned to Stuka flying during the French Campaign. He was promoted to Oberleutnant in September 1940. Service in the Balkans followed, but it was not to be until the German invasion of the Soviet Union that Rudel would begin his rise to fame. Until then he had made such a bad impression on his commanding officer that he was regarded as a liability and not allowed to take part in combat missions.

In September 1941, Rudel's squadron, Schlachtgeschwader 1 Immel-mann was ordered to attack elements of the Soviet fleet at Kronstadt. Rudel scored a hit on the battleship *Marat* and sank a Soviet cruiser. Subsequent reconnaissance flights established that *Marat*, though damaged, had made harbour and was under repair. A few days later Rudel's squadron made a further attack on her and despite a ferocious Flak barrage and defending Soviet fighters, Rudel, in an almost vertical dive, scored a direct hit with a 2,000lb bomb, breaking *Marat*'s back.

On 20 October 1941 Rudel was awarded the Luftwaffe Goblet of Honour for outstanding achievements and on 8 December became the first member of his squadron to win the German Cross in Gold. Less than one month later, on 6 January 1942, Rudel joined the ranks of the Ritterkreuzträger when his continued success as a dive-bomber pilot was recognized by the award of this coveted decoration. At this point Rudel had flown well over 400 missions. His pleasure in the award was to be temporarily offset by his enforced transfer to a reserve unit as an instructor in March 1942. Rudel was soon back in action on the Eastern Front, however, and rapidly clocked up many more missions, reaching the 500 mark in September 1942. Hospitalized with jaundice in early November 1942, Rudel discharged himself against the advice of the doctors so he could return to his squadron which was heavily involved in supporting Sixth Army at Stalingrad.

In February 1943 Rudel became the first flying officer to complete 1,000 missions. Once again, however, he was transferred away from the front, this time to a research establishment to investigate the possibility of mounting Flak cannon in the Junkers Ju 87 to provide a suitable 'tank-buster'. Rudel was impressed with the idea and soon returned to his unit eager to try out the new weapon. On 1 April 1943, he was promoted to the rank of Hauptmann.

During a Soviet assault across the River Don in the Kuban bridgehead, Rudel knocked out 70 landing craft using standard ammunition in place of the intended anti-tank shells in his tank-buster Ju 87. On 14 April 1943 he received the Oakleaves to his Knight's Cross from Hitler personally, for his continued success and bravery in action. Rudel only agreed to accept the honour if he was permitted to remain in action with his squadron. In July 1943 he finally had the opportunity to use his specially equipped Ju 87 in its intended role against armoured forces in the Bjelgorod and Kharkov regions. His personal score on the first day was twelve tanks. While normal bomb-carrying Ju 87s dealt with anti-aircraft defences, Rudel's tank-busters took their toll of the enemy's armour.

In September 1943 Rudel took command of III/Schlachtgeschwader 2. By 25 November he had scored a further triple success; his 100th tank destroyed, his 1,600th mission flown, and the award of the Swords to his Knight's Cross. At about this time he had recommended his rear-gunner, Erwin Henschel, for the Knight's Cross. Annoyed that this had not yet been approved, Rudel solved the problem by taking Henschel along with him to the ceremony for the investiture of the Swords and obtaining Göring's personal approval for Henschel's award. Henschel then received his Knight's Cross personally from Hitler at the same ceremony. On returning to the front, Rudel's amazing successes against Soviet armour continued and on 11 January 1944 his personal score had reached 150. Only five days later he had notched up his 1,700th mission. On 1 March 1944 he was promoted to Major.

On 20 March 1944, tragedy struck for Rudel. One of his comrades had been shot down behind Soviet lines after an attack on the bridge over the Dniester at Yampol. Rudel landed his own aircraft to attempt a rescue, but the soft boggy soil prevented him from taking off again. Abandoning the aircraft, all four crewmen set off across country for the German lines, eventually reaching the River Dniester. Swimming the 600 yards across the freezing waters quickly sapped their strength and Henschel drowned only 70 yards from safety. After many narrow escapes the fugitives finally reached safety.

A few days after his safe return, Rudel clocked up his 1,800th mission. On 26 March he personally knocked out seventeen tanks in a single day, an achievement which was mentioned in the Oberkommando der Wehrmacht daily dispatch on the following day. On 28 March Rudel added a further nine tanks to his tally, bringing his total score to more than 200. Rudel was decorated with his country's highest honour, the Diamonds to his Knight's Cross, on the following day.

On 3 June this was followed by the Pilot-Observers' badge with Diamonds and a few days later by a unique new award, the Flight Clasp for Schlachtflieger in solid gold and platinum with Diamonds. From the clasp was suspended a small pendant with the number '2000' picked out in small diamonds, celebrating Rudel's 2,000th mission. On 1 September 1944 Rudel was promoted to Oberstleutnant and on 1 October was given command of Schlachtgeschwader 2 Immelmann.

During the next few months Rudel's successes continued unabated, his tally of tanks destroyed growing steadily. This was not without cost however. In August 1944 he had been shot down and suffered a severe leg injury, and in November was wounded in the thigh. Rudel would allow nothing to interfere with his combat duties, however, and was invariably back in action before his wounds had properly healed. By December 1944 his score stood at 460 enemy tanks destroyed.

Rudel's achievements had been carefully monitored at Führerhauptquartier and as he already possess his country's highest award, Hitler decided that the introduction of a new award was justified. Thus on 29 December 1944 Hans Ulrich Rudel became the first and only recipient of the Golden Oakleaves Swords & Diamonds. The award was personally presented to him by Hitler at a ceremony on 1 January 1945. Rudel amazed all present by his audacity in refusing to accept the award unless Hitler authorized him to continue flying combat missions. Hitler initially agreed, but reversed his decision shortly afterwards. Nevertheless Rudel continued to fly, crediting his personal scores to the unit as a whole. This ruse was soon detected, however, and Rudel was given a severe reprimand and once again ordered to stop flying. Typically, Rudel ignored these restrictions and by the end of January 1945 his personal tally of enemy tanks destroyed stood at more than 500.

On 8 February 1945 disaster struck Rudel with a vengeance. While attacking a Soviet armoured breakthrough on the Oder front his Ju 87 was badly hit by Flak and he was seriously wounded. Despite his injuries, he managed to nurse his battered aircraft into a controlled crash-landing before passing out. Awakening in a hospital ward, Rudel was devastated to discover that his right leg had been amputated, having been so badly damaged that the doctors could not save it. So strong was his determination to return to flying, however, that by April he was back with his unit flying missions with a special artificial limb type device made up by his squadron mechanics. Rudel destroyed a total of 26 tanks while flying with only one leg. His war ended on 8 May 1945 when he became a prisoner of the Americans.

Rudel's achievements were truly unique. He had flown 2,530 missions and his score included more than 500 tanks destroyed, one battleship, one cruiser, one destroyer, 70 landing craft, four armoured trains, more than 800 military vehicles and a large number of artillery pieces, Flak guns, etc. Shot down thirty times himself, Rudel was involved in the rescue of six shot-down crews from his squadron.

Rudel was a true patriot who believed in his country to the bitter end and gave his undying loyalty to its leadership. Although his loyalty to the Nazi cause may reflect badly on him in some people's eyes, one thing is beyond any doubt; Rudel was an exceptionally brave and resourceful man, a true ace of aces whose place in history as the world's most successful and highly decorated military flyer is both assured and richly deserved.

Rudel died in 1982. The award document for his Knight's Cross came up for sale at auction in 1984 and fetched more than £20,000, a record price for such a document.

OBERLEUTNANT HANS-ARNOLD STAHLSSCHMIDT

Stahlsschmidt was born in Kreuztal on 15 September 1920. After completing his six-months period of compulsory labour service he enlisted in the Luftwaffe. His training was carried out at the flying school in Breslau and the Vienna military academy.

Stahlsschmidt's first posting was to Jagdgeschwader 27 in the spring of 1941. Serving in North Africa, he achieved his first victory in June 1941. This was not an enemy aircraft however, but a 3,000-ton cargo ship laden with essential ammunition for the Allied garrison in Tobruk. His first aerial victory came on 15 June when, after a long dogfight, he succeeded in shooting down an RAF Hurricane. It was to be the first of many successes for the young fighter pilot. He became an accomplished ace and a close friend of fighter virtuoso Hans-Joachim Marseille. Stahlsschmidt became the first fighter pilot in Africa to win the Flight Clasp for Fighters in Gold for 200 missions.

On 26 February 1942, whilst on a mission behind enemy lines, Stahlsschmidt had to make a forced landing. He was captured by Polish troops and was badly beaten, and had his decorations stolen. He was taken to a POW camp in Tobruk, but managed to evade his guards and made his way through 60 kilometres of enemy-held territory and no-mans-land, safely reaching his own lines.

On 20 April 1942, Stahlsschmidt was decorated with the German Cross in Gold. At this time he was Oberleutnant and Staffelkapitän in 2/ Jagdgeschwader 27. In one month alone, July 1942, he shot down 25 aircraft. On 20 August 1942, he was decorated with the Knight's Cross of the Iron Cross after scoring his 47th victory. On 7 September 1942, Stahlsschmidt scored his 59th, and his squadron's 500th, victory. It was to be his last. When his comrades returned and landed at their base, Stahlsschmidt was missing. His commander, Eduard Neumann, dispatched the 1st and 2nd Staffeln to search for the missing ace, but without success. Stahlsschmidt was officially reported missing in action on 7 September 1942. The Luftwaffe in Africa had lost one of its finest and most promising aces. On 3 January 1944, Oberleutnant Hans-Arnold Stahlsschmidt was posthumously decorated with the Oakleaves to the Knight's Cross, a fitting tribute to the memory of the young ace.

OBERST JOHANNES STEINHOFF

Of all Germany's top fighter aces, few are as admired and respected as much as the great 'Macki' Steinhoff. He was born on 15 September 1913 in Bottendorf and after completion of his academic studies he left the University of Jena in 1934 and joined the Navy as an officer cadet. A long-standing love of aviation, however, led to his transfer to the Luftwaffe in 1936. He trained as a fighter pilot and the outbreak of war found him as Staffelkapitän of 10/Jagdgeschwader 26. In February 1940 he was transferred to Jagdgeschwader 52 with the same appointment.

Steinhoff gained much valuable combat experience against the well-trained pilots of the RAF during the Battle of Britain before being posted to the Eastern Front. There he achieved considerable success against the pilots of the Red Airforce, who could not boast the fine aircraft such as the

Spitfires and Hurricanes of the British, at least not during the early campaigns. Although ultimately the Red Airforce would produce many fine aces of their own, and many excellent fighter aircraft, in 1941 they were to be easy prey for the eager young fighter virtuosi of the Luftwaffe. By 30 August 1941, Oberleutnant Steinhoff had achieved a score of 35 victories and was decorated with the Knight's Cross of the Iron Cross. On 2 September 1942, he added the coveted Oakleaves to his Knight's Cross following his 101st victory. He was the 115th recipient of this award and at the time held the rank of Hauptmann and Kommandeur of II/Jagdgeschwader 52.

After Russia, Steinhoff found himself posted to North Africa where he once again had to accustom himself to the fighting abilities of the RAF, being shot down on more than one occasion. Steinhoff went on to command Jagdgeschwader 77 in Italy following the defeat of Rommel's Afrika Korps. After the loss of Sicily and the Allied invasion of the Italian mainland, Steinhoff's unit was moved up into France where it was needed to help combat the Allied invasion forces in Normandy. On 28 July 1944, following his 167th victory, Steinhoff was decorated with the Swords to his Oakleaves. At this point he held the rank of Oberstleutnant.

In December 1944, Steinhoff took command of Jagdgeschwader 7 for a short period before joining Adolf Galland's Jagdverband 44, the 'Squadron of Experts' in January 1945. This amazing unit numbered one General, two Colonels, one Lieutenant-Colonel and three Majors among its combat pilots. By the last few days of the war Jagdverband 44 could field more than 70 jets available for combat, but lack of fuel and adequately experienced pilots meant that the unit could never achieve its full potential. With the limited strength it had, Jagdverband 44 made some devastating attacks on US daylight bombing raids. Firing a salvo of 24 rockets into the enemy formations, the Me 262 could wreak havoc among the enemy.

On 18 April 1945, Steinhoff and five of his comrades were awaiting orders to take off and intercept Allied bomber formations. Flying conditions were perfect. Ordered to scramble, Steinhoff and his Me 262 hurtled along the runway at a speed of 200kph. As his aircraft began to lift, his port wing suddenly dipped and the aircraft with its full load of fuel and armaments crashed. The jet immediately burst into flames and Steinhoff suffered horrendous burns, only just getting clear before it exploded. He spent the rest of the war in hospital. In his combat career he had flown nearly 1,000 missions and socred 176 victories, the last six of which were achieved with the Me 262. Spending two years in hospital undergoing many painful operations in an attempt to rebuild his disigured features, Steinhoff bore his fate with gallant determination. When he was finally discharged in 1947 he had to start to rebuild his life while coping with the twin disadvantages of his disfigurement and his now socially unacceptable military career. One day a glorious war hero, the next an unwanted militarist.

Eventually, he gained a post in an advertising firm, and remained in this job until 1952 when the new West German Bundeswehr was being reformed. Men of his calibre were desperately needed and Steinhoff once again donned the uniform of the Luftwaffe and prepared to serve his country. His career progressed well and by 1956 he had become Deputy Chief of Staff, Operations, of the Bundesluftwaffe. Steinhoff became a Brigadegeneral in 1958, and four years later was promoted to Generalmajor. He was appointed German Military representative to NATO, where he won the respect and admiration of his colleagues. When this tour of duty in Washington was over, he became Chief of Staff of NATO Air Forces, based now in Paris. Becoming Inspektor der Bundesluftwaffe in 1966, Steinhoff, insisted, despite his high rank, in maintaining his pilot qualification on all the current jet fighters introduced into the Luftwaffe. He finally retired in 1972. During his long military career, as well as becoming one of the worlds top aces, he was also one of the first jet aces and in addition had helped pioneer the German night fighter force, serving with Wolfgang Falck in the formation of Nachtjagdgeschwader 1.

Although Steinhoff is perhaps less well known than aces such as Galland or Mölders, his contribution to the history of the Luftwaffe is second to none. Indeed the Luftwaffe could have had no finer ambassador than this skilled and gallant airman, truly one of the great aces of all time.

GENERALMAJOR WALTER STORP

Walter Storp was born on 2 February 1910 in Schnecken, East Prussia. The son of a forester, he joined the Reichsmarine in 1928 as an officer cadet, on completion of his education. In 1933, he commenced flying training at Warnemünde, obtaining his pilot's licence in 1934.

Storp became a coastal reconnaissance pilot with Küstenaufklärungs-gruppe in Nordenay, flying the Heinkel He 60 before becoming a pilot of one of the catapult-launched floatplanes aboard the cruiser *Leipzig*. In 1936 he was promoted to Oberleutnant and took up duties as a pilot in various Luftwaffe experimental units. By the outbreak of war, Storp had reached the rank of Hauptmann and during the Polish Campaign flew the Messerschmitt Me 110 in Lehrgeschwader 1, winning the Iron Cross Second Class. Storp subsequently underwent conversion for bombers, joining the first Luftwaffe unit to receive the Junkers Ju 88 bomber for trials.

During the course of the Norwegian Campaign, Storp became the first pilot in his unit to win the Iron Cross First Class and achieved considerable successes, sinking the destroyer *Fafnir*. With Kampfgeschwader 30 and Kampfgeschwader 4 during the French Campaign, he succeeded in sinking a 10,000-ton troop transport during the evacuation from Dunkirk. His Geschwader sank more than 65,000 tons of merchant shipping plus a destroyer during this period, and was heavily engaged in attacks on railheads and airfields.

Storp was decorated with the Knight's Cross of the Iron Cross on 21 October 1940 at which point he was flying bombing missions against the United Kingdom. By April 1941 he had reached the rank of Major and was Kommodore of Schnellkampfgeschwader 210, serving on the central sector of the Eastern Front. In September of that year he was decorated with the Oakleaves to his Knight's Cross, only the 22nd recipient of this decoration. In early 1943, Major Storp was promoted to Oberstleutnant and by August to Oberst, becoming Commander of all Kampfflieger in the Mediterranean, with seven Geschwader under his command. In October 1944, Storp was promoted to Generalmajor and appointed General der Kampfflieger. The end of the war found him as Commander of 5 Fliegerdivision based in Norway.

One of the most respected figures in the Luftwaffe's bomber arm, Storp was an excellent tactician who had proved his own gallantry in hard combat. Taken prisoner by the British, he was held in captivity until 1948. He died in retirement at Goslar in August 1981.

HAUPTMANN WOLFGANG TONNE

Fighter ace Wolfgang Tonne was born in Moosbach, Thüringia on 28 February 1918. He joined the Luftwaffe in 1937 and went on to become one of Jagdgeschwader 53's most successful pilots.

Tonne joined the Geschwader in 1939, serving in 3/Jagdgeschwader 53 during the fall of France and the Battle of Britain. By the time his unit was withdrawn from the Battle of Britain to be posted to the Eastern Front, Tonne had qualified as an ace after achieving five victories.

As Staffelkapitän of 3/Jagdgeschwader 53, Tonne was awarded the Knight's Cross of the Iron Cross on 6 September 1942 after achieving his 54th victory. Two months later he was posted to the North Africa, serving in Tunisia. His successes continued here and on 24 September 1942 he was awarded the Oakleaves to his Knight's Cross, having increased his score to 101 victories in a very short time.

Tragedy befell this promising ace on 20 April 1943, when his aircraft crashed on landing at Protville, in Tunis. He had flown a total of 641 missions and scored 122 victories, 96 of which were achieved on the Eastern Front.

OBERFELDWEBEL ALOIS WOSNITZA

Born on 17 November 1914, Alois Wosnitza joined the Luftwaffe in 1935 and on completion of his basic military training, commenced his flying training in 1936. Once he had qualified as a pilot and gained his wings he was posted to a Stuka Gruppe.

On the outbreak of war, Wosnitza served during the Polish Campaign with Schlachtgruppe 77. Although the Junkers Ju 87 Stuka was already obsolescent at the start of the war, against the weaker Polish forces it achieved great success. The sight and sound of the Stuka in almost vertical dive, its siren screaming, has become synonymous with the term *Blitzkrieg*. During the French Campaign in 1940, the Stuka also proved an invaluable asset in the ground support role. On innumerable occasions, Stuka attacks on Allied troop concentrations helped win the day.

Wosnitza also served during the Battle of Britain. It was here that the Stuka's shortcomings were highlighted. Against the Spitfires and Hurricanes of the RAF it was far too slow and its manoeuvrability poor. Although its effectiveness against its targets remained high, fewer and fewer were able to reach their target areas, being intercepted by enemy fighters. Stuka losses reached such high levels that it was withdrawn from the battle.

After the Battle of Britain, Wosnitza and his Gruppe were transferred to the Balkans, seeing combat in Yugoslavia, Greece and Crete where the dive-bombing operations in support of the paratroop landings were an important factor in the German victory. During the early phase of the invasion of the Soviet Union, when Soviet air power was ineffectual, the Stuka once again came into its own. Schlachtgruppe 77 operated in the central and southern sector of the front. In December 1941, Wosnitza was awarded the Goblet of Honour for special achievement in the air war.

In 1942, Wosnitza's unit played an important part in the attack on Sevastopol, flying a total of nearly 8,000 missions. Stukas were still achieving considerable successes despite the increasing strength and effectiveness of the Red Airforce. Schlachtgruppe 77 also flew support missions at Stalingrad. On 7 September 1942, Wosnitza was decorated with the German Cross in Gold, shortly after having flown his 500th mission.

In October 1943, all Stuka-equipped units had their aircraft replaced by the excellent Focke-Wulf Fw 190 fighter. This superb fighter was infinitely superior to the elderly Stukas, and was indeed equal to any fighter that the Allies could field against it. As well as being used as a fighter, it had success as a fighter-bomber and even as a torpedo-bomber.

In May 1944, Wosnitza transferred to Schlachtgeschwader 102 at Deutsch-Brod for a short period before joining Schlachtgeschwader 10 for the remainder of the war. He was decorated with the Knight's Cross of the Iron Cross on 26 March 1944 after completing his 800th mission. By October 1944, Wosnitza, now flying the Fw 190, had increased his mission count to 1,000. Flying his last mission on 15 April 1945, he was shot down and seriously wounded.

Wosnitza flew a total of 1,217 missions of which around 150 were made with the Fw 190. He destroyed 104 tanks, two armoured trains, twelve bridges, one troop transport, several landing craft and about 180 other assorted enemy vehicles. As well as these ground-attack victories, Wosnitza shot down two enemy aircraft while flying the Fw 190. Oberfeldwebel Wosnitza was nominated for the Oakleaves to his Knight's Cross, but the war ended before the nomination could be processed and approved. This successful Stuka ace survived the war and died in retirement in December 1982.

THE SEA ACES

Although the Allies, especially the US Navy in the Pacific, did have some highly successful submarine aces, no other submarine force ever played such a major part in its country's fortunes as did the German U-Boat arm. Whereas Göring's boast that his Luftwaffe would bring Britain to its knees was shown to be empty, the U-boats under Karl Dönitz came within a hair's breadth of doing just that. Churchill himself admitted that if Britain were cut off, and the war at sea lost, nothing else would count.

Only a few weeks after the start of the war, the U-boat arm dealt a savage blow to British morale when *U 47* under Günther Prien slipped into the naval anchorage at Scapa Flow and sank the battleship *Royal Oak*. When France fell, giving the U-boats access to coastal bases, Dönitz's submarines could operate without having to take the time- and fuel-consuming, and very risky route around the north of Scotland.

Amazing though the achievements of the Kriegsmarine's U-boats were, on closer examination we can see that, as with the Luftwaffe, there were a number of contributing factors, not the least of which was the influence of Karl Dönitz. He had argued that Germany needed approximately 300 submarines in action before going to war with Britain with a good chance of success. In view of the fact that he had only about 60, and that peak U-boat strength even in 1944 was only 250, and still he almost brought Britain to her knees, it seems certain that if he had had 300, Britain would have had no chance. Few commanders have concerned themselves with the welfare of their men as much as did Dönitz. His men were an élite force; U-boat personnel received extra pay, extra rations, and more leave. Dönitz followed the fortunes of his commanders closely and was often on hand personally to greet them on their return from a war cruise. All of this contributed to the exceptionally high morale of the U-boat arm. Despite the fact that of some 40,000 men who went to sea in the U-boat service, about 30,000 perished, morale remained high to the very end.

In its early days the U-boat arm was equipped with the small coastal Type II. It was used mainly for minelaying duties in British waters and was withdrawn from front-line service and had been relegated to training duties by the end of 1939. The Type VII, in particular the VIIC model, became the backbone of the U-boat service with more than 600 being built. With a length of 66m and a displacement of approximately 800 tons, it carried a crew of about 50 men and was armed with fourteen torpedoes, a 3.5in deck gun and various combinations of anti-aircraft weapons. It was in this submarine that most of the U-boat aces achieved their fame.

The third most important U-boat type to see action was the Type IX of which the Type IXC saw most combat. A large boat of some 76m and with a displacement of well over 1,000 tons, it was intended for long-distance operations such as service in the Indian Ocean and the Pacific. It did not play a particularly significant part in the Battle of the Atlantic, only 143 being built.

The Type VIIC in its various improved forms was undoubtedly the best German U-boat to see widespread use, and certainly these boats were as good as those in use by any other nation. So, with sky-high morale and first-class equipment, the U-boat commanders went to war, fully confident in their ability to bring Britain to her knees.

One particular factor in the successes of the U-boat aces was of course the availability of targets. The German merchant marine did not operate large convoys of merchantmen over great distances, to provide targets for the submarines of the Royal Navy. Up to late 1940, the U-boats operated with near impunity against Allied shipping. Anti-submarine measures were totally inadequate and air cover poor. Lack of radio security, however, did allow Allied trackers some degree of success in establishing the positions of U-boats and thus avoiding them. As more disciplined convoy systems were introduced with escort destroyers and corvettes, U-boat successes suffered a definite decline.

Following the entry of the USA into the war, the U-boats once again enjoyed a period of great success. The Americans, unused to U-boat attacks, were in the same state of undisciplined disorganization as had been the British on the outbreak of war, and the U-boats took full advantage of the situation. Virtually unopposed, the U-boats inflicted horrendous losses on merchant shipping.

At first, incredibly, the US authorities did not believe the attacks were from U-boats but rather, losses through mines. Gradually, however, American anti-submarine measures grew in their effectiveness, and the U-boats were driven ever-farther afield in their search for targets. Moves into the Caribbean Sea and Indian Ocean brought new targets, but stretched the U-boats' range and communication lines to their absolute limits. This was initially overcome by the use of U-boat tankers, but these were soon all sunk, forcing an end to such long-distance patrols.

By 1943 the Battle of the Atlantic was reaching its climax as U-boat losses grew steadily, due to increasingly effective anti-submarine measures, while sinkings of Allied shipping decreased. While the U-boat arm remained aggressive and dangerous to the last, there was no longer any chance that Germany could win the war at sea. Towards the end of the war two new submarine types were introduced into service: the Types XXI and XXIII. The Type XXI was a superb vessel, some 76m long with a displacement of more than 1,600 tons. It carried 24 torpedoes and had two twin 20mm anti-aircraft guns in automated turrets. This ultra-modern vessel might well have swung the balance of the Battle of the Atlantic in Germany's favour had they been introduced early enough, but although a considerable number were built, only four had been commissioned by the end of the war, and of these only two went to sea on combat duty. The Type XXIII was a smaller coastal version of the type XXI, which, although some did see action, played no significant part in the war.

Naturally enough, the award of the Knight's Cross to a U-boat commander reflected credit on his entire crew. The Captain was in effect a figurehead and many commanders clearly felt that the award was worn on behalf of all his comrades. There does not appear to have been an exact tonnage target for the award of the Knight's Cross. The type of vessel sunk was highly significant. Some commanders might have received the Knight's Cross after sinking say 50,000 tons of shipping, others, after sinking just one ship, if the ship were a warship. This should be remembered when noting that a particular U-boat commander seems to have only a small tonnage to his credit. In view of the enormous losses suffered by the U-boats, it would indeed take great courage for a U-boat commander to attack a warship which might well have been purpose-built or equipped to destroy submarines. It should also be remembered that a small tonnage sunk in the latter part of the war may have taken as much courage and effort as a large tonnage sunk during the early days when anti-submarine measures were ineffective. Early and late submarine victories can be roughly equated with Eastern Front and Western Fighter victories.

While the high scores of the top aces do of course indicate an amazing level of skill and proficiency, it is totally wrong to base an estimate of a U-boat commander's status on tonnage sunk alone. A particular score may well have elevated a commander to ace status, but there were many other very gallant and daring commanders who risked and often lost their lives without achieving a high score. It was not only gallantry that brought success to an ace. Skill, a sound boat, an efficient crew and last but not least, luck, were also important.

A smaller, but highly important branch of the Kriegsmarine was the Schnellboote arm. These were the equivalent of the Allied motor torpedo-boats. The Schnellboote, usually abbreviated to S-Boote in German or to E-Boats in English, were extremely fast, well-armed vessels. With a very low profile, which made them a difficult target, these boats could approach the enemy at high speed, launch their torpedoes and be gone before the enemy could react effectively. In the English Channel, the Baltic, the Black Sea, and the Mediterranean, these boats proved their effectiveness. Certainly Grossadmiral Raeder was sufficiently impressed by their successes against Allied shipping that he introduced a special diamond-studded version of the E-Boat war badge for award to particularly successful commanders.

One vessel which caused considerable trouble to the Allies was the auxiliary cruiser. These were converted merchantmen with concealed guns and torpedoes, manned by regular naval personnel. Disguised by false superstructure and funnels to conceal their true identity, they would approach unsuspecting merchant ships before running the battle flag up the mast and uncovering their concealed armament. Often merchant ships caught in this way would surrender without further ado, but those that did put up a fight would soon be overcome by the superior armament of the auxiliary cruiser, most of which carried six 6in guns. Although not intended for action against warships, the power of these vessels was illustrated by the sinking of the cruiser *Sydney* by *Kormoran*. Although *Kormoran* herself was destroyed in the action, for a converted merchantman to take on and destroy a powerful modern cruiser was a considerable achievement. Part of the success of these auxiliary cruisers lay in the number of Allied ships tied down in the hunt for them, and which could be ill-spared from other essential duties.

One final section of the Kriegsmarine which deserves brief mention here was the Kleinkampfmittelverbande or small combat units. These encompassed frogmen, midget submarines, one-man torpedoes, etc. In the latter part of the war several midget submarines were introduced by the Kriegsmarine, including the *Neger*, *Biber* and *Molch* types. Several hundred of these were produced and put into service. With very limited range, these vessels could not play a significant part in the war. They were extremely unreliable and many crew were killed in them before they could reach their targets. It must be admitted though, that some successes were achieved by these vessels, sufficient to bring the award of the Knight's Cross to their crews.

In this section of the book, a selection of aces from the U-boats, E-boats and auxiliary cruisers is given. These are of course only representative and full lists are given in the appropriate appendices.

Above: Marine-Schreiber-Obergefreiter Walter Gerhold is decorated with the Knight's Cross of the Iron Cross by his commanding Admiral. Gerhold severely damaged the 5,000-ton cruiser *Dragon* in the waters off the Normandy coast with his Neger one-man torpedo. Making the award, in July 1944, is Admiral Hellmuth Heye, Admiral der Kleinkampfverbände.

KAPITÄNLEUTNANT KLAUS BARGSTEN

Born in Bad Oldesloe on 31 October 1911, Bargsten was a career submarine officer, spending his entire service career with the U-boat service. On the outbreak of war he was undergoing training at the U-Boat School in Neustadt. Shortly afterwards he was appointed as Wach Offizier in *U 99* under the ace of aces, Otto Kretschmer. Bargsten took part in most of *U 99*'s most successful cruises, gaining much invaluable experience under Kretschmer. Shortly before *U 99* was sunk, and her crew captured, Bargsten was given command of his own boat, *U 563* on 27 March 1941.

Soon, Bargsten was making his own reputation as a successful ace. On 24 October 1941, *U 563* attacked Convoy HG75, UK-bound from Gibraltar. Bargsten unleashed a salvo of torpedoes, sinking a steamer, and immediately fired again at a destroyer escort. The torpedoes missed their mark but, passing harmlessly by the escort, went on to strike another ship further into the convoy. The famous Tribal-class destroyer *Cossack* had been mortally stricken. Famed for her capture of the German supply ship *Altmark* in a Norwegian fiord, *Cossack* was now in dire straits and sank at about midnight on 26 October. *U 563* made further attacks on HG75 and although detonations were heard, no further conclusive evidence of sinkings was recorded. An attack on the corvette *Heliotrope* was likewise unsuccessful.

In the summer of 1942, Bargsten took command of *U 521*. In November of that year, he attacked yet another warship, this time the Canadian corvette *Moosejaw*, escorting Convoy SC107 UK-bound from Australia. Although the torpedo was heard to explode, *Moosejaw* was not sunk. However, from the same convoy the British steamer *Harlington* was sent to the bottom. This was in effect the *coup de grâce* as she had already been attacked by *U 552* and *U 438*. *Itahira*, an American steamer, was also sunk. In mid-November 1942, Bargsten attacked ONS144, outward-bound from the UK to North America, and despite the detonations of torpedoes being once again clearly heard, no actual sinkings were recorded.

Bargsten's next victories were scored in February 1943, against Convoy GIBR2, heading from the Canaries to Gibraltar. The auxiliary sub-chaser *Bredon* was sunk. The *U 521* also hit an oil tanker and it is thought that it was the fire spreading from the stricken tanker which engulfed and sank *Bredon*. On 25 February 1943, Bargsten again fearlessly attacked a destroyer escort, but once again he was dogged by bad luck and the enemy managed to evade his torpedoes. Bargsten's final success came on 18 March 1943 when the steamer *Molly Pitcher* from Convoy UGS6, Gibraltar-bound from the UK, was sent to the bottom. This brought his score to 23,523 tons of shipping sunk, and on 30 April 1943 he became the 164th naval recipient of the Knight's Cross of the Iron Cross. *U 521* was sunk off the US coast south-east of Baltimore by the US sub-chaser *PC565* on 2 June 1943. Bargsten and most of his crew were saved.

Bargsten's score, though appearing modest in comparison to some of his contemporaries, is none the less significant as it includes a powerful and important warship, one whose loss was a serious blow to the morale of the Royal Navy. Bargsten is still alive.

KORVETTENKAPITÄN ERNST BAUER

Ernst Bauer was born in Fürth, Bavaria on 3 January 1914. He joined the Navy in 1933 and on 22 March 1941 took his first command, *U 126*, to sea.

Bauer's first attack was on Gibraltar-bound Convoy OG69 on 27 July 1941. He fired four bow torpedoes and both stern tubes. The British steamer *Erato* of 1,300 tons exploded after a direct hit by one of Bauer's torpedoes and one other smaller ship behind her was also hit. The two stern torpedoes also scored hits on two other ships. Just eight days later *U 126* sank the steam trawler *Robert Max* by gunfire. A quiet spell of about ten days followed, broken on 14 August when the small Yugoslav steamer *Sud* of 2,600 tons was torpedoed and sunk. This was in fact a *coup de grâce* shot because she had already been disabled by the Italian submarine *Marconi* commanded by Lieutenant Mario Paolo Pollina. So ended Bauer's first sortie in *U 126*.

His second cruise saw its first success on 10 October 1941 when the 4,900-ton British steamer *Railsea Manor* was torpedoed and sunk, and nine days later the American *Lehigh*, also of 4,900 tons, was torpedoed. This was a dangerous move as the USA had not yet entered the war. On the following day, the British tanker *British Mariner*, a 7,000-tonner, was torpedoed and sunk. For more than three weeks after this Bauer could find no fresh victims, but on 13 November the 7,000-ton *Peru* was attacked and sent to the bottom.

During 1942, Bauer and *U 126* achieved their greatest victories, during his third cruise. The first victim of this patrol was the 2,300-ton Norwegian steamer *Gunny* on 5 March. Two days later, the 4,600-ton American steamer *Barbara* was torpedoed and the 5,100-ton *Cardonia* sunk by a combination of torpedo and gunfire. These successes continued on the following day when the large, 10,300-ton tanker *Esso Bolivar* was damaged by both torpedo and gunfire, and on 9 March the Panamanian tanker *Hanseat* of some 8,200 tons was sunk, also by a combination of torpedo and gunfire. Yet more success followed on 12 March when the American steamship *Texan* of 7,000 tons and the smaller *Olga* of 2,500 tons were both sunk. On 13 March, the 5,500-ton American steamer *Colabee* was badly damaged and had to be beached, though she was later salvaged. All the March victories were scored in the Caribbean area. On 16 March, in recognition of his considerable successes, Bauer was decorated with the Knight's Cross of the Iron Cross. He was presented with the award when *U 126* arrived home at the end of this highly successful cruise.

In the summer of 1942, Bauer took *U 126* back into American waters, operating off the coast of South America and the Caribbean. On 3 June he sank the large Norwegian tanker *Höegh Giant*, a 10,900-tonner which was sent to the bottom after an attack by torpedoes and gunfire. A lean period of nearly two weeks followed, but on 15 June the sailing ship *Nueva Alta Gracia* was sunk by gunfire. On the next day Bauer was luckier and sank the two American steamers *Arkansen* of 7,000 tons and *Kahuku* of 6,000 tons, the first by torpedo and the second by a combination of torpedo and gunfire. On 27 June, another large tanker, the 9,950-ton Norwegian *Leiv Eriksson* was sunk, to be followed two days later by the Canadian sailing ship *Mona Marie*, which was sent to the bottom by *U 126*'s 4.1in gun. July opened with a further victim on the 1st of the month when the large American 7,550-ton steamer *Warrior* was sunk, and two days later another large target, the American tanker *Gulfbelle* of 7,100 tons was damaged.

Bauer's final cruise with *U 126* was in the winter of 1942, when she was operating off the West African coast. On 1 November, the 7,100-ton American steamer *George Thacher* was sunk. On 4 November, the small British steamer *Oued Grou* was sunk, to be followed the next day by the 6.500-ton *New Toronto*, also British. On 22 November, *U 126* rendezvoused with the auxiliary cruiser *Atlantis* to take on fuel. While Bauer and some of his men were taking the opportunity of some hot food and coffee aboard *Atlantis* the British cruiser *Devonshire* was sighted. As *Atlantis* made ready to meet the enemy, *U 126* cut the fuel lines and crash-dived. Disabled by a faulty engine, *Atlantis* had no chance against the powerful cruiser and was soon sunk. The British, assuming that the U-boat was still lurking in the area, took no chances and sped off as soon as *Atlantis* had sunk. *U 126* surfaced and took on the survivors who included Ernst Bauer. This was to be Bauer's last cruise.

On his return to Germany, Bauer was appointed to the command of 26 Unterseebootsflotille, and ultimately of the training flotilla at Pillau. He ended the war with the rank of Korvettenkapitän and a total score of 108,513 tons, representing 24 ships, to his credit. A further four ships of 30,000 tons were damaged. Bauer survived the war and lived in retirement in Westerland until his death in 1988.

KORVETTENKAPITÄN HERMANN BÜCHTING

Hermann Büchting was born in Neumunster on 14 March 1916. His naval career began in April 1935 when he joined the Kriegsmarine and was enrolled into Schiffsstammabteilung 2 in Stralsund. On completion of his training he spent two months on seamanship training in the sail trainer *Gorch Fock*, followed by nine months on a world-wide goodwill tour in the light cruiser *Karlsruhe*. Then, with just over a year's service, Büchting was sent to the Marineschule Mürwick to undergo his officer training. This was completed in March 1937, and Büchting, by now a Fähnrich zur See, underwent a further series of courses at Torpedoschule, Nachrichtenschule, etc., before, on 15 October 1937 being posted as Wach Offizier with the Torpedo Boat Training Flotilla.

On 1 January 1938 Büchting was promoted to Oberfähnrich, and in April

1938 was commissioned Leutnant zur See. On completion of his torpedo-boat training in October 1938 he was given his first active posting. Joining 5 Torpedobootsflotille, he served in the Torpedoboot *Greif*, being promoted, in October 1939, to Oberleutnant zur See. From the outbreak of war until March 1940, Büchting served on minelaying and coastal security duties in the North Sea and Skagerrak.

In March 1940, Hermann Büchting transferred to the Schnellboote, joining 1 Schnellbootsflotille as commander of various boats including *S25*, *S21*, *S27* and *S51*. Until 1941, 1 Schnellbootsflotille was mainly active in Norwegian waters, in the English Channel and the mouth of the River Thames. These heavily armed and extremely fast vessels were a painful thorn in the side of the British Merchant Marine and Royal Navy. From mid-1941 until the end of the war, Büchting served off the Finnish Coast, then transferred to the Black Sea in early 1942. On 1 June 1942 he was promoted to Kapitänleutnant. 1 Schnellbootsflotille was extremely successful in its Black Sea operations; it was responsible for sinking huge amounts of shipping and also shot down several aircraft. On 22 April 1943 Büchting was decorated with the Knight's Cross of the Iron Cross for his successes as an E-boat commander and shortly thereafter was given command of the Flotilla. In the closing stages of the war, Büchting and his flotilla served in the Danzig-Gotenhafen area and the Kurland coast, defending the evacuation of vast numbers of military and civilian refugees from certain Soviet captivity. Hermann Büchting survived the war and became a very successful businessman. He lives today near Hamburg.

KAPITÄN ZUR SEE THEODOR DETMERS

Theodor Detmers was born in Witten on 22 August 1902. He joined the Navy in 1921 and on commissioning his duties included overseas tours with the cruiser *Köln*. Detmers also served in torpedo-boats for a spell before being appointed to command Z7, a modern, 2,200-ton destroyer *Hermann Schoemann*, built by Deschimag of Bremen. Detmers commanded her until June 1940 when he was posted to command a new vessel, the auxiliary cruiser *Schiff 41*, *Kormoran*.

Kormoran had been built for the Hamburg-Amerika Line as *Steiermark*. She never saw merchant service, having been requisitioned by the Kriegsmarine as soon as her trials were completed. The 8,736-tonner was then fitted out with six 5.9in guns, two 37mm and five 20mm Flak guns, two 21in torpedo tubes and 360 mines. She carried two Arado Ar 196 floatplanes.

Breaking out via the Denmark Strait on 13 December 1940, she had reached the tropics by the end of the month. Her first victim, the 4,800-ton Greek freighter *Antonis*, with a cargo of coal, was sunk on 6 June 1941. Two days later the 6,987-ton *British Union*, a fully laden tanker, was sent to the bottom. On 29 June Detmers encountered *Afric Star* of 11,900 tons and had no sooner disposed of her when the 5,700-ton *Eurylochus* appeared on the scene and was rapidly attacked and sunk.

Plagued by engine trouble, Detmers spent a fruitless two months searching for new victims until 22 March 1941 when he encountered the small, 3,560-ton tanker *Agnita* and sank her without loss of life. Three days later the much larger 11,300-ton *Canadolite* was captured undamaged. On 9 April, the British freighter *Craftsman*, an 8,000-tonner refused to stop after a warning shot and was swiftly dealt with. Three days later the Greek 5,500-ton *Nicolaos D.L.* was captured intact with her entire crew. On the evening of 1 May, Detmers rounded the Cape and entered the Indian Ocean. These new waters appeared to be devoid of traffic and it was not until 26 June that Detmers met his next victim, the 4,150-ton Yugoslav freighter *Velebit*. The freighter refused to stop despite repeated signals from *Kormoran*, and heavy shelling. She was soon ablaze from stem to stern, and was left adrift. She eventually beached in the Andaman Islands. Later that same day, the Australian merchantman *Mareeba* of 3,470 tons, carrying a cargo of sugar, was caught and sunk after her crew had been taken off.

A very lean time followed for Detmers, his ship now the sole raider in the Indian Ocean. His constant patrolling was fruitless until 23 September when the small Greek freighter *Stamatios G. Embiricos* of 3,930 tons was encountered. After she had surrendered without a fight, Detmers had her scuttled. On 19 November 1941, Detmers luck ran out when he was intercepted by the cruiser HMAS *Sydney*. With one troublesome engine, Detmers had no chance of outrunning the fast cruiser. He could only hope to bluff his way for as long as possible then fight it out. Amazingly, *Sydney* was at first taken in by *Kormoran*'s attempts to pass herself off as a Dutch freighter and allowed herself to come well within range of *Kormoran*'s guns. When Detmers felt he could no longer sustain his bluff, he uncovered the guns and opened fire on the unsuspecting cruiser, smashing her bridge and putting both forward turrets out of action. Then a torpedo smashed into *Sydney*'s hull level with her forward turrets, but her after turrets poured fire into *Kormoran*, hitting the engine room and setting her on fire. Both *Kormoran*'s engines stopped and as she lay floundering, Detmers saw the blazing hull of *Sydney* slowly disappear over the horizon. Detmers abandoned his ship and just half an hour after the last man left, the flames reached her magazine and her mines exploded, blasting the ship to pieces.

Detmers and his crew were eventually picked up by an Australian ship and spent the rest of the war in captivity. While held by the Australians, Detmers was advised that he had been promoted to Kapitän zur See and on 4 December 1941 was awarded the Knight's Cross of the Iron Cross. He had sunk eleven ships totalling 68,250 tons, including a powerful warship. He was released in 1947 and returned to Germany. Theodor Detmers died in November 1976.

KAPITÄNLEUTNANT ALFRED EICK

Alfred Eick was born in Essen on 9 March 1916. After completing his six months' obligatory *Reichsarbeitsdienst* service from October 1936 to March 1937, he entered the Kriegsmarine as a potential officer cadet. Like most of his contemporaries he completed a period of sail training in *Gorch Fock*, the beautiful three-masted barque. This was followed by a period of about seven months in a capital ship, in this case the old battleship *Schlesien* from September 1937 until April 1938. Thereafter he attended the Marineschule at Flensburg-Mürwick, undergoing weapons and signals training before being commissioned Leutnant zur See on 1 August 1939.

From 1 September 1939 to 1 November 1940, Eick served with the minesweeping branch before commencing his U-boat training at Pillau in November 1940. On completion of his training in October 1941 Eick was posted to *U 176* as Wach Offizier. *U 176* was a Type IX6, a powerful 1,200-tonner armed with 22 torpedoes and a 4in cannon.

Eick was promoted to Oberleutnant zur See on 1 September 1941. Ultimately he was given command of his own boat, *U 510*, a Type IXC, which he took over from Karl Neitzel. In July 1942 he sailed on his first cruise, during which he attacked and sank the 10,000-ton Norwegian tanker *B.P. Newton* as well as disabling a smaller, 1,400-ton steamer.

In January 1943, *U 510* was sent to the Indian Ocean where Eick scored considerable successes despite several times being subjected to furious depth-charge attacks by escort destroyers. On 16 March 1944 he was decorated with the German Cross in Gold, and this was followed on the 31st of that month by the Knight's Cross of the Iron Cross. Eick saw action in the South Atlantic, off the South American coast, in the Gulf of Aden, off Singapore and in Japanese waters. On 1 April 1944 he was promoted to Kapitänleutnant. He had sunk a total of ten ships, totalling 57,220 tons, and damaged or disabled many more.

He was recalled from the Pacific in the closing stages of the war and returned safely to home waters, itself no mean feat, given the Allied air and sea superiority at this juncture. Having safely covered such a vast distance, she ran out of fuel just off St-Nazaire and was captured. Used by the French after the war, *U 510* was renamed *Bouan*, being finally scrapped in 1958. France in fact utilized several captured U-boats during the early post-war years, including the Type IXB *U 123* which was scrapped in 1957, the type VIIC *U 471* which, as the French *Mille*, was not scrapped until 1963, and a Type XXI which served in the French Navy as *Roland Morillot*. It is an indication of the quality of German U-boat design that some of the Kriegsmarine's U-boats were still in service some twenty years after the end of the war. Alfred Eick was also taken prisoner by the French, and was held as a POW until 1947. He is still alive.

KORVETTENKAPITÄN KARL EMMERMANN

Karl Emmermann was born in Hamburg on 6 March 1915 and joined the Navy in 1934. The outbreak of war found him in a posting at the Marineschule at Mürwick. From November 1940 to August 1941, he served as Wach Offizier in the U-boat *U-A*. This was a 1,300-ton vessel built in Germany for the Turkish Navy under the name *Batiray*. On the outbreak of war, however, she was taken over by the Kriegsmarine. A lucky ship, she survived the war, to be scuttled in May 1945.

On 5 August 1941, Emmermann took command of his own boat, *U 172*, a Type IXC. This was a new boat, built by the Deschimag yard in Bremen. After the usual trials and working-up period, *U 172* set off on her first cruise in April 1942. It was uneventful and was followed by a second, longer cruise to the Caribbean.

Emmermann's first success was the sinking of the British tanker *Athel Knight* on 27 May. This was followed on 1 June by the steamer *Illinois* and on 3 June *Delfind* was added to *U 172*'s score. On 8 June 1942 *Sicilien* and on 14 June *Lebore* were sent to the bottom. Emmermann's successes continued unabated; on 15 June the steamer *Bernetsvet* was sunk. The small tanker *Motorex* was sunk by gunfire on 18 June and both torpedoes and gunfire were used to sink the larger steamer *Santa Rita* on 9 July. This successful cruise was followed by a welcome month-long break in Lorient, before setting off for the South Atlantic. Emmermann's next victim was the 6,200-ton *Chicksaw City*, sunk on 7 October, followed by *Freihorn* and *Pantelu* within 24 hours.

A major success followed on 10 October when the large troopship *Orcades* of some 23,500 tons was hit by a total of four torpedoes and sank three hours later. *Orcades* was carrying 1,067 passengers and crew of whom some 1,021 were saved. On 31 October, the 5,000-ton British *Aldington Court* was sunk, followed on 2 November by another 5,000-tonner, *Llandilo*. *U 172* surfaced and seeing that the lifeboats were waterlogged, took the survivors on board until the lifeboats could be baled out and made ready. The next ship to fall victim to *U 172* was the 6,600-ton *Ben Lomond*, off the Brazilian coast. One survivor, a steward, was adrift on a life-raft for more than four months before being rescued. On 27 November 1942, Carl Emmermann was decorated with the Knight's Cross of the Iron Cross in recognition of his successes. On the same day that his award was approved, Emmermann sank another 5,300-ton steamship, *Alaskan*. After refuelling at sea from one of the Type XIV tanker U-boats known as *Milch Kuh* (milk cows), *U 172* sailed for home and reached Lorient on 27 December 1942.

Emmermann's fourth cruise was to the US coast, setting sail on 21 February 1943. *U 172*'s first success was *City of Pretoria* on 4 March. On 6 March *Thorstrand* followed. On 13 March, *U 172* was involved in an attack on Convoy UGS6, and sank the steamer *Keystone*. On 16 March *Benjamin Harrison* followed. At the end of this month in an attack on another convoy, RS3, the steamer *Silverbeach* was sunk. It was the last victory of this cruise.

On his return, Emmermann was posted to command 6 Unterseeboots-flotille at St-Nazaire and served in this capacity until August 1944. From then until March 1945, he served on the staff of the commander of U-Boat Training. In March 1945, for just one month, he took command of one of the new Type XXI, built by Deschimag. In April 1945, he became Commander of 31 Unterseebootsflotille before, in the last few days of the war, commanding a Marine Infanterie Bataillon in the defence of Hamburg. Taken prisoner at the end of the war, he was released in September 1945.

Emmermann's boat, *U 172* was sunk on 12 December 1943 in the mid-Atlantic, west of the Canaries, by the US destroyers *Clemson*, *Dupont*, *George E. Badger*, and *George W. Ingram*, and by aircraft from the carrier *Bogue*. *U 172*'s new commander and 34 of his crew were saved. Carl Emmermann's final score of tonnage sunk was 152,904 representing 27 ships. He became the 256th recipient of the Oakleaves on 4 July 1943, in recognition of his successes against shipping.

KAPITÄNLEUTNANT HEINZ FRANKE

A Berliner, born on 30 November 1915, Heinz Franke began his career in U-boats as Wach Offizier in *U 262*, taking over command from Kapitän-leutnant Schiesbauch. Franke's first success as a commander was on 17 November 1942 in the Atlantic during an attack on Convoy ONS144. He fired a spead of three torpedoes at a 7,000-ton freighter. Although the detonations were clearly heard, there are no Allied records of a ship being sunk. It may well be that the torpedoes exploded prematurely, the Kriegsmarine being plagued by faulty torpedoes for a considerable time. On the following day, however, the same North America-bound convoy was attacked and the corvette *Montbretia* was sunk, having received direct hits from two torpedoes. On the 26th, the British steamer *Ocean Crusader* of some 7,100 tons was torpedoed and sunk. No further successes were scored until 5–6 February 1943 when an attack on Convoy SC118 from Sydney to the United Kingdom was launched. The Polish steamship *Zagloba* of 2,800 tons was sunk and three hits were made on an unidentified tanker which broke her back and sank in twenty minutes.

In October 1943, *U 262* attacked the joint convoy MKS28 and SLI38. The Norwegian steamer *Hallfried* of approximately 3,000 tons was sunk. A destroyer was also attacked using T-5 Zaunkönig and Flächenabusch or FAT torpedoes. The T-5 was an acoustic torpedo designed to home in on propeller noise and the FAT a special design intended to zigzag its way through a convoy until hitting a target. On this occasion detonations were heard as were the sounds of the sinking vessel breaking up. Once again, however, no losses were recorded by the Allies and the destroyer was never identified.

On 9 November 1943 an attack was made on a destroyer which was escorting Convoy MKS29A. Again an acoustic T-5 was used, but the results were inconclusive. On 28 November, *U 262* was involved in an attack on Convoy MKS31/SKI40. Yet again the three torpedoes launched were heard to detonate. One was thought to be an end of run detonation, but no confirmation of sinkings could be made for the other two. Franke's total confirmed score was 13,935 tons, including the corvette *Montbretia*.

The Knight's Cross of the Iron Cross was awarded to Franke on 30 November 1943 and he was subsequently given command of *U 2502*, one of the superb Type XXI boats, built by the Hamburg firm of Blohm & Voss. These huge boats had a displacement of about 1,800 tons, could travel at sixteen knots and had a range of 11,150 nautical miles. They were armed with four 30mm Flak guns in twin turrets and carried 23 torpedoes. These were ocean-going vessels which could almost certainly have swung the Battle of the Atlantic in favour of Germany had they been put into service at an earlier stage. Production was so delayed, however, that despite a considerable number being completed, only two (*U 2511* and *U 3008*) had actually put to sea by the time the war ended.

Franke sailed from Horten in Norway to England to surrender his vessel during Operation 'Deadlight' in May 1945, never having had the opportunity to take her into battle. Franke is still alive and lives in retirement near Sasbach.

KAPITÄNLEUTNANT FRIEDRICH GUGGENBERGER

Born on 6 May 1915 in Munich, Friedrich Guggenberger took command of his first boat, *U 81*, on 26 April 1941, with the rank of Oberleutnant zur See. Having completed its trials by mid-July, the Type VIIC set off on its first cruise which was completed without incident. On 27 August, *U 81* sailed again, and on 9 September scored her first victory, sinking *Empire Springbuck*, a 5,000-ton British steamer. At dawn on the following day, *Sally Maersk* was also sent to the bottom.

In November 1941, *U 81* was one of twenty U-boats which Hitler had promised Mussolini to send to the Mediterranean to protect the Axis supply routes to North Africa. Entering the Mediterranean through the Straits of Gibraltar on 11 November, *U 81* was ordered to seek out and attack units of the Mediterranean Fleet. Just two days later, *U 81* intercepted a major British naval unit, Force H, which included the aircraft carrier *Ark Royal* and the battleship *Malaya*. At just after 1540 hours, *Ark Royal* was struck by a torpedo from *U 81*. Hit in the starboard boiler room, she started to flood, developing a heavy list. The destroyer *Legion* was summoned from Gibraltar and took off *Ark Royal*'s crew. The remaining destroyer escorts from Force H fell upon *U 81* with a vengeance, dropping more than 180 depth-charges, but she escaped unscathed. *Ark Royal*, pride of the Royal Navy, sank during the early hours of 14 November. When Guggenberger discovered that he had sunk the carrier he was delighted but amazed – he had actually aimed his torpedoes at *Malaya*. On 10 December 1941, he was decorated with the Knight's Cross of the Iron Cross for his achievement.

A quiet period then followed for *U 81* until the spring of 1942 when the British tanker *Caspia* was sunk and eight small sailing ships were sunk by gunfire. At this point in his career, Kapitänleutnant Guggenberger was given command of a new boat, *U 513*, operating off the coast of South America. On 8 January 1943, Guggenberger was decorated with the Oakleaves, one of only 28 U-boat men to be so honoured. In South American waters, Guggenberger sank three more freighters before he himself fell victim to enemy forces when *U 513* was bombed and sunk off Santos. He and his crew were saved and spent the rest of the war in internment. After the war, Guggenberger rejoined the Navy and became an Admiral in the West German Bundesmarine.

KORVETTENKAPITÄN REINHARD HARDEGEN

Reinhard Hardegen was born in Bremen on 18 March 1913. He joined the Reichsmarine in 1933 and his basic seaman's training was carried out in the three-masted barque *Gorch Fock*, one of the three sail trainers used by the navy. He later served in the cruiser *Karlsruhe*, and visited India, Sumatra, Java, Australia, Honolulu, Pearl Harbor, New York and Boston.

Hardegen trained for the Naval Air Service and in fact several wartime photographs of him in his service uniform show the Luftwaffe's Beobachter-abzeichen being worn beside his U-boat Kriegsabzeichen. During the Polish Campaign he flew coastal recce missions and on the conclusion of that campaign was sent for U-boat training in November 1939.

Oberleutnant zur See Hardegen was given his first U-boat posting as Wach Offizier in *U 124*. He served in this boat for a year, gaining valuable experience before obtaining his own command, *U 147* in December 1940. *U 124* was a large Type IXB, of more than 1,000 tons displacement, armed with 22 torpedoes and a 4in cannon. *U 147*, however, was a small coastal craft of just 360 tons, carrying only six torpedoes. With this diminutive craft, however, Hardegen sank a large, 9,000-ton merchantman in the North Sea on his first patrol. Following this success, Hardegen handed over command to his First Officer and in turn took command of a new boat, *U 123*, from Karl-Heinz Moehle, himself a future Knight's Cross-winning ace. *U 123* was also a large Type IXB, and was to be a lucky ship for Hardegen and his crew.

On his first cruise with *U 123*, Hardegen met with considerable success, sinking more than 30,000 tons of shipping. This represented five ships, including the auxiliary cruiser *Rio Azul*. On his next cruise, Hardegen intercepted a small, heavily escorted convoy of four large merchantmen. He fired two torpedoes and was rewarded with a hit on the starboard side of one of the largest ships. Hardegen now took to the depths, to avoid the attention of the convoy escorts. When the enemy had left and Hardegen surfaced, he discovered the identity of the ship he had hit. It was no

Left: One of the great personalities of the Fighter Arm, Josef Pips Priller was decorated with the Knight's Cross during the Battle of Britain as an Oberleutnant with 6./J.G. 51. Ultimately, he gained the rank of Oberst and served as Inspector of Jagdflieger West. He flew more than 300 missions, gaining 101 victories.

Below: One of the Luftwaffe's best fighter aces, Günther Rall scored his first victory in France in May 1940 and from then until the end of the war amassed a total score of 275 victories. The photograph shows him as Hauptmann and Kommandeur of III./J.G. 52 in which post he subsequently won the Swords to his Oakleaves in September 1943. He ended the war as Kommodore of J.G. 300 with the rank of Major, having flown 621 missions.

Above left: Major Hubert Rauh. In an eventful ten-year flying career beginning in the Austrian Air Force in 1935, Rauh flew a total of 150 combat missions, and, as a night fighter pilot, scored 31 victories. At the end of the war Rauh was Kommandeur of II./N.J.G.4. The photograph was taken shortly before the surrender. (Hubert Rauh)

Above: The most highly decorated German soldier of the Second World War was Oberst Hans Ulrich Rudel. This photograph of him as an Oberleutnant, shortly after the award of the Oakleaves in April 1943, shows him in full flying kit. By the end of the war, Rudel had flown an amazing 2,500 plus, missions. His biography *Stuka Pilot* has sold more than one million copies. (Josef Charita)

Left: Hans-Arnold Stahlschmidt. A close friend of fighter virtuoso Hans-Joachim Marseille, Oberleutnant Stahlschmidt scored all of his 59 victories in North Africa with J.G. 27. He flew more than 400 missions before being reported missing in action in September 1942, three weeks before the death of his friend. Shown here as a Leutnant, Stahlschmidt had Oakleaves added posthumously to his Knight's Cross in January 1944.

Left: Hauptmann Johannes Steinhoff pictured on the Eastern Front in 1942. 'Macki' Steinhoff went on to reach the rank of Oberst and Commander of JV-44. He downed a total of 176 enemy aircraft before crashing in his Me 262. Horribly disfigured by burns, with great personal courage he overcame his injuries, undergoing intensive plastic surgery, and returned to active service, reaching the rank of Generalmajor in the West German airforce. Macki Steinhoff is one of the most admired and respected of all German airmen.

Right: Major Walter Storp ned the ranks of the akleaves winners in July 1941 Kommodore of S.K.G. 210, ving earned the Knight's Cross ne nine months earlier with G. 76. Storp's Knight's Cross th Oakleaves is particularly arly seen here, as is his Flight asp in Gold for Bomber Pilots. te also the high-quality silver llion wire insignia, on a llow base for flying personnel, d the early-style droop-tailed east eagle.

Major Walter STORP

Opposite page:

Top left: Kapitänleutnant Klaus Bargsten. Commander of *U 521*. He was decorated with the Knight's Cross in April 1943. *U521* was finally sunk by a US sub-chaser, but Bargsten and his crew were saved. (Klaus Bargsten)

Top right: This photograph shows U-boat ace Ernst Bauer as a Kapitänleutnant and Commander of *U 126* in 1942. His U-boat service badge can just be seen below the Iron Cross 1st Class. Of special interest are the individual U-boat and flotilla badges pinned to the hat band and peak of his cap. These unofficial badges were widely worn within the U-boat service. The white cap cover was the distinctive sign worn only by the commander of a U-boat. (Ernst Bauer)

Bottom: E-boat ace Korvettenkapitän Hermann Büchting. Decorated with the Knight's Cross in April 1943, he was Commander of 1. S-Boot Flotille. Note that in the photograph Büchting wears the First Pattern E-Boat War Badge next to his Iron Cross 1st Class. These badges were highly prized by their owners who generally continued to wear them even after the introduction of the later pattern. (Hermann Büchting)

Above: A superb portrait photograph of Oberleutnant Wolfgang Tonne. His Oakleaves are particularly clearly seen here, as is the Flight Clasp for Fighter Pilots with pendant. Before his death in a crash he had achieved 122 victories, 96 of which were scored in the east.

Right: Oberfeldwebel Alois Wosnitza. A Pilot with 6./S.G. 77, he was decorated with the Knight's Cross of the Iron Cross in March 1944 after having flown 800 missions. Among the decorations visible in this photograph are the Knight's Cross, German Cross in Gold, Iron Cross First Class, Pilot's Badge, Flight Clasp with Pendant, Krim Schild and Kurland cuffband. His early-model tunic has yellow flight section Waffenfarbe piping around the collar next to the NCO tresse. (Josef Charita)

Left: Fregattenkapitän Theodor Detmers, commander of the Auxiliary Cruiser *Kormoran*. An extremely successful officer, Detmers was awarded the Knight's Cross of the Iron Cross in December 1941.

Below: Kapitänleutnant Alfred Eick. Awarded the Knight's Cross as Commander of *U 510* in March 1944, Eick sank ten ships totalling 57,200 tons. The photograph shows Eick wearing the naval officers' summer dress white tunic. All the insignia on these tunics were removable for cleaning purposes. His Iron Cross First Class is just visible on the left breast pocket as is the German Cross on the right. (Josef Charita)

Above left: Korvettenkapitän Karl Emmermann. As Commander of *U 172*, Emmermann won the Knight's Cross in November 1942, and the Oakleaves in July 1943. He sank 27 ships totalling some 153,000 tons. He commanded 6 U-Flotille for a period before becoming a Staff Officer on Grandadmiral Dönitz's staff. At the end of the war he was again on an active service posting as Commander of 31 U-Flotille.

Above: A fine candid shot of U-boat ace Heinz Franke. In this photograph Kapitänleutnant Franke has just been awarded the Knight's Cross on 8 December 1943 when *U 262* returned from La Pallice. The award was actually approved on 30 November 1943 while he was still at sea. Franke had sunk the British corvette *Montbretia*. Note once again the white brim to the cap. Franke is wearing a battledress blouse closely modelled on the British Army pattern, highly popular with U-boat crews. His rank is indicated by the two gilt pips on his silver braid shoulder-straps. (Heinz Franke)

Left: Kapitänleutnant Friedrich Guggenberger. This young U-boat commander achieved lasting fame by sinking the British aircraft carrier *Ark Royal* in November 1941. He sank a total of ten ships of approx. 68,500 tons, and was decorated with the Oakleaves in January 1943. In July 1943, his U-boat was sunk in South American waters, but he and many of his crew were saved.

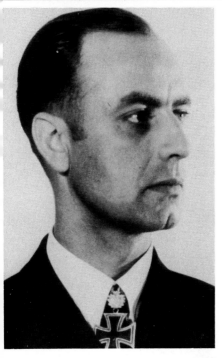

Opposite page: A fine portrait photograph of U-boat ace Korvettenkapitän Reinhard Hardegen, clearly showing his Knight's Cross with Oakleaves. (Reinhard Hardegen)

Above: Highly successful E-boat commander Friedrich Kemnade was decorated with the Knight's Cross in July 1942 as Commander of 3 S-Boot Flotille. The Oakleaves followed in May 1943 and shortly thereafter Korvettenkapitän Kemnade was decorated with the solid silver version of the E-Boat war badge with diamond-studded swastika. Only a handful of these badges was ever awarded, as a personal token of esteem from Grossadmiral Raeder to particularly successful E-boat aces. (Friedrich Kemnade)

Above right: Commander of *U 616*, Kapitänleutnant Siegfried Koitschka sank only two merchantmen totalling 17,750 tons, but he also sank the US destroyer *Buck*. (Siegfried Koitschka)

Right: Hans Werner Kraus. As Kapitänleutnant in command of *U 83*, Kraus was decorated with the Knight's Cross in June 1942. (Hans Werner Kraus)

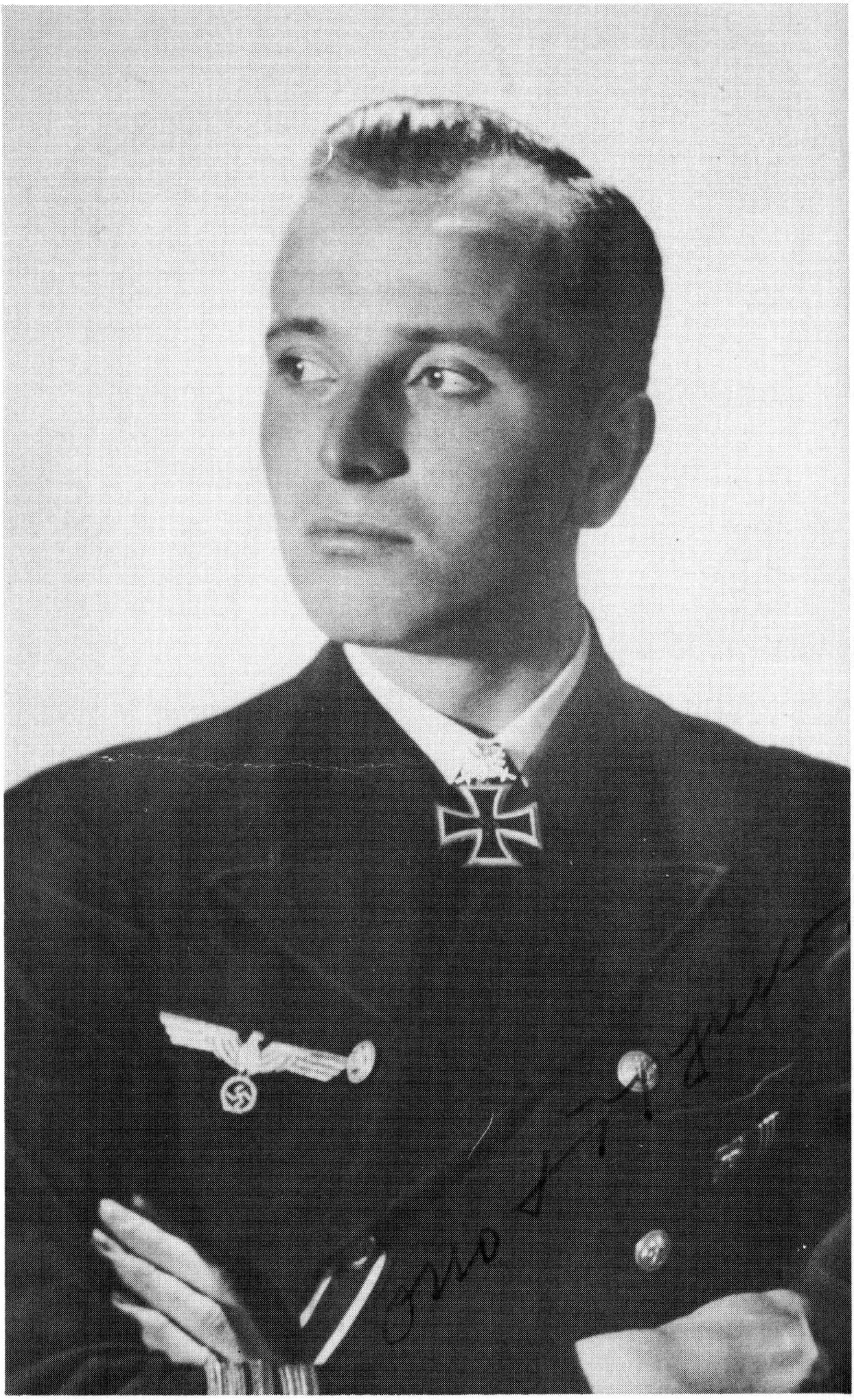

Opposite page: Korvettenkapitän Otto Kretschmer. The greatest of the U-boat aces, he received his Swords after his capture in March 1941. The photograph has been retouched from one showing Kretschmer with his Oakleaves.

Above: Kapitänleutnant Karl-Heinz Marbach. A U-boat Commander who had torpedoed a number of destroyers, Marbach was bedevilled by lack of confirmation of sinkings. He is officially credited with only one ship of just 1,900 tons, a score which belies the skill and tenacity of this ace.

Above right: Kapitänleutnant Waldemar Mehl, Commander of *U 371* from 1942 to 1944. Mehl sank nine ships totalling more than 43,000 tons. He ended the war with the rank of Korvettenkapitän as a Staff Officer with the High Command of the Navy. Mehl's German Cross in Gold can just be seen on the lower right breast of his tunic. (Waldemar Mehl)

Right: Kapitän zur See Karl-Friedrich Merten, a highly successful ace, who claimed 29 enemy ships totalling more than 180,000 tons while Commander of *U 68*. This photograph shows Merten wearing the Spanish Cross for service in Spanish waters during the Civil War. He also wears the Iron Cross First Class, U-Boat Service Badge, and High Seas Fleet Service Badge, earned during his time in the cruiser *Königsberg*. Unusually, his Iron Cross Second Class ribbon is worn on the ribbon bar rather than in the buttonhole. (Paul Anderson)

Above: Korvettenkapitän Jost Metzler. As Commandant of *U 69* with the rank of Kapitänleutnant, Metzler was awarded the Knight's Cross on 28 July 1941. He sank ten ships, totalling some 50,750 tons. Ultimately he became Commander of a U boat flotilla and it is in this command that the photograph shows him inspecting his men. He is dressed in parade dress with brocade belt and carrying his dagger. (Jim Marcks)

Left: Korvettenkapitän Adolf Piening. As Commander of *U 155* Piening sank some 26 ships totalling 141,500 tons. he was awarded the Knight's Cross in August 1942. In March 1944 he became Commander of 7 U-Flotille, a post which he held until the end of the war.

Above: The most successful of all the auxiliary cruiser commanders was Vizeadmiral Bernhard Rogge. With the famed *Atlantis* he sank more than 157,000 tons of shipping in a 602-day cruise. He was decorated with the Oakleaves in December 1941. He is the only verified recipient of the Auxiliary Cruiser War Badge with Diamonds. The photograph shows Rogge as a Kapitän zur See. Of interest are the Bars to both Second and First Class Iron Crosses, as well as the Auxiliary Cruiser War Badge with its Viking ship motif. (Jak P. Mallmann Showell)

Above right: One of the U-boat service's best-known personalities, Korvettenkapitän Adalbert Schnee, The photograph shows him as a Kapitänleutnant at the time of the award of his Oakleaves as Commander of *U 201*. (Adalbert Schnee)

Right: Kapitänleutnant Heinrich Schroeteler, Commander of *U 667* was awarded the Knight's Cross in May 1945. Schroeteler's Iron Cross First Class can be seen on the lower left breast of the tunic; the ribbon of the Second Class is in the buttonhole. (Heinrich Schroeteler)

Above: Oberleutnant Gerd Suhren. Brother of U-boat ace Reinhard Suhren, Gerd was one of the few Knight's Cross winners in the U-boat service who were not commanders. He received his award in October 1940 as the Engineering Officer in *U 37*. Ending the war with the rank of Korvettenkapitän, he served in the new Type XXI *U 2511*, under command of U-boat ace Adalbert Schnee. An expert engineering officer who could extract maximum performance in the most difficult circumstances was essential to a successful boat. (Gerd Suhren)

Above: Fregattenkapitän Reinhard Suhren, one of Germany's top U-boat aces with almost 100,000 tons of shipping sunk, and a winner of the Swords and Oakleaves. This photograph shows him in the early part of his career, as Wachoffizier in *U 48* under Heinrich Bleichrodt. (Jak P. Mallmann Showell)

Left: Kapitänleutnant Hans Dietrich von Tiesenhausen. Another of those who had sunk only a handful of ships, but who included a warship in their tally. In his case it was the British battleship *Barham*. For this he was awarded the Knight's Cross on 27 January 1942. Von Tiesenhausen's *U 331* was attacked and sunk by British aircraft in November 1942. He and a handful of his crew were saved.

Left: Fregattenkapitän Erich Topp. One of only a handful of U-Boat recipients of the Swords, Erich Topp was Kapitänleutnant in command of *U 552* at the time of the award. He sank a total of 35 ships totalling some 192,600 tons. His last commission was as Commander of the Type XXI *U 2513*. The photograph shows Topp wearing his Swords and Oakleaves. He is dressed in the naval officers' greatcoat. His rank banding is shown by the wide row of Oakleaves to the peak of his cap, and specific rank by the shoulder-straps. (Jak P. Mallmann Showell)

Right: Oberleutnant zur See Otto Westphalen. As commander of *U 968*, this young officer sank only six ships, but among them were three escort destroyers. For this considerable achievement he was decorated with the Knight's Cross on 23 March 1945. The photograph was taken before the award was made. The finely hand-embroidered gilt wire cap insignia are seen to good advantage here. (Otto Westphalen)

Left: As Commander of the auxiliary cruiser *Orion*, Kurt Weyher was decorated with the Knight's Cross in August 1941. In this photograph he wears the Admirals' peaked cap with white summer-issue cover. Note the double row of peak oakleaves and the wide gold braid cuff rings. His German Cross in Gold can be seen just below the breast Eagle on the right breast of the double-breasted jacket.

Left: Korvettenkapitän Helmut Witte. As Commander of *U 159*, Witte achieved considerable success, sinking 21 ships totalling 114,000 tons. He was awarded the Knight's Cross in October 1942. He ended the war as a Staff Officer in Naval High Command. The photograph shows Witte as a Kapitänleutnant. His rank is shown by the two pips on the silver braid shoulder-straps worn on the naval officers' greatcoat. (Helmut Witte)

merchantman but the 14,000-ton auxiliary cruiser *Aurania*, which sank one hour after being torpedoed, as the result of a magazine explosion.

Following the German declaration of war on the United States, the rich pickings in American coastal waters were open to Dönitz's U-boats. Christmas 1941 saw Hardegen in *U 123* arrive off the coast of New York. On 12 January 1942, *U 123* torpedoed the 9,000-ton freighter *Cyclops*. Not wishing to waste valuable torpedoes, Hardegen surfaced and finished off the vessel with *U 123*'s deck gun. Two days later, still off New York harbour, Hardegen scored a direct hit on the fully laden tanker *Norness*, a ship of some 9,500 tons. The American did not believe that a U-boat would dare to operate so close to the shore, and the loss of *Norness* was put down to mines. On 15 January, Hardegen sank yet another tanker, and a large freighter. Four days later, during the night of 19 June, three more freighters and yet another tanker were sunk. Hardegen had now sunk eight ships totalling some 50,000 tons since arriving in American waters. For this achievement he was decorated with the Knight's Cross of the Iron Cross on 23 January 1942. On 24 January, the German people learned of Hardegen's success in a special communiqué:

'German U-boats have, since their first appearance in American and Canadian waters, caused serious losses to enemy merchant shipping. Immediately off the enemy coast, they have sunk 18 merchant ships totalling 125,000 tons. A further ship and an escort were damaged. In these battles, the U-boat of Kapitänleutnant Hardegen specially distinguished itself. He alone has sunk 8 ships, including 3 tankers, off New York.'

His supply of torpedoes expended, Hardegen decided to stay on and use up his 4in gun's ammunition. On 25 January the steamer *Culelua* was sent to the bottom. During the following night, the tanker *Pan Norway*, a large vessel of 9,200 tons, was also sunk by gunfire. With his torpedoes and ammunition expended, Hardegen returned home.

After a brief period for rest and resupply, *U 123* was soon back in American waters. On 22 March 1942, the 7,000-ton tanker *Muskogee* was sunk and two days later the 8,100-ton *Empire Steel* followed her to the bottom. On 25 March, *U 123* intercepted a small, 3,000-ton freighter. The crew of this vessel were determined to fight back and when *U 123* approached on the surface to sink her with gunfire rather than torpedoes, the crew opened fire with rifles and a machine-gun, killing one of *U 123*'s midshipmen. Hardegen played safe, and withdrew to a safe distance to sink her by torpedo.

On 26 March, the tanker *Liebre* was sunk, and on 8 April two more tankers, the 9,500-ton *Esso Baltic* and the 10,500-ton *W. B. Walker*. On 9 April the refrigerator ship *Esparta* and a 12,500-ton tanker were sunk. Hardegen's last torpedo was used to sink a 5,500-ton freighter and once again he was left with only 4in artillery shells. A heavily laden tanker was attacked but not sunk, though a smaller freighter, *Point Brava* was less lucky and was sent to the bottom by Hardegen's 4in gun. *U 123*'s second cruise in American waters had netted eleven ships totalling 79,000 tons. In recognition of his achievements he was decorated with the Oakleaves on 23 April 1942.

On his return Hardegen was obliged to relinquish *U 123* to a new commander. Aces such as he were considered too valuable to risk their loss on combat operations; he was to be given a shore posting. No doubt Hardegen's crew were sad to see their successful commander go, but they were to be fortunate. *U 123* remained a lucky boat; she survived the war and in 1945 was taken into the French Navy as the *Blaison* before being scrapped in 1957.

Hardegen's experience and knowledge were to be put to good use to train new U-boat commanders. The help and practical advice from a successful ace such as he could make the difference between success and failure, life or death to an inexperienced commander. Hardegen had survived many depth-charge attacks and attacks by aircraft and could pass on as many tips about survival as about successful attacking. In October 1944, he was posted to the Torpedo Weapons Inspectorate of the Naval High Command.

During the closing stages of the war, large numbers of German sailors, whose ships were immobilized through damage or lack of fuel, were formed into Marine Infantry units, and thrown into the battle on land. Hardegen's last command was as Korvettenkapitän and Bataillon Kommandeur in 2 Marine Infanterie Division. Reinhard Hardegen survived the war and after being released from a POW camp returned to his native Bremen. He went into politics and became chairman of his local parliamentary group of the CDU. He is still alive.

KORVETTENKAPITÄN FREDRICH KEMNADE

One of the Kriegsmarine's top Schnellboot or E-boat aces, Kemnade was born on 12 December 1911 in Schwarmstedt and joined the Reichsmarine in 1931. By the outbreak of war, he was the Torpedo Officer in the cruiser *Emden*. On 15 May 1940, he transferred to E-boats, serving with 3 Schnellbootsflotille in Kiel.

After initial service in the English Channel, 3 Schnellbootsflotille was transferred to the Baltic, the Gulf of Riga and the Mediterranean Sea. His considerable successes against shipping brought the award of the Knight's Cross of the Iron Cross on 23 July 1942 while serving as Kapitänleutnant in command of the flotilla. The award was for successes achieved from 1940 to 1942.

Kemnade's success in command of the flotilla continued and was further rewarded on 27 May 1943 by his becoming the 249th recipient of the coveted Oakleaves. The award was personally presented by Hitler at a special ceremony at Führerhauptquartier in December of the same year. As well as the Oakleaves, Kemnade was further honoured by the award of the special version of the E-Boat War Badge with Diamonds, a personal token of esteem from the Oberbefehlshaber der Kriegsmarine. Kemnade's was one of only eight recipients of this award.

On 1 January 1944, Korvettenkapitän Kemnade was removed from sea duties and posted as a staff officer and representative of the S-Boote at Oberkommando der Marine, where his experience and combat knowledge were invaluable. He remained in this post until the end of the war. When peace came to German again, Kemnade took up a career in commerce, but the call of the sea was strong and when the West German Navy was being formed, Kemnade returned to military service. He served a tour of duty in Washington DC, as a NATO representative. In 1968 he reached the rank of Konteradmiral. This highly skilled and daring naval officer is still alive and lives in retirement near Hamburg, after many years of service to his country.

KAPITÄNLEUTNANT SIEGFRIED KOITSCHKA

Siegfried Koitschka was born on 6 August 1917 in Bautzen and joined the Kriegsmarine in 1937. He took command of his first boat in 1943. This was *U 616*, a type VIIC and in March of that year he sailed on his first cruise. *U 616* went into action against Convoys HX229 and SC122 which were heavily screened by destroyer escorts, and had no success on these occasions.

In May 1943, *U 616* was sent to the Mediterranean to operate out of the Italian base at La Spezia. By this stage in the war, U-boat operations in the Mediterranean were suffering grievous losses for little success, but there were a few notable exceptions. Dönitz could ill afford to waste his invaluable resources in this way, but his objections were overruled. Koitschka's cruise led him into the waters off the Algerian Coast. Once again, it was a fruitless patrol. An unsuccessful attack on a British cruiser and its escorting destroyer led to a savage depth-charge attack from which *U 616* was extremely fortunate to escape.

In October 1943, *U 616* was operating against the Allied landing forces at Salerno. Here at last Koitschka found success. On 19 October he attacked the US destroyer *Buck* which was supporting the landings and sent her to the bottom. He also torpedoed and damaged a tank-landing ship and a merchantman. During Koitschka's cruises in the following two months, only one more ship was torpedoed and damaged. On 27 January 1944, Koitschka was decorated with the Knight's Cross of the Iron Cross, principally for the sinking of *Buck*.

In May 1944, *U 616* caught and torpedoed the 10,600-ton tanker *G. S. Walden* and the 7,000-ton steamer *Ford Fiedler*. It was to be his last victory; on his next operation Koitschka was caught by US forces off Cartagena. The destroyers *Nields*, *Cleaves*, *Ellyson*, *Hilitary P. Jones*, *Macomb*, *Hambleton*, *Rodman* and *Emmons* as well as a number of aircraft proved far too great an opposition for *U 616* and she was fatally damaged. Koitschka and his crew escaped from the U-boat and were taken prisoner by the Americans, and spent the rest of the war in captivity. Koitschka is still alive.

KAPITÄNLEUTNANT HANS WERNER KRAUS

Hans Werner Kraus was born on 1 July 1915 in Beulwitz-Saalfeld. He was, like Klaus Bargsten, fortunate to spend some time as a Wach Offizier under one of the truly great aces. In the case of Kraus, this was to be Günther Prien, the hero of Scapa Flow. Kraus was to serve in *U 47* with Prien for a year before, on 8 February 1941, taking command of his own boat, *U 83*.

On 12 October 1941, Kraus achieved his first success. The Portuguese steamer *Corte Real* was stopped and searched, being destroyed when it was discovered that she was carrying contraband material. On 21 October, Kraus attacked Convoy HG75, and the British steamer *Ariguani* was hit and damaged. Two other hits on unidentified ships were also registered. In October 1941, Kraus also attacked the British aircraft carriers *Eagle* and *Furious*, but neither was hit.

Kraus and his U-boat were subsequently transferred to the Mediterranean theatre and on 14 February 1942 attacked a steamer under escort by a corvette. Both were hit but no sinkings were claimed. During the next month, *U 83* was once again involved in an attack against another merchantman escorted by a warship. In both cases detonations were heard, but no sinkings could be confirmed. On 14 March a steamer was attacked and left damaged, though a *coup de grâce* shot missed. Three days later the British ship *Crista* was torpedoed and damaged. On 7 June 1942, Kraus attacked and torpedoed a steamer which sank in twenty minutes. On the following day, two sailing vessels, one of which was the Egyptian *Said*, were sunk by gunfire, followed by the Palestinian *Typhoon* which was also sunk by gunfire, on 9 June. In mid-June, the British sailing ship *Farouk* was sunk by gunfire off the Palestinian coast. Shortly afterwards, on 19 June 1942, Hans Werner Kraus was decorated with the Knight's Cross of the Iron Cross. He was the 114th naval recipient. After several weeks of small sailing vessels sunk by gunfire, the next sizeable vessel to fall victim to *U 83* was the Canadian *Princess Marguerite*, which was torpedoed on 17 August.

Kraus was thereafter transferred to take command of *U 199* in the Atlantic and is recorded as having attacked the US steamer *Charles Wilson Peale* off Rio de Janeiro on 27 June. The Brazilian merchantman *Pelotasloide* was sunk on 4 July 1943, despite a strong escort of destroyers. Two days later another Brazilian vessel, this time a small sailing freighter was sunk by gunfire off Rio de Janeiro. The last of *U 199*'s successes came on 24 July 1943 when the steamer *Henzada* of 4,160 tons was torpedoed and sunk.

One week later, on 31 July 1943, *U 199* was attacked and sunk by aircraft, still in the waters off Rio. Kraus and his crew, however, were saved and spent the rest of the war in captivity. His total score was 10,386 tons, representing six ships confirmed sunk and five ships of 10,800 tons damaged.

KORVETTENKAPITÄN OTTO KRETSCHMER

Otto Kretschmer, greatest of all Germany's U-boat aces in the Second World War, was also the second highest-scoring ace in history, beaten only by the Korvettenkapitän Lothar Arnauld de la Perriere of the Kaiserliche Marine during the First World War. Kretschmer was born on 1 May 1912 in Heidau, Lower Silesia, the son of a local teacher. He came to the U-boat service in 1936 as a Leutnant zur See in *U 35* and by the outbreak of war in September 1939 he had his own command, *U 23*, a small Type IIB vessel of some 300 tons. With its limited range and offensive capability, *U 23* was to be used principally for minelaying duties, a much less glamorous although equally important form of warfare, than the daring torpedo attacks of such contemporaries as Prien. Kretschmer's first wartime operation involved laying mines in the Firth of Forth. During this operation he launched two torpedoes at an enemy ship, both of which failed to explode. These were but two in a lengthy catalogue of faulty torpedoes which were to plague the U-boat service.

In October 1939, Kretschmer scored his first victory when he torpedoed and sank the coaster *Glen Farg*, after having allowed the crew to get clear. This victory was scored in the dangerous waters of the approaches to Scapa Flow. In December the steamer *Deptford* and the coaster *Magnus* were sunk, both in the waters off the Shetlands. For his success in these sinking and for his minelaying duties Kretschmer received both the Second and First Class Iron Crosses. A more important victory came on 12 June 1940 when *U 99* located the 10,000-ton tanker *Denmark* in Inganes Bay in the Shetlands. Kretschmer entered the bay under the cover of darkness, passing under the very noses of the tanker's escorts. With a single torpedo, he sent the tanker to the bottom, and escaped past the escorting patrol boats. On his return voyage, he sank the freighter *Polzella* and the coaster *Baltanglia*.

During her next voyage, *U 23* sank a destroyer escort and shortly afterwards a convoy straggler the freighter *Tiberton*, was also sent to the bottom. Three days later Kretschmer sank yet another freighter, *Loch Maddy*, expending the last of his torpedoes. He then returned to base. His next war cruise was completed without a single attack being made, but on return to Kiel, he handed over *U 23* to a new commander. *U 23* was to be a lucky ship, surviving until September 1944 when, long obsolete, she was scuttled by the Germans in the Black Sea. In *U 23* Kretschmer had made a total of nine war cruises, sinking nine ships including a destroyer, for a total of 30,000 tons.

On 30 April 1940, Kretschmer took command of his new boat, *U 99*. This vessel was a type VIIB of some 800 tons, with a much greater offensive capability. His new First Officer was Klaus Bargsten who would later become a Knight's Cross-winning ace in his own right. During *U 99*'s first war cruise she was attacked by mistake by a floatplane from the battlecruiser *Scharnhorst*, having been mistaken for a British submarine. She had to return to Wilhelmshaven for repairs. After this inauspicious start, however, *U 99* began to run up a considerable tally of successes which would take its commander into the record books.

On 5 July 1940, Kretschmer sank the steamer *Magog*. Before leaving the scene, however, he ensured that the survivors had directions to the nearest landfall and gave them a bottle of brandy to help them on their way. Two days later the Swedish coaster *Bissen* was also sent to the bottom. During the early hours of the next day, *U 99* encountered its first convoy, and Kretschmer struck quickly. The freighter *Humber Arm* was sent to the bottom although the hit on the ship was somewhat of an accident as Kretschmer had been aiming at a totally different ship. Retribution was soon to come, however, as *U 99* suffered a depth-charge attack in which more than 120 charges were dropped during a 14-hour period.

On the following day, *U 99* attacked and sank the 4,500-ton *Petsamo* off the coast of Ireland and on the next day captured the Estonian steamer *Merisaar* which was sent on its way to Bordeaux as a Prize. The next three days passed quietly, but on the fourth the steamer *Budoxia* was spotted off the coast of Eire and sunk, followed the next morning by the *Woodbury*. Always a humane and considerate man wherever possible, Kretschmer ordered all *U 99*'s spare blankets, plus a keg of rum to be given to the survivors before leaving the area to return to the French port of Lorient.

During *U 99*'s stay in this major U-boat base, Kretschmer took the opportunity to have the boat completely cleaned out. It still reeked of foetid air and damp after the lengthy depth-charge attack. The crew's uniforms were also in a terrible state. It was at this point that Kretschmer started what was to become a popular fashion among U-boat personnel when he had his men kitted out in captured British battledress blouses. This was a particularly suitable form of dress for the close confines of a submarine, being smart and functional. This dress became so popular that when captured British stocks were exhausted, the Germans began to manufacture their own copies.

U 99 put to sea again on 24 July 1940. Only five days later the steamer *Auckland Star* was spotted. Kretschmer sank her with a spread of three torpedoes. Shortly after this, *Clan Menzies* and *Jamaica Progress* were attacked and destroyed. Several hours later, Kretschmer intercepted a convoy of 15–20 ships. He attacked and sank a straggler, *Jersey City*, but came under a severe depth-charge attack. The enemy were unable to locate him, however, and by the time he was able to surface the convoy had gone. When he caught up with it again, he decided on a night attack on the surface. He was the first U-boat commander to use this tactic.

In the middle of the convoy, Kretschmer attacked and sank the 9,000-ton tanker *Baron Recht*, the 6,500-ton *Lucerna* and the *Alexia*, an 8,000-ton tanker. When the convoy's escorting destroyers began to close in, he broke off the action and set a course for his Lorient base, well satisfied with his successes.

On his return, Kretschmer was decorated with the Knight's Cross of the Iron Cross on 4 August 1940. The award was made by Grossadmiral Raeder personally. Ironically, Raeder complimented Kretschmer on the smartness of his crew, apparently unaware that they were wearing British battledress. At this point Kapitänleutnant Kretschmer had sunk a total of 117,000 tons of shipping, of which 50,000 tons were sunk in a single cruise. During *U 99*'s next patrol, Kretschmer attacked Convoy HX72, destroying the Norwegian steamer *Hird*, the freighter *Crown Arum*, the 9,000-ton tanker *Invershannon*, the *Elmbank* and *Baron Blythwood*. All these successes proved the worth of Kretschmer's tactics of surface attack.

On her next cruise, *U 99* took part in a wolf-pack attack on Convoy SC7, together with six other U-boats. A total of seventeen Allied ships were sunk, nine of them falling victim to *U 99*. On his return to port a mere nine days later, *U 99* was received with an elaborate welcome by a full turn-out of brass bands, admiring crowds and eager war correspondents. There to meet Kretschmer was Karl Dönitz, the Befehlshaber der U-Boote.

On 3 November 1940, in a single night's engagement, Kretschmer sank the small freighter *Casanove* and the two auxiliary cruisers *Laurentic* and *Patroclus*, a total of more than 30,000 tons. On the next day, Kretschmer expended his last torpedo in an attack on yet another convoy, sinking the tanker *Scottish Maiden*, before returning again to Lorient. On 4 November 1940, Hitler approved the award of the Oakleaves to Kretschmer's Knight's Cross in recognition of his score having passed the 200,000-ton mark. At the same time, his Wach Offizier Stabsobersteuermann Heinrich Petersen was awarded the Knight's Cross. Kretschmer's Oakleaves were personally presented by Hitler at a ceremony at the Reichskanzlei.

Late November found *U 99* at sea again. Her first victim was yet another auxiliary cruiser, *Forfar*, followed by the Norwegian merchantman *Sananger*, the tanker *Conch* and the Dutch steamer *Farnsum*. *U 99* then suffered another intensive depth-charge attack and on her return to port it was decided that a refit would be necessary, which would put her out of action for at least a month. This would be a welcome rest for Kretschmer and his crew.

U 99's next war cruise began on 25 February 1941. In co-operation with *U 47* under Günther Prien, *U 100* under Joachim Schepke and Scheiber's *U 95*, Kretschmer was hunting yet again as part of a wolf-pack. On 7 March, the huge, 20,000-ton whale factory ship *Terje Viken* was sunk followed swiftly by the tanker *Athelbeach*. On 16 March, in a single engagement, Kretschmer sank the tankers *Fern*, *Bedouin* and *Franche Conte* and the fighters *Venetia* and *J. B. White*.

These were to be Kretschmer's last successes however, as retribution was about to strike in the form of the escorts *Walker* and *Vanoc*. Earlier the same night, Schepke's *U 100* had been rammed and sunk by *Vanoc*. Battered by a ferocious depth-charge attack, Kretschmer's *U 99* was forced to the surface. Her crew successfully evacuated the stricken U-boat. The engineer returned to the boat to flood the ballast tanks and scuttle her before she could be boarded. He was never seen again. Kretschmer and all but two of his crew were picked up by *Walker*.

After a period of captivity in England, Kretschmer was taken to Canada where he was held in the POW camp at Bowmanville. On 26 December 1941 at a full parade in the camp, the award of the Swords to Kretschmer's Oakleaves was announced. His total score had exceeded 250,000 tons in a period of just eighteen months.

After the war, Kretschmer returned to the service of his country when the new West German Bundesmarine was formed. He eventually retired with the rank of Flotillenadmiral and is still alive.

KAPITÄNLEUTNANT KARL-HEINZ MARBACH

Born on 5 July 1917 in Kolberg, Karl-Heinz Marbach served as Wach Offizier in *U 101* under U-boat ace Fregattenkapitän Fritz Frauenheim and also his successor Korvettenkapitän Ernst Mengersen during *U 101*'s most successful voyages, gaining, in the process, invaluable experience under the tutelage of those great aces. He took part in attacks on Convoy HX90 in December 1940 under Mengersen when *U 101* sank five ships: *Aracataca*, *Appalachee*, *Lady Glanely*, *Kavak* and *Stirlingshire*. He was also involved in the sinking of the destroyer *Broadwater* in October 1941.

Marbach's first command was *U 953*, a Type VIIC built by Blohm & Voss in Hamburg. From May 1943 to July 1944, he made six operational cruises in the North Atlantic, the west coast of Africa and the North Sea. On 8 June 1944, Marbach attacked a destroyer escort group including the destroyers *Qu'Appelle*, *Restigouche* and *Skeena*. Marbach launched four acoustic T-5 Gnat torpedoes. Unfortunately all of the torpedoes detonated in the wakes of their intended victims. All the destroyers, from Escort Group 12, escaped. Marbach's bravery in attacking such dangerous warships was shown again during the following month. In July he attacked and sank the British 1,900-ton steamer *Glendinning* and five days later a 9,000-ton freighter escorted by a destroyer was also attacked. Marbach reported the freighter sunk and a T-5 Gnat which was fired at the destroyer was heard to detonate. As this was not an end of run detonation, the destroyer was assumed hit and sunk. No confirmation of the sinkings could be made. Marbach's gallantry and aggressiveness in attack while in command of *U 953* and his service in *U 101* were rewarded on 22 July 1944 when he was decorated with the Knight's Cross of the Iron Cross.

On 17 December 1944, Marbach was given command of a new boat, *U 3014*, one of the formidable modern-type XXI vessels, but the surrender came before Marbach's new command had completed its trials and could be readied for combat. To prevent its capture by the enemy, Marbach took his new vessel to sea and scuttled her on 3 May 1945.

Marbach was a typical example of a U-boat ace with a very small score of confirmed tonnage sunk – only one vessel of 2,000 tons. This illustrates the error of equating only high tonnage sunk with the award of the Knight's Cross of the Iron Cross and ace status. His share of the credit for the successes of *U 101* would no doubt have gone a long way towards the approval of his award, but equally, his fearless attacks on powerful warships during a period when U-boat losses to such ships were so heavy is particularly significant. There is no difference in the gallantry of a commander who sinks a warship, and one whose attempts to do so are foiled only by faulty torpedoes, and it speaks volumes for the fairness with which the Knight's Cross was awarded that such deserving cases as Marbach's received the award. Karl-Heinz Marbach survived the war and is still alive.

KORVETTENKAPITÄN WALDEMAR MEHL

Waldemar Mehl was born on 7 September 1914 in Usingen. His first commands had been *U 62*, a Type IIC and *U 72* a Type VIIC. Both were lucky ships, surviving the hostilities. *U 62* was scuttled in Wilhelmshaven in May 1945, and *U 72* sank at her moorings in March 1945. Mehl's next command was *U 371*, another Type VIIC built at Howaldts Werke in Kiel. Displacing 800 tons and carrying fourteen torpedoes, she was also armed with a 3.5in cannon and three anti-aircraft guns. Mehl took over command of this boat from Kapitänleutnant Driver and commenced his first war cruise with her in the late autumn of 1942.

In the relatively confined waters of the Mediterranean Mehl's first success did not come until 7 January 1943 when *U 371* attacked and sank the British fleet auxiliary *Jura* and damaged the 7,000-ton steamer *Ville de Strasbourg*. The next ship to fall victim to *U 371* was the small 2,000-ton steamer *Fintra* on 23 February 1944 and five days later the American 7,000-ton steamer *Daniel Carrol* was also sent to the bottom. On 27 April Mehl sank the small 1,100-ton Dutch vessel *Merope* off Cape Bengut.

A quiet period followed for Mehl until on 10 July the American freighter *Matthew Maury* of some 7,000 tons and the tanker *Gulf Prince* of 6,500 tons were both torpedoed and damaged but not sunk. On 7 August 1943, the 6,000-ton British merchant ship *Contractor* was torpedoed and sent to the bottom. Two days later Mehl attacked an Allied cruiser off Cap de Fer but the torpedoes missed. Once again a quiet period ensued but this was followed by a considerably successful October.

On the 11th *U 371* sunk the minesweeper *Hythe*. Two days later the US destroyer *Bristol* followed her to the bottom and on 15 October the 7,000-ton freighter *James Russel Lowel* was also torpedoed and sunk. Mehl's last successes came on 17 March 1944 when he made contact with an Allied convoy. The straggler *Malden Creek*, a 5,000-ton US steamer was sunk. A further two ships were attacked. Hits were observed on the Dutch *Dempo*, a 17,000-tonner and she was sent to the bottom. A further detonation was heard, but no sinking was confirmed. On 28 March 1944, Mehl was decorated with the Knight's Cross of the Iron Cross, his score standing at nine ships totalling 43,000 tons sunk, and four ships of 28,000 tons damaged.

The Mediterranean was an unlucky hunting-ground for the U-boats. Although the occasional triumphs such as the sinking of *Ark Royal* and *Barham* raised morale, U-boat losses were very heavy. Mehl's successes, though low in terms of tonnage sunk, were substantial considering that they included three warships. After the award of the Knight's Cross, Mehl was taken off combat duties and assigned as a staff officer. He ended the war on the operations staff of the Befehlshaber der U-Boote.

Mehl's boat, *U 371* was handed over to Oberleutnant zur See Horst Arno Fenski, also a Ritterkreuzträger. She was sunk off the Algerian coast on 4 May 1944 by the British destroyer *Blankney*, the US destroyer escorts *Pride* and *Campbell* and the French frigate *Senegalis*. Most of her crew were saved, including the Captain. Korvettenkapitän Mehl also survived the war, and lives in retirement near Wiesbaden.

KAPITÄN ZUR SEE KARL-FRIEDRICH MERTEN

Born in Posen on 15 August 1905, Merten joined the Reichsmarine in 1926. On completion of his basic training as an officer cadet and his commissioning as Leutnant zur See, he served as weapons officer in the cruiser *Königsberg*, a modern 6,650-ton vessel which was armed with nine 5.9in guns in three triple turrets. Subsequently, he served in *T157*, a rather elderly torpedo-boat, and in the escort boat *F7*. In the German Navy, a torpedo-boat was a fairly large vessel, more like a small destroyer and not at all comparable to what was known as a torpedo-boat in the British or American Navies. Thereafter, Merten became a cadet training officer in the training ship *Schleswig-Holstein*, an old 13,000-ton battleship from the First World War, based in Wilhelmshaven before the outbreak of war.

In early 1940, Merten transferred to the U-boat service and his rise to the status of a U-boat ace of the highest calibre began. His first posting was to *U 38* under command of Heinrich Liebe. Having served his time as a Wach Offizier, he was given his own command in February 1941. This was *U 68*, a large, Type IXC built by Deschimag of Bremen. It was a powerful, 1,200-ton ocean-going boat, equipped with 22 torpedoes and a 4in gun.

During the summer of 1941 Merten began to build his score. On 28 July *U 68* made an attack on the ships of Convoy OG69, bound for Gibraltar from the United Kingdom. Although torpedoes were launched, no detonations were recorded though a vivid jet of flame was seen on the side of an escorting corvette. On 22 September it was the turn of Convoy SL87 from Sierra Leone to the UK. The 5,300-ton British merchantman *Silverbelle* was sunk. A tanker was also hit and was spotted again on the following day with a heavy list and under protective escort by two warships. On 22 October, the 5,300-ton British tanker *Darkdale* was sunk off St Helena and six days later the steamer *Hazelside* of similar tonnage was also sent to the bottom. During November the last victim of that cruise, the 4,950-ton *Bradford City*, was attacked and sunk.

U 68 returned to port and after a welcome break began her next cruise, this time to the South Atlantic, off the coast of South Africa, and in the Caribbean. The first victim was the 7,360-ton steamer *Helenus* on 3 March 1942. Five days later the 7,000-ton *Baluchistan* was sunk by a combination of torpedoes and gunfire. March was to be a particularly successful month for Merten. On the 16th, the small, 3,380-ton steamer *Baron Newlands* was added to the list of *U 68*'s victims. On the next day three more ships were sunk, these being the 5,750-ton *Ile de Batz* and the 4,900-ton *Scottish Prince*, sunk by a combination of torpedo and gunfire, and the 5,000-ton steamer *Allende* sunk by torpedo later the same day. A quiet spell then ensued for almost two full weeks, broken on 30 March by the sinking of the 5,850-ton *Muncaster Castle*.

Merten's next major success was the large Panamanian tanker *C. O. Stillman* of 13,000 tons, sunk on 6 June 1942. On the previous day the tanker *L. J. Drake* of some 6,690 tons was reported missing in the same area. Although not claimed as a kill, she was thought to have been sunk by *U 68*. A particularly successful day was 10 June 1942 when the 5,580-ton *Surrey*, the 5,000-ton *Ardenvohr* and the 5,880-ton *Port Montreal* were added to Merten's list of kills. All were sunk by torpedoes.

On 13 June, Merten's achievements were rewarded by the Knight's Cross of the Iron Cross. Merten held the rank of Korvettenkapitän at this time. *U 68* was still at sea when Merten learned of his award. On 15 June he celebrated his decoration with the sinking of the 9,240-ton tanker *Frimaire* in the Caribbean. The final success of this cruise was another tanker, the *Arriaga*, of 2,500 tons, sunk by a combination of torpedo and gunfire on 23 June.

Merten's next cruise was to see several more sinkings. On 12 September 1942, the British *Trevillay* was sunk, followed three days later by the 6,860-ton Dutch steamer *Breedijk*. On 8 October, in the Indian Ocean, *U 68* destroyed four ships: the Greek *Koumoundouros* of 3,600 tons, the Dutch *Gaasterkerk* of 8,700 tons, the US tanker *Swiftsure* of 8,200 tons and the British *Sarthe* of 5,270 tons. All were sunk by torpedo. On the following day the US *Examelia* of 5,000 tons and the Belgian *Belgian Fighter* of 5,400 tons were added to Merten's ever-growing score. This represented some 36,000 tons in just two days. On 6 November, the British *City of Cairo*, an 8,000-tonner was also sent to the bottom, sunk by a torpedo from *U 68*. On 16 November, Merten's achievements were further recognized by the award of the coveted Oakleaves to his Knight's Cross. After this, Merten was given command of 26 Unterseebootsflotille in Pillau, then 24 Unterseebootsflotille in Memel. Here his greatest achievements were not to be in sinking ships but in saving lives. In the closing months of the war, Merten assisted in the evacuation of more than 50,000 refugees from the advancing Russians.

Merten ended the war with the rank of Kapitän zur See under command of the Marine Oberkommando West. He had sunk a total of 180,870 tons of shipping. After the war he went into French captivity where in 1948 attempts were made to try him on fabricated war crimes charges. These allegations were totally unsubstantiated and he was released in March 1949. This accomplished U-boat ace is still alive and lives in retirement near Waldshut.

KORVETTENKAPITÄN JOST METZLER

Born on 16 February 1909 in Altshausen, Jost Metzler joined the Reichsmarine in 1932. On completion of his training he was commissioned Leutnant zur See and served as Wach Offizier in various torpedo-boats and minesweepers. Thereafter he also served in the yacht *Aviso Grille*.

In November 1940, Metzler took command of his first U-boat, *U 69*, a Type VIIC built by Germania Werft in Kiel. His first victory came on 17 February 1941 in the North Atlantic when he torpedoed and sank the 8,450-ton *Siamese Prince*. On 18 February the freighter *Blanda* became his second victim. On 23 February, just five days later, yet another Allied merchantman, *Temple Moat* was sent to the bottom. This was the final victory of Metzler's first cruise.

The second cruise began in May 1941 and saw the sinking of *Coultarn*. On 21 May the 5,000-ton *Robin Moore* was hit and sunk. Although an American vessel and strictly speaking neutral, she was carrying contraband goods. Later that same day Metzler attacked and sank *Tewkesburg*. On 31 May the freighter *Sangara* was sunk in Accra harbour. In addition, *U 69* had been busy laying mines and some of these accounted for the loss of *Robert Hughes*. Metzler was next in action against Convoy SL76 from which he torpedoed three more merchantmen. This brought his score to ten ships sunk totalling 50,750 tons and one ship of 5,450 tons damaged. This achievement brought Metzler the award of the Knight's Cross of the Iron Cross on 28 July 1941 while he was still at sea.

In mid-August, Metzler became seriously ill with kidney troubles and *U 69* had to return to base, Metzler being hospitalized. This brought his promising career as a U-boat commander to an end; he was told he could not return to sea. Metzler was to remain with the U-boat service, however, and was given a shore posting in command of a U-boat training flotilla and subsequently took command of 19 Unterseebootsflotille in Pillau. Metzler's boat, *U 69* was lost on 17 February 1943 in the North Atlantic after an attack by the British destroyer *Viscount*. 19 Unterseebootsflotille was subsquently moved to Kiel and it was here that Metzler was taken prisoner at the end of the war.

KORVETTENKAPITÄN ADOLF PIENING

Born on 16 September 1910 in Süderende, Adolf Piening joined the Reichsmarine in 1930. His first posting to a U-boat was to *U 48*. This was a fortunate posting as *U 48* was commanded by one of the greatest aces, Heinrich Bleichrodt, and in fact *U 48* herself was the Kriegsmarine's most successful boat of the whole war.

On 23 August 1941, Piening was given his own command, the Type IXC *U 155*. This was a brand-new boat and Piening had to see her through the usual trials before, in February 1942, she set off on her first cruise. Operating off the US coast, *U 155* attacked Convoy ONS67. On this, his first operation, Piening sank the 1,800-ton Norwegian freighter *Sama*, and the tanker *Adellen*. On 7 March the Brazilian merchantman *Arabitan*, of some 7,800 tons was torpedoed and sunk off Cape Hatteras.

U 155 then returned to Lorient to refuel and rearm, but quickly returned to combat patrol and was in action again on 14 May when, in a night attack in the waters near Trinidad, the Belgian freighter *Brabant* was sunk. On 17 May the British tanker *San Victoria* was hit with two torpedoes and left sinking. Shortly afterwards the American freighter *Challenger* joined the list of *U 155*'s victims. Three days later the 7,700-ton Panamanian *Sylvan Arrow* was torpedoed and sunk, and on 23 May the 2,200-ton *Watsonville* was left sinking after a night attack. A few days later two smaller freighters totalling just over 5,000 tons were to be *U 155*'s last sinkings before returning to Lorient.

At the start of July, Piening began his next cruise. Again in US waters, on 28 July the 4,700-ton *Barbacona* was sent to the bottom and later on that same day she was joined by the 2,300-ton *Piave*. On 29 July, *Bill*, a Norwegian steamer of just over 2,000 tons was torpedoed and sunk, to be followed the next day by the 6,000-ton *Cranfurd*. Piening was increasing his score rapidly in these lucrative waters. Only hours after *Cranfurd* had been sent to the bottom, she was joined by *Kentar* and *Macnaughton*, adding nearly 12,000 tons to Piening's tally.

The 7,000-ton *Empire Arnold* was sunk by torpedo on 4 August. The crew took to the boats and were given medical assistance by *U 155*'s crew. On 5 August the Dutch *Draco* was sunk by gunfire and three days later the 8,000-ton tanker *San Emiliano*, carrying a full load of aviation fuel, was torpedoed. On 13 August 1942, just one year after taking command of *U 155*, Piening was decorated with the Knight's Cross of the Iron Cross in recognition of his successful operations off the US coast.

A change of scene followed when Piening took his U-boat into the Mediterranean to attack Allied ships involved in Operation 'Torch', the landings in North Africa. During the night of 15 November 1942, Piening launched a three-torpedo salvo against a convoy of ships and was rewarded with hits on *Almaack*, *Ettrick* and the escort carrier *Avenger*. *Almaack* was damaged and was successfully towed into Gibraltar, but both *Ettrick* and *Avenger* sank. Another freighter, the 8,500-ton *Seroonskerg*, was sunk on 6 December, the last victory of Piening's fourth cruise.

Piening took *U 155* back to US waters for her fifth cruise. Things had changed since his last visit, however. Successes were no longer so easily obtained. Only two ships totalling just under 8,000 tons were sunk on this patrol. US anti-submarine measures were becoming far more effective and these were now dangerous waters for any U-boat.

U 155's sixth cruise was aborted when she was attacked and damaged by an RAF aircraft in the Bay of Biscay. The seventh was also totally unsuccessful, although Piening did manage to pioneer a new and safer route to the Atlantic via Spanish waters. Losses among U-boats operating from French ports had been horrendous; boat after boat fell victim to the mines and enemy aircraft attacks in the Bay of Biscay.

Piening and *U 155* undertook an eighth patrol, again to US waters, but sank only one ship, the 5,400-ton *Siranger*. On his return to Lorient, Korvettenkapitän Piening was appointed to a shore command, that of 7 Unterseebootsflotille at St-Nazaire. He held this post from March 1944 until the end of the war. Adolf Piening sank a total of 141,520 tons of shipping representing some 26 vessels. He was the sixteenth highest-scoring U-boat ace.

Note. *U 155* had three other commanders after Piening. She survived the war to be scuttled by her final commander, Oberleutnant Friedrich Altmeier.

VIZEADMIRAL BERNHARD ROGGE

Bernhard Rogge, the most successful of the auxiliary cruiser commanders, was born in Schleswig on 4 November 1899. The son of a government official, he had joined the Kaiserliche Marine in July 1915, and served in several surface ships. Discharged in 1919, he applied to re-enlist and was one of the fortunate few to be accepted into the tiny Navy permitted to the Weimar Republic. Rogge served as commander of the sail trainers *Gorch Fock* and *Albert Leo Schlageter*.

On mobilization for war Rogge was appointed to command the auxiliary cruiser, *Schiff 16*, better known as the notorious *Atlantis*. This ship, a 7,860-ton merchantman, was built in 1937 for the Bremen Hansa Line as the *Goldenfels*. Under Rogge's personal supervision she was gutted and re-fitted for her wartime role. She was given increased fuel capacity and greater crew accommodation, hangars for her seaplane and much more. She was armed with six 5.9in guns, one 75mm gun, four 20mm Flak guns, four 21in torpedo tubes and 92 mines.

Rogge took *Atlantis* to sea on 11 March 1940, at the same time as fellow auxiliary cruisers *Orion* and *Widder*. Rogge had his ship disguised as a Soviet freighter, the *Kim*. Rogge felt that as a Soviet ship he would be less likely to be interfered with by any British naval patrols encountered. With a U-boat escort as far as the Denmark Strait, Rogge broke out successfully into the Atlantic. Crossing the Equator into the South Atlantic, *Atlantis* was re-camouflaged as the Japanese *Kasii Maru*. His first action came on 3 May 1940. *Atlantis* encountered the 6,200-ton freighter *Scientist* which ignored Rogge's order to stop and sent a 'QQQQ' warning message, indicating attack by a raider. Fortunately for Rogge this signal was not picked up by an Allied receiver. Accurate shooting from Rogge's 5.9in guns soon had the freighter ablaze and after evacuating her crew to *Atlantis*, Rogge sank her with a torpedo.

The next task for *Atlantis* was to lay mines off Cape Aguilhas, a mission which was achieved without incident and which was later to reap benefits for Rogge. A new disguise followed for *Atlantis* and she became the Dutch *Abbekerk*, a very successful ruse which resulted in the capture of the 7,230-ton Norwegian *Tirranna*. Completely taken in by the disguise until it was too late, the Norwegian allowed *Atlantis* to get too close before attempting to speed off – not to escape a suspected enemy Rogge believed, but through vanity, in not wishing this Dutchman to overtake his new ship of which he was most proud. *Atlantis* then opened fire and at last the *Tirranna* realized the danger and returned fire with her sole 4.7in stern gun. Only after 150 shells had been fired by *Atlantis* did the plucky Norwegian heave to and surrender. Rogge took off the crew and substituted a prize crew under Leutnant zur See Waldmann. He set off for home with his prize ship and also took some 270 of the prisoners held in *Atlantis*. Waldmann's ship reached home waters before being torpedoed by HMS *Tuna* and sinking with considerable loss of life.

Rogge's next victim was the 7,500-ton *City of Baghdad* which stopped after a warning shot. An attempt to use her radio, however, brought a shell from *Atlantis* into her radio room. Once the crew had been taken aboard *Atlantis*, explosive charges were set and the elderly freighter sank. On 13 July 1941 the 7,770-ton liner *Kemmendine*, *en route* from Glasgow to Rangoon, became *Atlantis's* next victim. She was carrying 147 passengers and crew who swelled Rogge's complement of prisoners to 347. On 2 August the 6,730-ton *Talleyrand* blundered into *Atlantis* while she was transferring prisoners to the *Tirranna* before Waldemann set off. Unaware of what was happening, *Talleyrand* was quickly captured. She was sunk by the tiny Arado seaplane carried by *Atlantis*.

Just after midnight on 24 August, *Atlantis* encountered and quickly sank the 4,740-ton *King City*. September saw the tanker *Athelking* and the freighter *Benarty* added to Rogge's score. The *Commissaire Ramel* followed on 19 September. Rogge's next prize, the Yugoslav *Durmitor* was used as a prison ship, because *Atlantis* was once again being overrun with prisoners, rapidly using up her food supplies. *Durmitor* was sent off with nearly 300 prisoners aboard and reached port on 22 November.

Operating in the Gulf of Bengal, the next success for *Atlantis* was the 6,750-ton Norwegian tanker *Teddy*, which was captured intact on the night of 8/9 November. On the following day the tanker *Ole Jacob* was also captured with 10,000 tons of aviation spirit aboard. Yet another victim, the freighter *Automedon*, was captured one day later. On 7 December 1940, Kapitän zur See Rogge was decorated with the Knight's Cross of the Iron Cross in recognition of his achievements.

In January 1941, the 5,140-ton *Mandasur* fell victim to the 5.9in guns of *Atlantis*. On the 31st of that month, the British steamer *Speybank* of some 5,144 tons was captured intact and a prize crew put aboard. With the capture of this ship the total score for Rogge and his men so far was in excess of 100,000 tons. On 3 February, the elderly tanker *Ketty Brövig*, totally unarmed, fell into Rogge's clutches with its useful cargo of 6,370 tons of oil and 4,125 tons of diesel. The next victim appeared on 17 April. The Egyptian *Zam Zam* was carrying many civilian passengers who would put an intolerable strain on *Atlantis*'s resources. These prisoners were put aboard the prize ship *Dresden* and safely reached port.

A very quiet spell ensued and *Atlantis* was not to achieve her next victory until 14 May when the 5,610-ton steamer *Rabaul* was sunk. *Atlantis* did try to stop her without using violence, but the *Rabaul*'s Second Officer, who had seen the signal from Rogge to stop, did not understand the signal so simply ignored it hoping *Atlantis* would just go away. On 17 May Rogge's luck almost ran out when *Atlantis* spotted the shadows of two large ships in the night. These shadows turned out to be the battleship *Nelson* and an aircraft carrier. *Atlantis* escaped unseen.

One week later, Rogge encountered the British freighter *Trafalgar*, a 4,530-tonner with a cargo of coal. Battered by gunfire she was quickly sent to the bottom with a torpedo.

In the middle of June, *Atlantis* added to her list of victims the British *Tottenham*, loaded with military supplies. Time, however, was running out for the German raider. Rogge's penultimate victim was the British freighter *Balzac*, a 5,370-tonner with a mixed cargo of foodstuffs and wood. On 10 September, Rogge met his last victim, the 4,800-ton *Silvaplana* which, being captured intact with a valuable cargo, was taken as a prize.

Having been at sea for eighteen months, six months longer than planned, Rogge decided it was time to sail for home. He had achieved everything that could be asked of him and he and his men would now see Christmas at home. Rounding the Cape at the end of October, Rogge re-entered the Atlantic. He had been ordered to rendezvous and refuel *U 68*, commanded by his old friend, Karl-Friedrich Merten. Having successfully carried out this task, he was rather annoyed to receive orders to undertake another refuelling mission, this time for *U 162* under Ernst Bauer. On 22 November 1941, Rogge and Bauer rendezvoused north of the Ascension Islands. Bauer and some of his men came over to *Atlantis* to have a hot meal, and while the refuelling was taking place Rogge used the opportunity to carry out essential repairs to one of his engines. Shortly after the refuelling operation commenced, the lookouts in *Atlantis* spotted a three-funnelled ship. Rogge recognized her as the *Devonshire*. As soon as the fuel lines were detached, Rogge turned his stern towards the enemy to show as small a target as possible. Bauer had no time to return to his U-boat, and *U 162* dived with the First Officer in command.

With a damaged engine Rogge had no chance to escape. His only hope was that he could lure the enemy into range of *U 162*. *Devonshire*'s first salvo was taken by the U-boat for depth-charges and instead of attacking she dived even deeper seeking to escape. *Atlantis* had no chance and Rogge was forced to abandon ship. When *U 126* finally surfaced the enemy had departed and Bauer rejoined his U-boat together with the wounded survivors from *Atlantis*. Taking the life-boats in tow, *U 126* headed towards the coast of Brazil, eventually meeting the supply ship *Python*.

History repeated itself. On 4 December, while refuelling U-boats, *Python* was attacked by *Dorsetshire*, sister of *Devonshire*. The survivors from *Atlantis* were again shipwrecked as *Python* was scuttled. Again U-boats picked up the survivors after the enemy had departed. Rogge and his crew eventually reached St-Nazaire on 25 December 1941.

Rogge had sunk 145,000 tons of shipping, an achievement rewarded with the Oakleaves to his Knight's Cross on 31 December 1941. He was also the only confirmed recipient of the diamond-studded version of the Auxiliary Cruiser War Badge, presented by Grossadmiral Raeder.

Rogge was appointed Chief of Staff of the Naval Education Inspectorate and in 1943 was promoted to Konteradmiral, being responsible for the selection of officer candidates. In 1944 he was promoted to Vizeadmiral and given command of Marine Kampf Gruppe III with the heavy cruiser *Prinz Eugen* as his base. *Prinz Eugen* was used in fire support missions against Soviet forces around the beleaguered German positions near Danzig. After the war Rogge re-joined the navy, serving as a Konteradmiral in the Bundesmarine until he retired in 1962.

Bernhard Rogge was one of the most respected of all Germany's great sailors. His war was fought with the maximum of chivalry and regard for human life. He was well known for the respect with which his prisoners were treated. On one occasion he court-martialled one of his own men for stealing a pair of binoculars from a British officer prisoner. Despite the victim's plea for leniency, Rogge sentenced the thief to two years' imprisonment, and the sentence was carried out. Bernhard Rogge died in Hamburg in 1982.

KORVETTENKAPITÄN ADALBERT SCHNEE

One of the true greats of the U-boat service, Adalbert Schnee was born in Berlin on 31 December 1913. He joined the Navy in 1934 and after his basic training and commissioning he served as Leutnant zur See in the light cruiser *Leipzig*, taking part in the non-intervention patrols in Spanish waters during the Civil War.

On 20 May 1938, he transferred to U-boats and received his first posting as Wach Offizier in *U 23* under none other than Otto Kretschmer, destined to become the greatest of all U-boat aces. Shortly after the outbreak of war, Schnee was given his own command. This was *U 6*, a small Type IIA coastal submarine of some 250 tons. He commanded this vessel until July 1940 when he took over command of a new boat, *U 60*, from Georg Schewe.

Schnee's first victory came on 13 August 1940 when he sank the Swedish steamer *Nils Gorthon*, north of Malin Head. She was a small, 1,700-ton freighter straggling from the Halifax, Nova Scotia – UK Convoy HX62. On 31 August 1940, Schnee attacked the Dutch merchantman *Volendam*, a large, 15,400-ton freighter from Convoy OB205, sailing from Liverpool to the USA. His torpedo struck and damaged the ship, but she was not sunk. On 3 September 1940, the British steamer *Ulva* of some 1,400 tons became Schnee's next victim when she was torpedoed and sunk. It was the final success of the cruise and Schnee's last with *U 60*. This small Type IIB U-boat survived the war, to be scuttled at Wilhelmshaven in May 1945.

Schnee's next command was *U 201*. This was a much larger, ocean-going Type VIIC, an 800-tonner of the type which formed the backbone of the U-boat service. She was built by Germania Werft in Kiel. Schnee's first cruise with *U 201* was in May 1941. On the 2nd of that month he encountered the tanker *Capulet*. This 8,100-ton vessel from Convoy HX121 had been torpedoed by *U 552* under Erich Topp, and left a blazing wreck. Schnee administered the *coup de grâce* and sent the stricken vessel to the bottom. Six days later Schnee encountered a passenger ship which he torpedoed, and although he observed the torpedo strike the ship, it failed to explode. Faulty torpedoes were to be the bane of many U-boat commanders. On 9 May the British steamer *Gregalia* of 5,800 tons was torpedoed and sunk, and the 5,900-ton *Empire Cloud* was damaged. Both ships were from Convoy OB318, outward-bound from Liverpool to the USA.

In August 1941, on his next cruise, Schnee operated against the Gibraltar convoys and on the 19th the British steamer *Ciscar* of 1,800 tons and *Aguila* of 3,250 tons from Convoy OG71, bound for Gibraltar from the UK, were both sunk by torpedoes. Schnee observed other hits during this attack, but no sinkings. On 23 August a further attack was made on the same convoy, and *Stork* of 787 tons and the steamer *Aldergrove* of 1,900 tons were both sunk. On 30 August 1941, Schnee's successes were rewarded with the Knight's Cross of the Iron Cross.

Schnee's next cruise was also against the Gibraltar convoys. On 21 September during an attack on Gibraltar-bound Convoy OG74, three ships were sunk by *U 201*: the 1,570-ton *Runa*, the 1,500-ton *Lissa* and the 1,380-ton *Rhineland*. On 27 September Schnee attacked another convoy, HG73, homeward-bound from Gibraltar, twice on the same day. In the first attack, the 5,150-ton *Springbank* and the 2,400-ton Norwegian steamer *Siremalm* were sunk. In the second attack the 3,100-ton British steamer *Margareta* was struck by a torpedo and broke in half. A second ship was also observed as being hit, but at this point Schnee had to crash-dive to avoid the escorts and was unable to identify her.

On 18 April the Argentinian tanker *Victoria* of 7,400 tons was hit and damaged, but she was successfully taken under tow and reached New York escorted by the destroyers *Nicholson* and *Swanson*. Three days later a more successful attack was made on the Norwegian steamer *Bris*, a 2,000-tonner, which was torpedoed and sunk. On 22 April two more Allied ships fell victim to *U 201* when the 5,000-ton American merchantman *San Jacinto* was sunk by torpedo and gunfire, and the British *Derryheen* of 7,200 tons was sunk by torpedo.

Schnee's next area of operations was the South Atlantic where on 6 July 1942 he torpedoed and sank the large British merchantman *Avila Star* of 14,400 tons. On 12 July he attacked Convoy OS33, which had scattered.

The 7,000-ton British steamer *Cortona* and the smaller, 5,200-ton *Siris* were sunk by combined torpedo and gunfire. *Cortona* had also been struck by torpedoes from *U 116*, but it was Schnee in *U 201* who struck the mortal blow. On the following day, an attack was made on the 6,700-ton British steamer *Sithonia* which was a straggler from the same dispersed convoy. She was torpedoed and sunk. On 15 July the 6,990-ton tanker *British Yeoman* was also sunk, by a combination of torpedoes and gunfire. Schnee's achievements brought the award of the Oakleaves to his Knight's Cross on 15 July 1942. Schnee's final victory came on 25 July 1942 when he sank the British *Laertes*, a fleet auxiliary which was hit by a torpedo and sank. On his return to base Schnee was posted to shore duties and went on to serve as a staff officer with the Oberkommando der Marine, as an acknowledged expert on the tactics of attacking convoys.

Towards the end of the war, Schnee was once again given command of a U-boat. He was one of the few fortunate enough to take one of the new Type XXI boats to sea on combat duties. This was *U 2511*, which sailed in May 1945. While at sea awaiting suitable targets, Schnee received orders that in view of the imminent cessation of hostilities, he was not to carry out any attacks. Schnee had, however, spotted the British cruiser *Norfolk* and could not resist making a dummy run against her. Schnee confirmed that he could easily have sunk her with his superb new boat, but kept to his orders and allowed her to pass unmolested.

Adalbert Schnee survived the war and went on to become a leading figure in the U-Boat Veterans Association. A son-in-law of Grossadmiral Dönitz, Schnee was one of the pallbearers at Dönitz's funeral. Schnee died in Hamburg in November 1982.

Note. Schnee's U-boat, *U 201*, was sunk on 17 February 1943, off Newfoundland by the British destroyer *Fame*.

KAPITÄNLEUTNANT HEINRICH SCHROETELER

Heinrich Schroeteler was born on 10 December 1915 in Essen. His naval career began in the minesweeping service and he also served as an officer on the staff of the Befehlshaber der U-Boote before being given his own command in 1942.

Schroeteler's first cruise began on 20 October 1942 with *U 667*. His early years in this boat were less than fruitful. It was not until 16 April 1944, six days after Schroeteler had been decorated with the German Cross in Gold, that his first success was achieved. *U 667* attacked a destroyer escort with a T-5 acoustic torpedo and the detonation was heard twelve minutes later. Despite this successful attack, no sinking was observed, and it was assumed that either the torpedo was faulty or the explosion was an end-of-run detonation. Subsequently, Schroeteler handed over command of *U 667*, a Type VIIC, and took over a new vessel, *U 1023*. It was a fortunate move because *U 667* was mined and sunk of La Rochelle in the Bay of Biscay on 25 August 1944.

Schroeteler next found action on 9 April 1945 when, with *U 1023*, he attacked Convoy SC171 sailing from Sydney to the United Kingdom. Schroeteler fired a spread of three FAT torpedoes and two detonations were heard. These were also recorded by the escorting frigate *Capilano*, so although no sinkings were registered, Schroeteler at least had the satisfaction of damaging two enemy vessels. Ten days later, on 19 April, Schroeteler attacked another convoy, firing three torpedoes, and recorded a detonation after 50 seconds and another just afterwards in the centre of the convoy. On 23 April, *U 1023* attacked the UK coastal Convoy TBC135 and damaged the British steamer *Riverton*, a 7,000-tonner. During the last month of the war, *U 1023* attacked and sank the Norwegian minesweeper *Nyms* with a T-5 acoustic torpedo. On 2 May 1945, Schroeteler was decorated with the Knight's Cross of the Iron Cross. Schroeteler was still at sea with *U 1023* when, on 10 May 1945, the instructions for surrender came through. Schroeteler's last communication, was a signal to Grossadmiral Dönitz:

> 'In the last 46 days of schnorkel operations against convoys, have sunk one steamer of 8,000 tons and one Destroyer [actually the Minesweeper *Nyms*]. A large freighter of 10,000 tons torpedoed . . . In complete faith and confidence in you Herr Grossadmiral, we now carry out our gravest orders.'
>
> Schroeteler *U 1023*

Schroeteler's heavy heart at having to surrender was by no means unusual. Despite the most dreadful losses, the U-boat service kept its *esprit de corps* to the last. *U 1023* was surrendered to the Royal Navy at Weymouth in 1945 and was used for a time by the British under the number *N.83*.

Schroeteler survived the war and now lives in retirement in Bochum.

FREGATTENKAPITÄN REINHARD SUHREN

Reinhard Teddi Suhren was born on 16 April 1916 in Langenschwalbach, the son of a cavalry officer. He joined the Navy in April 1935 and was commissioned Leutnant zur See in 1938. On the outbreak of war, he was serving as Wach Offizier in *U 48* under Kapitänleutnant Schultze who himself was to become an Oakleaves winning ace with 28 ships to his credit.

Suhren gained a great deal of combat experience under Schultze and is reckoned to have actually fired more torpedoes at the enemy than any other man in the German Navy. He completed nine war cruises in *U 48* as Wach Offizier and his share of the credit for the sinking of between 200,000 and 250,000 tons of shipping brought him the award of the Knight's Cross of the Iron Cross on 3 November 1940.

In the following year, Suhren gained his own command, *U 564*, a Type VIIC boat of about 800 tons, armed with a 3.5in gun and fourteen torpedoes. On 3 April 1941, *U 564* began combat duty. On her first attack, against Convoy HX133 she scored a resounding success, sinking two large freighters of about 8,000 tons and damaging a third. Suhren's experiences in *U 48* had stood him in good stead. During his next convoy attack, on OG76, Suhren torpedoed and sank the corvette *Zinnia* on 23 August 1941, as well as two smaller merchant ships. On 31 December 1941, Oberleutnant zur See Suhren became the 56th recipient of the Oakleaves to the Knight's Cross in recognition of his success.

On Suhren's next war cruise, during an attack on Convoy HG75, he sank two more merchantmen. The 11,000-ton tanker *Victolite* was a major success for Suhren when she was sunk by *U 564* in February 1942. His next war cruise saw three more ships sunk as well as others damaged. Suhren's final major success was against Convoy OS34 when the 8,000-ton tanker *Vardaas* was sunk, along with two 5,000-tonners and two smaller merchantmen.

On 1 September 1942, Kapitänleutnant Suhren became the eighteenth recipient of the Swords and one of only five naval personnel to win this coveted decoration. Suhren's personal score amounted to 95,000 tons of shipping sunk and a further 31,000 tons disabled. Added to the near quarter of a million tons of shipping lost to *U 48* while he was Wach Offizier, these totals made him one of Germany's most experienced U-boat aces. This wealth of experience was put to good use when he was posted as an instructor to 2 U-Boot Lehrdivision in Gotenhafen.

In the early part of 1944, Suhren was posted as Commander of U-Boats in Norway with his base in Narvik. With this post came promotion to Fregattenkapitän. He commanded U-boats operating out of Trondheim, Narvik and Bergen, tasked with attacking Allied convoys carrying Lend-Lease material to the Soviet Union from the USA and Great Britain.

At the surrender, Suhren became a prisoner of the British and was released in 1946. He was notoriously outspoken and would speak his mind no matter who was present. U-boat Ace Heinrich Bleichrodt, under whom Suhren had served, described him and his friend Erich Zurn as being the toughest lads in the whole navy, a real handful for the Kriegsmarine, let alone the enemy. Reinhard Teddi Suhren died in August 1984.

Suhren's elder brother Gerd was also a U-boat ace who was decorated with the Knight's Cross of the Iron Cross on 21 October 1940 as Engineering Officer in *U 37* before being transferred to the staff of Grossadmiral Dönitz. He returned to combat service in May 1945, however, with one of the few Type XXI boats to see service, *U 2511* under command of Adalbert Schnee.

KAPITÄNLEUTNANT HANS DIETRICH VON TIESENHAUSEN

Hans Dietrich Freiherr von Tiesenhausen was born in Riga on 22 February 1913. He joined the Navy in 1934 and like so many of his peers, his basic seaman's training was carried out in the barque *Gorch Fock*. Next came a world-wide goodwill tour in the cruiser *Karlsruhe*, before attending the Flensburg Marineschule. Freiherr von Tiesenhausen saw service during the Spanish Civil War in the cruiser *Nürnberg* on non-intervention patrol. He was subsequently posted as Adjutant to 5 Marine Artillerie Abteilung in Pillau. In 1940, he transferred to the U-boat service. His first appointment was as Wach Offizier in *U 23* under Otto Kretschmer and thereafter under Korth in *U 93*. After a year's Wach Offizier service, he was given his own command, *U 331*, a Type VIIC, on 31 March 1941.

U 331's first cruise was fairly uneventful. Only one attack was made and all the torpedoes launched missed their target. The second cruise was to be in the dangerous waters of the Mediterranean. The hazardous passage through the Straits of Gibraltar was made safely and *U 331* was based at Salamis. Von Tiesenhausen's first task was to land a party of the élite Brandenburgers at Ras el Gibecia. *U 331* then went on to patrol the waters off Mersa Matruh in an attempt to prevent supplies being landed for the beleaguered garrison at El Alamein.

On 25 November 1941, von Tiesenhausen encountered a powerful British naval force comprising three battleships escorted by eight destroyers. He launched four torpedoes and scored hits on the battleship *Barham*. At one point the conning tower of *U 331* broke surface, but she was in fact too close to the British ships for their guns to be depressed low enough to engage her. *U 331* crash-dived and almost miraculously escaped the attention of the strong escort force. The stricken *Barham* capsized and exploded with the loss of more than 860 crew members. For various reasons the British withheld admission of the loss, and although von Tiesenhausen knew that he had hit the battleship he was unaware that she had actually sunk. When the loss was finally announced, von Tiesenhause was immediately decorated with the Knight's Cross of the Iron Cross. *U 331*'s subsequent patrols were uneventful until 9 November 1942 when he was on patrol off Algeria, searching for victims among the flotilla of merchantmen bringing troops and supplies for the 'Torch' landings. The USS *Leedstown*, a 9,000-ton transport ship laden with troops and landing craft had been attacked and damaged by torpedo-bombers when she was spotted by *U 331*. Immediately, von Tiesenhausen launched two torpedoes which struck the troopship amidships She sank just over an hour later. Three days later *U 331* suffered a severe depth-charge attack after having been spotted during an attack on an Allied convoy.

On 17 November, *U 331* was spotted by a Hudson bomber of RAF Coastal Command. She dived before the aircraft could attack, but the Hudson's pilot was no amateur. When *U 331* surfaced two hours later, the Hudson was still waiting, and this time pounced before the U-boat could dive again, dropping depth-charges which straddled her, causing damage to the main gun and jamming the hatch open. Two more aircraft appeared and dropped more depth-charges which damaged the U-boat still further. Unable to dive, von Tiesenhausen ordered his crew to prepare to abandon ship and hoisted the white flag of surrender. His problems were not over yet however. Three torpedo-bombers from the carrier *Formidable* appeared on the scene, escorted by fighters. The Hudson, still patrolling, witnessed the fighters brutally machine-gun the survivors despite the white flag. A torpedo from one of the attacking torpedo-bombers struck *U 331* killing many more of the crew. A total of seventeen of *U 331*'s crew were saved, including von Tiesenhausen and his Wach Offizier. The pilot of the Hudson received the DSO for his part in the action, but the pilot of the torpedo-bomber was court-martialled for attacking the U-boat while she was flying the white flag. In the Mediterranean, where victories for the U-boats were few and far between, the sinking of *Barham* by Dietrich von Tiesenhausen was one of only a handful of major successes.

FREGETTENKAPITÄN ERICH TOPP

Erich Topp, one of the U-boat service's most highly decorated aces, was born in Hanover on 2 July 1914. He joined the Navy in 1934, and was transferred to U-boats just before the outbreak of war. Initially he served as Wach Offizier in *U 46*. In June 1940, Topp took over command of *U 57* from Klaus Korth. *U 57* was a small, Type IIC coastal craft of some 340 tons with a crew of 25 and equipped with a mere three torpedo tubes.

On his first major cruise with *U 57*, Topp sank, on 17 July 1940, the first of his many victims. This was the Swedish steamer *Atos* of 2,160 tons. Three weeks passed before his third victim, the 5,860-ton British steamer *Saint Dunstan* was hit and sunk. She was part of the North America-bound Convoy OB202 out of Liverpool. On the same day the 10,900-ton freighter *Cumberland* was torpedoed and sunk. A third vessel, *Havildar* was also hit, but the 5,400-tonner was only damaged. On the following day, the British tanker *Pecten*, of 7,500 tons, a straggler from Convoy HX65, was added to Topp's growing list of victims. A second victim, the 8,650-ton British *Manipur* was sunk on the same day. She was from the UK-bound Convoy HX55A our of Halifax, Nova Scotia.

With a score in excess of 30,000 tons sunk, using such a small coastal U-boat, Topp's first cruise was a resounding success. Disaster was to strike, however; on the return passage *U 57* was sunk in a collision with the Norwegian freighter *Rona* in the lock at Brunsbüttel. Six crew members were lost. *U 57* was eventually raised and recommissioned, serving safely throughout the war, to be scuttled at Kiel in May 1945.

Topp's new command was *U 552*, a large Type VIIC built by Blohm & Voss in Hamburg. Topp took over the new boat on 4 December 1940. His first success with her was on 1 March 1941 when the British tanker *Cadillac* of some 12,000 tons, sailing with Convoy HX109 from Canada to the UK, was torpedoed and sunk. On 10 March the Icelandic trawler *Reykjaborg* was sunk by a combination of torpedoes and gunfire.

On Topp's next cruise the British *Commander Horton*, a fleet auxiliary, and the 10,160-ton freighter *Beacon Grange* were sunk on 27 April 1941. On the following day the 8,100-ton tanker *Capulet, en route* to the UK from Canada was torpedoed, to be finished off later by *U 201*. In May the 5,500-ton British freighter *Nerissa* was sent to the bottom. June 1941 was to be a particularly successful month for Topp, with the 4,860-ton steamer *Ainderby* being sunk on the 10th. Two days later the large freighter *Chinese Prince* of 8,600 tons went to the bottom and on the 18th the 10,000-ton steamer *Norfolk* joined them. His successes brought Topp the award of the Knight's Cross of the Iron Cross on 20 June while still at sea. He was the 75th naval recipient.

Topp's next cruise brought some of his greatest successes. It began modestly enough when Topp administered the *coup de grâce* to the small Norwegian steamer *Spind* which had been damaged earlier by *U 564*. Topp sent her to the bottom on 23 August 1941. Almost a month passed before his next success, the British tanker *T. J. Williams*, an 8,200-tonner, was sunk on 20 September. A second salvo of torpedoes fired shortly afterwards sank the 4,100-ton Panamanian steamer *Pink Star* and later the same day the Norwegian *Barbo*, of 6,300 tons was hit with two torpedoes and quickly sank. On 31 October, Topp joined that august band of aces who had sunk warships when *U 552* attacked and sank the US destroyer *Reuben James*. She was escorting UK-bound Convoy HX156. It was the last sinking of a highly successful cruise.

U 552 began her next cuise at the beginning of 1942. On 15 January she found her first victim, the 4,100-ton steamer *Dayrose* which was sunk by torpedo. Three days later the small American steamer *Frances Salmar* was added to Topp's score. On 25 March, the Dutch tanker *Ocana*, a 6,250-tonner was torpedoed and set on fire. April was to become another of Topp's particularly successful months when the waters off the American east coast seemed littered with his victims. On 3 April the American steamer *David H. Atwater* was sunk by gunfire. Two days later the 7,950-ton tanker *Byron T. Benson* was sent to the bottom. On 7 April the 7,130-ton tanker *British Splendour* and the Norwegian factory ship *Lancing* of some 7,860 tons were both sunk. On 9 April, the US tanker *Atlas* of 7,100 tons was sunk, to be followed just two days later by yet another US tanker, the 6,940-ton *Tamaulipas*. This cruise had so far netted five tankers totalling nearly 35,000 tons in sixteen days. On 11 April 1942, Kapitänleutnant Topp had his achievements recognized by the award of the Oakleaves to his Knight's Cross.

Topp seemed unstoppable. His next cruise in the summer of 1942 was against the Gibraltar convoys and on 15 June 1942 in two separate attacks on Convoy HG84, he sank five ships: the British steamer *Etrib* of 1,950 tons, the *Pelayo* of 1,350 tons, the Norwegian tanker *Slemdal* of 7,370 tons, the steamer *City of Oxford* of 2,760 tons and the 2,430-ton *Thurso*. On 25 July 1942, Topp attacked Convoy ON113 bound for the USA from the UK. The 5,130-ton British steamer *Broompark* was sunk and the 8,000-ton tanker *British Merit* damaged. On 3 August Convoy ON115 bore the brunt of Topp's attack when the Belgian steamer *Belgian Soldier* of 7,160 tons was sunk and the 10,600-ton British tanker *G. S. Walden* was damaged. This was Topp's last cruise. On his return to base he was decorated with the Swords to his Oakleaves, the seventeenth recipient of this rare award and the second of only three naval recipients, all of whom were U-boat aces.

Topp was given command of a U-Boat Flotilla at Gotenhafen until a few weeks before the end of the war when he once again took command of a U-boat. This was the Type XXI *U 2513*. She never had an opportunity for combat, however, and was scuttled at Horten on 8 May 1945. She was later raised by the Americans and used for experimental work. Topp's *U 552* also survived the war, being scuttled by her crew in May 1945.

Erich Topp ended the war with the rank of Fregattenkapitän, and a total of 35 ships to his credit. Depending on the sources consulted, estimates of Topp's total tonnage sunk range from 192,000 to just under a quarter of a million tons. After the war, Topp joined the West German Bundesmarine, and reached the rank of Admiral.

OBERLEUTNANT ZUR SEE OTTO WESTPHALEN

A U-boat ace from the latter part of the Second World War, Otto Westphalen was born in Hamburg on 12 March 1920. He joined the Navy in 1938 and initially served with the surface fleet. As Wach Offizier in Torpedoboot *Kondor* from 1939 to 1940, he served in Norwegian and French waters, winning the Iron Cross Second Class.

Transferring to U-boats, Westphalen became Wach Offizier in *U 566*, serving in the Atlantic and off the American coast during 1941, winning the Iron Cross First Class. In 1942, Leutnant Westphalen underwent training as a U-boat commander in *U 121* at Pillau and on 18 March 1943, took command of his own boat, *U 968*. Serving principally in the North Atlantic against Allied convoys to the Soviet Union, on 1 April 1944, Westphalen attacked Convoy JW58 and fired torpedoes at an escort destroyer. Explosions were heard but as no sinkings were recorded it is assumed these must have been torpedoes which had reached the end of their run.

In January 1945, *U 968* attacked a Soviet convoy sailing from the White Sea to Kola Fiord. The Norwegian tanker *Norfjell*, of 8,100 tons was sunk. On 17 February, Convoy RA64 was attacked and the US steamer *Thomas Scott* was hit and damaged. She was taken under tow by a Soviet destroyer, but eventually sank. The escort sloop *Lark* was hit in the bows by an acoustic torpedo and had to be towed into Kola Fiord where she was beached, never to sail again. On 20 March Westphalen scored another success on a British warship, sinking the sloop *Lapwing* and the US Liberty freighter *Thomas Donaldson*, from Convoy JW65. On 23 March, he became the 297th naval recipient of the Knight's Cross of the Iron Cross. He had already received the German Cross in Gold in February 1944. On 29 April Westphalen once again attacked a warship, sinking the British destroyer escort *Goodall*.

At the surrender, Otto Westphalen had achieved a score of 26,396 tons of shipping sunk. Not a huge score, but in view of the fact that it included three warships specifically equipped as anti-submarine escorts, this was a considerable achievement. Westphalen was obliged to hand over his boat in Operation 'Deadlight', the surrender of Germany's remaining U-boats, on

16 May 1945. After the war, he became a hotelier in Hamburg and is still alive.

KONTERADMIRAL KURT WEYHER

Kurt Weyher was born in Graudenz on 30 August 1901 and joined the Imperial Navy as a 17-year-old Cadet on 1 April 1918. He served in a Freikorps unit after the armistice in 1918, but rejoined the Reichsmarine in 1922. His training and experience was varied and included torpedo-boats, sail trainers, U-boats and cruisers. Shortly before the outbreak of war he was given command of *Schiff 36*, the auxiliary cruiser *Orion*. She was a 7,000-ton freighter built in 1930 by Blohm & Voss of Hamburg, armed with six 5.9in guns, one 75mm gun plus one 37mm and four 20mm Flak guns. She also carried torpedoes and 228 mines, plus a seaplane. Despite her armament, however, the ship was not mechanically suitable for war operations and this was to cause her commander much trouble later.

Orion sailed on 1 April 1940 and on the 24th of that month scored her first success, when the 5,200-ton *Huxby* fell victim to her guns and sank after just six minutes of action. Weyher then sailed south and rounded Cape Horn on 21 May. By mid-June he was in New Zealand waters engaged in minelaying. Those mines were responsible for the sinking of the 13,400-ton *Niagara*, carrying a huge sum in gold bullion. On 19 June, the Norwegian *Tropic Sea* was taken without a fight. Several weeks passed before *Orion* met her next victim, *Notou*, a French ship of some 2,500 tons. The refrigerated cargo ship *Turakina* with a cargo of food bound for the UK next fell victim to *Orion* and was followed by *Ringwood* which surrendered to Weyher on 13 October. In late November Weyher temporarily joined forces with the auxiliary cruiser *Komet* and, working together, the two raiders sank the tiny 550-ton *Holmwood* and the huge 16,700-ton *Rangitane*. On 8 December, Weyher sank *Triadic* and *Traister* before parting company with *Komet* and heading for home via the Indian Ocean.

The return passage was uneventful in terms of action, but was fraught with mechanical troubles. If any Allied warships had appeared while *Orion* was so continually beset by engine trouble she would have been doomed. Weyher and his men had a terrible time of it until July 1941 when she actually succeeded in sinking *Chaucer*, despite her bad state of repair. *Orion* finally reached French waters in August 1941, having covered 127,337 nautical miles and sunk 73,500 tons of shipping. Her cruise had lasted 510 days.

Weyher's achievements were considerable in view of the unsuitability of his ship for combat operations and the mechanical troubles which had dogged her. Fregattenkapitän Weyher was decorated with the Knight's Cross of the Iron Cross on 21 August 1941, when he reached port.

Weyher subsequently became an officer on the Naval Staff, serving in Roumania and Greece. From November 1944 until the end of the war, he was Commander of Sea Defences in Ostfriesland, reaching the rank of

Konteradmiral. He was taken into British captivity and on his release started a ships' chandlery business in Emden and Wilhelmshaven. In July 1977 he was decorated with the Bundesverdienstkreuz.

KORVETTENKAPITÄN HELMUT WITTE

One of Germany's top U-boat aces, and a truly chivalrous warrior, Helmut Witte was born in Bojendorf in Holstein on 6 April 1915. He enlisted in the Navy in 1934 and saw action at the Battle of Narvik with the destroyer *Z22 Anton Schmitt*. When the destroyer was sunk in the battle, Witte and his comrades found themselves on shore fighting alongside the infantry. In common with many destroyer crewmen whose ships were lost at Narvik, Witte transferred to the U-boat service in 1940. In October 1940 after completing his U-boat training, he was posted as Wach Offizier in *U 107* under Kapitänleutnant Günther Hessler. On *U 107*'s first cuise, four ships were sunk. From 29 March to 2 July 1941, in the course of a single cruise, *U 107* sank fourteen ships totalling 86,699 tons.

Witte had become a very experienced officer, having served in the cruiser *Köln*, in torpedo-boats, and in the destroyer *Anton Schmitt* prior to his U-boat training. He undertook a training course in preparation for his first U-boat command and on 4 October 1941 became Commander of *U 159*. His first cruise was a quiet affair, being a hand-over trip in combination with laying weather buoys.

Witte's second cruise as commander, however, found *U 159* lying off the Panama Canal and here the new commander was to find great success as ship after ship fell victim to *U 159*'s torpedoes. On 21 May 1942, the British steamer *New Brunswick* was sent to the bottom, the first of two ships sunk on that day. On 3 June, the American *City of Alna* was sunk, followed swiftly by *Edith*, *Fort Good Hope*, *Sixaloa*, *Flora*, the Yugoslav *Ante Matkovik*, *E. J. Sadler* and *Salon Turman*. A total of ten ships totalling 50,354 tons.

On his third cruise, Witte exceeded even this remarkable level of success. Operating off the South African coast from 24 August to 16 November 1942, Witte sank eleven ships totalling 63,730 tons. The sinking of one of these ships in particular gives a good insight into the chivalrous nature of this fine seaman. On 13 November 1942, *U 159* torpedoed and sank the US merchant ship *Star of Scotland*, operating out of California. Witte took the lifeboat with the eighteen surviving crew members of the sunken ship in tow, despite the great danger to his own vessel and its crew by staying on the surface. The American Captain, Constantine Fink, was taken aboard the U-boat and found Witte to be a kind and considerate captor, who supplied medicines, food and blankets, and allowed Fink to return to his men. *U 159*'s medics treated two of *Star of Scotland*'s wounded survivors. A lasting friendship was formed between the two Captains which survives to this day.

Helmut Witte was decorated with the Knight's Cross of the Iron Cross on 22 October 1942. The award was presented when *U 159* returned to Lorient from her cruise on 5 January 1943. *U 159* had spent 135 days at sea, and covered 21,650 nautical miles. Witte missed the next cruise of *U 159* through illness, which was fortunate for him because his boat was sunk on 15 July 1943 by US aircraft in the Caribbean. After his recovery Witte attended the Naval Academy and thereafter served on the Ship Construction Commission before becoming a staff officer at the Seekriegsleitung of the Oberkommando der Marine. Witte served as the representative of Vizeadmiral Heye, commander of the Kleinkampfverbände.

After the war, Witte was employed by several major manufacturing firms, becoming director of Ruhrkohle AG. He is still alive in retirement in Duisburg.

APPENDICES

The number of German pilots alone who qualified technically as aces was in excess of 5,000. This book can only give a representative selection, so these Appendices should not be taken as complete. Only fighter, night fighter and support pilots are listed for the Luftwaffe; for the navy, only the U-boat Service, the E-boats, the auxiliary cruisers and the human torpedoes; for the Army, only the Panzertruppen, the tank destroyers, and the assault guns.

In all cases it has been attempted to include only those who won their Knight's Cross in action as a pilot-submariner/tank crewman, etc. Therefore the reader will not find many of the famous generals and commanders who technically had belonged to the branches of service described but whose awards were usually given for their skill as leaders and tacticians. Rommel is probably one of the best-known Panzer generals in history; he was not however a tank ace in the sense that this book requires, though he may have been an ace strategist.

It is hoped that the reader will not be too disappointed if he does not find his own particular favourite ace listed here. Those who wish to study more extensive tables of data are referred to the many excellent works mentioned in the Bibliography.

HIGHEST DECORATED PANZERTRUPPEN PERSONNEL

Rank	Name	Unit	Date
SWORDS WINNERS			
Oberstleutnant	Franz Bäke	Pz Rgt 11	
SS-Obersturmführer	Michael Wittmann	schw SS Pz Abt 501	
SS-Standartenführer	Kurt Meyer	SS Pz Rgt 12 Hitlerjugend	
SS-Obersturmbannführer	Jochen Peiper	SS Pz Rgt 1 Leibstandarte Adolf Hitler	
OAKLEAVES WINNERS			
Oberleutnant	Ernst-Georg Buchterkirch	2/Pz Rgt 6	31 Dec 41
Hauptmann	Adalbert Schulz	1/Pz Rgt 25	31 Dec 41

Rank	Name	Unit	Date
Hauptmann	Johannes Kümmel	1/Pz Rgt 8	11 Oct 42
Hauptmann	Helmut Hudel	1/Pz Rgt 7	2 April 43
Hauptmann	Hans-Günther Stotten	1/Pz Rgt 8	10 May 43
Major	Bernhard Sauvant	schw Pz Abt 505	28 July 43
Major	Hans-Detlev von Cassel	1/Pz Rgt 35	29 Aug 43
SS-Hauptsturmführer	Erwin Meierdress	1/SS Pz Rgt 3	12 Oct 43
SS-Sturmbannführer	Christian Tychsen	II/SS Pz Rgt 2	10 Dec 43
Hauptmann	Josef Rettemeier	Pz Abt 5	13 Mar 44
Hauptmann	Georg Grüner	1/Pz Rgt 2	26 Mar 44
Oberfeldwebel	Hans Strippel	4/Pz Rgt 1	4 June 44
Hauptmann	Clemens Graf von Kageneck	schw Pz Abt 503	26 June 44
Major	Erich Löwe	schw Pz Abt 501	8 July 44
Leutnant	Otto Carius	schw Pz Abt 502	27 July 44
SS-Obersturmführer	Karl Kloskowski	7/SS Pz Rgt 2	11 Aug 44
SS-Obersturmbannführer	Max Wünsche	SS Pz Rgt 12	11 Aug 44
Leutnant	Johannes Bölter	schw Pz Abt 502	10 Sept 44
Major	Rudolf Haen	Pz Abt 103	21 Sept 44
SS-Obersturmbannführer	Otto Meyer	SS Pz Rgt 9	30 Sept 44
Oberleutnant	Jörg Burg	7/Pz Rgt 'GD'	4 Oct 44
Major	Fritz-Rudolf Schultz	Pz Rgt 35	28 Oct 44
Major	Wilhelm Weidenbrüch	Pz Abt 104	16 Nov 44
SS-Sturmbannführer	Fritz Biermeier	II/SS Pz Rgt 3	26 Dec 44
Major	Karl Rossmann	Pz Rgt 1 'HG'	1 Feb 45
Leutnant	Hans-Babo von Rohr	2/Pz Rgt 25	24 Feb 45
SS-Sturmbannführer	Werner Potschke	1/SS Pz Rgt 1	15 Mar 45
SS-Obersturmbannführer	Otto Paetsch	SS Pz Rgt 9	5 April 45
SS-Obersturmbannführer	Paul-Albert Kausch	SS Pz Rgt 11	23 April 45

TOP FIGHTER ACES OF THE LUFTWAFFE

A complete list of all Luftwaffe personnel who achieved ace status by bringing down five or more enemy aircraft would take a book in itself, an amazing 5,000 Luftwaffe pilots having qualified during the Second World War. This list is confined to the pilots who achieved a score of 75 or more

'kills', a figure which in any other airforce would have been deemed
fantastic. The list shows the ultimate rank achieved during the war, the unit
in which the pilot was serving at the surrender, and the score achieved.

Rank	Name	Unit	Score
Major	Erich Hartmann	JG52	352
Major	Gerhard Barkhorn	JV44	301
Major	Günther Rall	JG300	275
Oberleutnant	Otto Kittel	JG54	267
Major	Walter Nowotny	JG54	258
Major	Wilhelm Batz	JG52	237
Major	Erich Rudorffer	JG7	222
Oberstleutnant	Heinz Bär	JV44	220
Oberst	Hermann Graf	JG11	212
Major	Theodor Weissenberger	JG7	208
Oberstleutnant	Philipp Hans	JG1	206
Oberleutnant	Walter Schuck	JG7	206
Major	Heinrich Ehrler	JG7	204
Oberleutnant	Anton Hafner	JG51	204
Hauptmann	Helmut Lipfert	JG53	203
Major	Walter Krupinski	JV44	197
Major	Anton Hackl	JG300	192
Hauptmann	Joachim Brendl	JG51	189
Hauptmann	Max Stotz	JG54	189
Hauptmann	Joachim Kirschner	JG27	188
Major	Kurt Brändle	JG3	180
Oberleutnant	Günther Josten	JG51	178
Oberst	Johannes Steinhoff	JV44	176
Hauptmann	Günther Schack	JG3	174
Hauptmann	Ernst-Wilhelm Reinert	JG27	174
Hauptmann	Heinz Schmidt	JG52	173
Hauptmann	Emil Lang	JG26	173
Major	Horst Ademeit	JG54	166
Oberst	Wolf-Dietrich Wilcke	JG3	162
Hauptmann	Hans-Joachim Marseille	JG27	158
Hauptmann	Heinrich Sturm	JG52	157
Oberleutnant	Gerhard Thyben	JG54	157
Oberleutnant	Hans Beisswenger	JG54	152
Leutnant	Peter Düttmann	JG52	152
Oberst	Gordon M. Gollob	JG77	150
Leutnant	Fritz Tegtmeier	JG7	146
Oberleutnant	Albin Wolf	JG54	144
Leutnant	Kurt Tanzer	JG51	143
Oberstleutnant	Friedrich-Karl Müller	JG3	140
Major	Heinrich Setz	JG27	138
Hauptmann	Rudolf Trenkel	JG52	138
Oberleutnant	Karl Gratz	JG2	138

Rank	Name	Unit	Score
Oberleutnant	Franz Schall	JG7	137
Hauptmann	Walter Wolfrum	JG52	137
Oberst	Adolf Dickfeld	JG52	136
Hauptmann	Horst-Günther von Fassong	JG11	136
Oberleutnant	Otto Fönnekold	JG52	136
Hauptmann	Karl-Heinz Weber	JG1	136
Major	Joachim Müncheberg	JG51	135
Oberleutnant	Hans Waldmann	JG7	134
Hauptmann	Alfred Grislawski	JG53	133
Major	Johannes Wiese	JG77	133
Major	Adolf Borchers	JG52	132
Major	Erwin Clausen	JG11	132
Hauptmann	Wilhelm Lemke	JG3	131
Oberst	Herbert Ihlefeld	JG1	130
Oberleutnant	Heinrich Sterr	JG54	130
Major	Franz Eisenach	JG54	129
Oberst	Walter Dahl	JG300	128
Hauptmann	Franz Dörr	JG5	128
Oberleutnant	Rudolf Rademacher	JG7	126
Oberleutnant	Josef Zernemann	JG11	126
Leutnant	Gerhard Hoffmann	JG52	125
Oberst	Dietrich Hrabak	JG54	125
Oberst	Walter Oesau	JG1	125
Oberleutnant	Wolf-Udo Ettel	JG27	124
Hauptmann	Wolfgang Tonne	JG53	122
Oberfeldwebel	Heinz Marquardt	JG51	121
Major	Heinz-Wolfgang Schnaufer	NJG4	121
Hauptmann	Robert Weiss	JG54	121
Oberleutnant	Friedrich Obleser	JG52	120
Oberstleutnant	Erich Leie	JG77	118
Leutnant	Franz-Josef Beerenbrock	JG51	117
Leutnant	Hans-Joachim Birkner	JG52	117
Leutnant	Jakob Norz	JG5	117
Leutnant	Heinz Wernicke	JG54	117
Oberleutnant	August Lambert	SG77	116
Oberst	Werner Mölders	JG51	115
Leutnant	Wilhelm Crinius	JG53	114
Major	Werner Schroer	JG3	114
Leutnant	Hans Dammers	JG52	113
Leutnant	Berthold Korts	JG52	113
Oberstleutnant	Kurt Bühlingen	JG2	112
Oberst	Helmut Lent	NJG3	110
Major	Kurt Ubben	JG2	110
Oberleutnant	Franz Woidich	JG400	110
Major	Reinhârd Seiler	JG104	109
Hauptmann	Emil Bitsch	JG3	108

Rank	Name	Unit	Score
Major	Hans Hahn	JG54	108
Oberst	Günther Lützow	JV44	108
Oberleutnant	Bernhard Vechtel	JG51	108
Oberst	Viktor Bauer	EJG1	106
Hauptmann	Werner Lucas	JG3	106
Generalleutnant	Adolf Galland	JV44	104
Leutnant	Heinz Sachsenberg	JV44	104
Major	Hartmann Grasser	JG210	103
Major	Siegfried Freytag	JG7	102
Hauptmann	Friedrich Geisshardt	JG26	102
Oberstleutnant	Egon Mayer	JG2	102
Oberleutnant	Max-Hellmuth Ostermann	JG54	102
Oberleutnant	Herbert Rollwage	JG53	102
Major	Josef Wurmheller	JG2	102
Hauptmann	Rudolf Miethig	JG52	101
Oberst	Josef Priller	JG26	101
Leutnant	Ulrich Wernitz	JG54	101
Oberfeldwebel	Heinrich Bartels	JG27	99
Major	Wolfgang Späte	JG7	99
Leutnant	Leopold Steinbatz	JG52	99
Hauptmann	Paul-Heinrich Dähne	JG1	98
Oberleutnant	Horst Hannig	JG2	98
Oberst	Gustav Rödel	JG27	98
Oberfeldwebel	Helmut Rüffler	JG51	98
Oberleutnant	Hans Schleef	JG4	98
Hauptmann	Helmut Mertens	JG3	97
Major	Diethelm von Eichel-Streiber	JV44	96
Hauptmann	Heinrich Höfmeier	JG51	96
Hauptmann	Franz Hrdlicka	JG2	96
Hauptmann	Siegfried Lemke	JG2	96
Leutnant	Hermann Schleinhege	JG54	96
Oberleutnant	Leopold Münster	JG3	95
Leutnant	Anton Döbele	JG54	94
Oberleutnant	Heinrich Klöpper	JG1	94
Oberfeldwebel	Rudolf Müller	JG5	94
Major	Rudolf Resch	JG51	94
Leutnant	Edmund Rossmann	JG52	93
Major	Siegfried Schnell	JG54	93
Oberstleutnant	Helmut Bennemann	JG53	92
Oberleutnant	Gerhard Loos	JG54	92
Oberleutnant	Oskar Romm	JG3	92
Oberleutnant	Anton Resch	JG52	91
Hauptmann	Eberhard von Boremski	EJG1	90
Oberleutnant	Georg Schentke	JG3	90
Oberleutnant	Heinz Kemethmüller	JG26	89
Leutnant	Josef Jennewein	JG51	86

Rank	Name	Unit	Score
Oberstleutnant	Anton Mader	JG54	86
Leutnant	Friedrich Wachowiak	JG3	86
Leutnant	Ulrich Wöhnert	JG54	86
Leutnant	Gerhard Köppen	JG52	85
Leutnant	Walter Zellot	JG53	85
Leutnant	Heinz Ewald	JG52	84
Oberleutnant	Peter Kalden	JG51	84
Oberfeldwebel	Werner Quast	JG52	84
Leutnant	Walter Ohlrogge	JG7	83
Oberfeldwebel	Emil Pusch	NJG2	83
Major	Prinz Heinrich zu Sayn-Wittgenstein	NJG100	83
Oberleutnant	Otto Weissling	JG3	83
Hauptmann	Hans Götz	JG54	82
Oberleutnant	Hans Grünberg	JV44	82
Oberfeldwebel	Helmut Missner	JG54	82
Major	Franz Beyer	JG3	81
Leutnant	Hugo Broch	JG54	81
Oberleutnant	Max-Hermann Lücke	JG51	81
Leutnant	Willi Nemitz	JG52	81
Oberfeldwebel	Wilhelm Phillip	JG54	81
Leutnant	Rudolf Wagner	JG51	81
Leutnant	Herbert Bachnik	JG52	80
Leutnant	Otto Würfel	JG51	79
Major	Georg-Peter Eder	JG2	78
Major	Wolfgang Ewald	JG3	78
Hauptmann	Heinrich Krafft	JG51	78
Oberst	Karl-Gottfried Nordmann	JG51	78
Oberfeldwebel	Alexander Preinfalk	JG53	78
Major	Hubertus von Bonin	JG54	77
Hauptmann	Josef Haiböck	JG52	77
Leutnant	Johann-Hermann Meier	JG51	77
Leutnant	Hans-Joachim Kroschinski	JG54	76
Hauptmann	Maximilian Mayerl	JG1	76
Oberleutnant	Alfred Teumer	JG7	76
Hauptmann	Edwin Thiel	JG51	76
Leutnant	Johann Bunzek	JG52	75
Leutnant	Helmut Grollmus	JG54	75
Leutnant	Johann Pichler	JG77	75
Hauptmann	Hans Röhrig	JG53	75
Hauptmann	Joachim Wandel	JG54	75

TOP NIGHT-FIGHTER ACES OF THE LUFTWAFFE

Rank	Name	Unit	Score
Major	Heinz Wolfgang Schnaufer	NJG4	121
Oberst	Helmut Lent	NJG3	110
Major	Prinz Heinrich zu Sayn-Wittgenstein	NJG100	83
Oberst	Werner Streib	NJG1	66
Hauptmann	Manfred Meurer	NJG5	65
Oberst	Günther Radusch	NJG5	64
Hauptmann	Heinz Rökker	NJG2	64
Major	Rudolf Schönert	NJG10	64
Oberstleutnant	Walter Borchers	NJG5	63
Major	Paul Zorner	NJG5	59
Hauptmann	Gerhard Raht	NJG2	58
Hauptmann	Martin Becker	NJG6	57
Major	Wilhelm Herget	JV44	57
Oberleutnant	Gustav Fransci	NJG100	56
Hauptmann	Josef Kraft	NJG1	56
Hauptmann	Heinz Strüning	NJG1	56
Hauptmann	Hans-Dieter Frank	NJG1	55
Feldwebel	Heinz Vinke	NJG1	54
Hauptmann	August Geiger	NJG1	53
Oberstleutnant	Herbert Lütje	NJG6	53
Major	Martin Drewes	NJG1	52
Major	Prinz Egmont zu Lippe-Weissenfeld	NJG5	51
Major	Weiner Hoffmann	NJG5	52
Oberleutnant	Kurt Welter	NJG1	50
Hauptmann	Hermann Greiner	NJG1	50

JET FIGHTER ACES OF THE LUFTWAFFE

The following Luftwaffe fighter pilots qualified as aces by shooting down at least five enemy aircraft while flying jet fighters.

Rank	Name	Score
Oberstleutnant	Heinz Bär	16
Hauptmann	Franz Schall	14
Oberfeldwebel	Hermann Buchner	12
Major	Georg Peter Eder	12
Major	Erich Rudorffer	12
Leutnant	Karl Schnarrer	11
Feldwebel	Buttner	8
Oberleutnant	Lorenz And	8
Oberleutnant	Heinz Lennartz	8

Rank	Name	Score
Oberleutnant	Rudolf Rademacher	8
Oberleutnant	Walter Schuck	8
	Gunther Wegmann	8
Major	Theodor Weissenberger	8
Generalleutnant	Adolf Galland	7
	Fritz Müller	6
Oberst	Johannes 'Macki' Steinhoff	6
Feldwebel	Baudach	5
Major	Heinrich Ehrler	5
Oberleutnant	Hans Grunberg	5
Hauptfeldwebel	Heim	5
Major	Klaus Neumann	5
Leutnant	Schreiber	5
Hauptmann	Wolfgang Spaete	5

THE LUFTWAFFE'S MOST HIGHLY DECORATED PILOTS

Rank	Name	Unit
DIAMONDS WINNERS		
Generalleutnant	Adolf Galland	JV44
Oberst	Gordon M. Gollob	JG77
Oberst	Hermann Graf	JG11
Major	Erich Hartmann	JG52
Oberst	Helmut Lent	NJG2
Hauptmann	Hans-Joachim Marseille	JG27
Oberst	Werner Mölders	JG51
Major	Walter Nowotny	JG54
Oberst	Hans-Ulrich Rudel	SG2
Major	Heinz Schnaufer	NJG4
SWORDS WINNERS		
Oberstleutnant	Heinz Bär	JV44
Major	Gerhard Barkhorn	JV44
Major	Wilhelm Batz	JG52
Oberstleutnant	Kurt Buhlingen	JG2
Major	Anton Hackl	JG300
Oberst	Hajo Hermann	1 Jagd-Div
Oberstleutnant	Herbert Ihlefeld	JG1
Oberleutnant	Otto Kittel	JG54
Oberst	Günther Lützow	JV44
Oberstleutnant	Egon Mayer	JG2
Major	Joachim Müncheberg	JG77
Oberst	Walter Oesau	JG1
Oberleutnant	Max Oestermann	JG54

Rank	Name	Score
Oberstleutnant	Hans Philipp	JG1
Oberst	Josef Priller	JG26
Major	Günther Rall	JG300
Hauptmann	Ernst-Wilhelm Reinert	JG27
Major	Erich Rudorfer	JG7
Major	Prinz Heinrich zu Sayn-Wittgenstein	NJG2
Major	Werner Schroer	JG3
Leutnant	Leopold Steinbatz	JG52
Oberst	Johannes Steinhoff	JV44
Oberst	Werner Streib	NJG1
Oberst	Wolf-Dietrich Wilcke	JG3
Major	Josef Wurmheller	JG2
Hauptmann	Werner Baumbach	KG30
Hauptmann	Joachim Hellbig	KG1
Hauptmann	Alfred Druschel	SG1
Major	Alwin Boerst	SG2
Oberst	Dr Ernst Kupfer	SG2
Major	Friedrich Lang	SG1
Major	Theodor Nordmann	SG1
Hauptmann	Hermann Hogeback	KG6

U-BOAT RITTERKREUZTRÄGER

This list shows the U-boat Ritterkreuzträger with the last rank achieved, the command with which they were best associated and the date of the award of the Ritterkreuz. Several of course subsequently won the Oakleaves and higher awards. These are noted in a separate Appendix. It will be noted that a number of winners are not in fact U-boat captains, but in some cases watch officers or engineers. These awards recognized the essential part played by these men to a U-boat's successful performance.

Rank	Name	Boat	Date
Korvettenkapitän	Albrecht Achilles	U 161	16 Jan 43
Kapitänleutnant	Klaus Bargsten	U 521	30 April 43
Korvettenkapitän	Ernst Bauer	U 126	16 Mar 42
Kapitänleutnant	Gerhard Bigalk	U 751	26 Dec 41
Kapitänleutnant	Gerhard Bielig	U 177	10 Feb 43
Korvettenkapitän	Heinrich Bleichrodt	U 48	24 Oct 40
Fregattenkapitän	Albrecht Brandi	U 617	21 Jan 43
Kapitänleutnant	Paul Brasack	U 737	31 Oct 44
Korvettenkapitän	Otto von Bülow	U 404	20 Oct 42
Korvettenkapitän	Nicolai Clausen	U 129	13 Mar 42
Korvettenkapitän	Peter Erich Cremer	U 333	5 June 42
Stabsobermaschinist	Heinrich Dammeier	U 270	12 Aug 44

Rank	Name	Boat	Date
Kapitän zur See	Kurt Dobratz	U 1232	23 Jan 45
Grossadmiral	Karl Dönitz		21 April 40
Fregattenkapitän	Wilhelm Dommes	U 178	2 Dec 42
Kapitänleutnant	Alfred Eick	U 510	31 Mar 41
Korvettenkapitän	Carl Emmermann	U 172	27 Nov 42
Kapitänleutnant	Engelbert Endrass	U 47	5 Sept 40
Oberleutnant zur See	Horst Arno Fenski	U 410	26 Nov 43
Kapitänleutnant	Karl Fleige	U 18	18 July 44
Oberleutnant zur See	Hans Joachim Förster	U 480	18 Oct 44
Kapitänleutnant	Ulrich Folkers	U 125	27 Mar 43
Korvettenkapitän	Siegfried Freiherr von Forstner	U 402	9 Feb 43
Kapitänleutnant	Heinz Franke	U 262	30 Nov 43
Korvettenkapitän	Wilhelm Franken	U 565	30 April 43
Fregattenkapitän	Fritz Frauenheim	U 101	29 Aug 40
Kapitänleutnant	Harald Gelhaus	U 107	26 Mar 43
Kapitänleutnant	Friedrich Guggenberger	U 81	10 Dec 41
Korvettenkapitän	Robert Gysae	U 98	31 Dec 41
Korvettenkapitän	Reinhard Hardegen	U 123	23 Jan 42
Korvettenkapitän	Werner Hartenstein	U 156	17 Sept 42
Kapitän zur See	Werner Hartmann	U 37	9 April 40
Korvettenkapitän	Ernst Hechler	U 870	21 Jan 45
Kapitänleutnant	Hans Heidtmann	U 559	12 April 43
Kapitänleutnant	Hans-Jürgen Hellriegel	U 543	3 Feb 44
Korvettenkapitän	Werner Henke	U 515	17 Feb 42
Oberleutnant zur See	Hans-Georg Hess	U 995	11 Feb 45
Fregattenkapitän	Günther Hessler	U 107	24 June 41
Kapitänleutnant	Günther Heydemann	U 575	3 July 43
Korvettenkapitän	Ulrich Heyse	U 128	21 Jan 43
Obersteuermann	Horst Hoffmann	U 672	20 May 44
Obersteuermann	Otto Ites	U 94	
Obersteuermann	Karl Jäckel	U 907	28 May 45
Korvettenkapitän	Gunter Jahn	U 596	30 April 43
Kapitänleutnant	Hans Jenisch	U 32	7 Oct 40
Oberleutnant (Ing)	Hans Johannsen	U 802	31 Mar 45
Leutnant zur See	Walter Kaeding	U 123	15 May 44
Kapitän zur See	Ernst Kals	U 130	1 Sept 42
Kapitänleutnant	Gerd Kelbling	U 593	19 Aug 43
Korvettenkapitän	Eitel-Friedrich Kentrat	U 74	31 Dec 41
Kapitänleutnant (Ing)	Reinhard König	U 123	8 July 44
Kapitänleutnant	Siegfried Koitschka	U 616	27 Jan 44
Korvettenkapitän	Claus Korth	U 93	29 May 41
Kapitänleutnant	Hans Werner Kraus	U 83	19 June 42
Kapitänleutnant	Günther Krech	U 558	17 Sept 42
Fregattenkapitän	Otto Kretschmer	U 99	4 Aug 40
Leutnant (Ing)	Heinz Krey	U 752	4 Sept 43

Rank	Name	Boat	Date
Korvettenkapitän	Günther Kuhnke	U 28	19 Sept 40
Kapitänleutnant	Herbert Kuppisch	U 94	14 May 41
Kapitänleutnant (Ing)	Karl August Landfehrmamm	U 181	27 Oct 43
Kapitänleutnant	Hans-Günther Lange	U 711	26 Aug 44
Korvettenkapitän	Georg Lassen	U 160	10 Aug 42
Kapitänleutnant (Ing)	Willi Lechtenbörger	U 847	4 Sept 43
Kapitänleutnant	Hans Lehmann	U 997	8 June 45
Fregattenkapitän	Heinrich Lehmann-Willenbrock	U 96	26 Feb 41
Kapitänleutnant	Fritz-Julius Lemp	U 30	14 Aug 40
Kapitänleutnant	Philipp Lichtenberg	U 516	31 Mar 45
Fregattenkapitän	Heinrich Liebe	U 38	14 Aug 40
Oberleutnant zur See	Johann Limbach	U 181	6 Feb 45
Korvettenkapitän	Siegfried Lüdden	U 188	11 Feb 44
Kapitän zur See	Wolfgang Lüth	U 138	24 Oct 40
Kapitänleutnant	Karl Heinz Marbach	U 953	22 July 44
Kapitänleutnant	Friedrich Markworth	U 66	8 July 43
Kapitänleutnant	August Maus	U 185	21 Sept 43
Korvettenkapitän	Waldemar Mehl	U 371	28 Mar 44
Korvettenkapitän	Ernst Mengersen	U 101	18 Nov 41
Kapitän zur See	Karl-Friedrich Merten	U 68	13 June 42
Korvettenkapitän	Jost Metzler	U 69	28 July 41
Korvettenkapitän	Karl-Heinz Moehle	U 123	26 Feb 41
Korvettenkapitän	Helmut Möhlmann	U 571	16 April 43
Korvettenkapitän	Johann Mohr	U 124	27 Mar 42
Oberbootsmannsmaat	Rudolf Mühlbauer	U 123	10 Dec 44
Korvettenkapitän	Günther Müller-Stockheim	U 67	27 Nov 42
Kapitänleutnant	Rolf Mützelburg	U 203	17 Nov 41
Kapitän zur See	Karl Neitzel	U 510	27 Mar 43
Fregattenkapitän	Victor Oehrn	U 37	21 Oct 40
Korvettenkapitän	Jürgen Oesten	U 106	26 Mar 41
Oberleutnant (Ing)	Georg Olschewski	U 66	23 April 44
Kapitänleutnant (Ing)	Herbert Panknin	U 106	4 Sept 43
Oberleutnant zur See	Heinrich Petersen	U 99	5 Nov 40
Korvettenkapitän	Adolf Piening	U 155	13 Aug 42
Kapitänleutnant	Gustav Poel	U 413	21 Mar 44
Kapitän zur See	Fritz Poske	U 504	6 Nov 42
Obermaschinist	Heinz Prassdorf	U 1203	21 April 45
Korvettenkapitän	Günther Prien	U 47	18 Oct 39
Kapitänleutnant	Günther Pulst	U 978	28 Dec 44
Kapitänleutnant	Hermann Rasch	U 106	29 Dec 42
Kapitänleutnant	Reinhard Reche	U 255	17 Mar 43
Kapitän zur See	Hans Rudolf Rösing	U 48	29 Aug 40
Korvettenkapitän (Ing)	Hellmut Rohweder	U 514	14 Nov 43

Rank	Name	Boat	Date
Fregattenkapitän	Wilhelm Rollmann	*U 34*	31 July 40
Korvettenkapitän	Helmut Rosenbaum	*U 73*	12 Aug 42
Korvettenkapitän	Erwin Rostin	*U 158*	28 June 42
Kapitänleutnant	Gerd Schaar	*U 957*	1 Oct 44
Fregattenkapitän	Harro Schacht	*U 507*	9 Jan 43
Kapitänleutnant	Joachim Schepke	*U 100*	24 Sept 40
Korvettenkapitän	Georg Schewe	*U 105*	23 May 41
Korvettenkapitän	Egon Freiherr von Schlippenbach	*U 453*	19 Nov 43
Korvettenkapitän	Adalbert Schnee	*U 60*	30 Aug 41
Kapitänleutnant	Herbert Schneider	*U 522*	16 Jan 43
Oberleutnant zur See	Dietrich Schöneboom	*U 431*	20 Oct 43
Fregattenkapitän	Klaus Scholtz	*U 108*	26 Dec 41
Korvettenkapitän	Heinrich Schonder	*U 77*	19 Aug 42
Kapitänleutnant	Heinrich Schroeteler	*U 667*	2 May 45
Kapitänleutnant	Horst von Schroeter	*U 123*	1 June 44
Kapitän zur See	Victor Schütze	*U 103*	11 Dec 40
Korvettenkapitän	Otto Schuhart	*U 29*	16 May 40
Korvettenkapitän	Heinz Otto Schultze	*U 432*	9 July 42
Korvettenkapitän	Herbert Schultze	*U 48*	1 Mar 40
Korvettenkapitän	Georg Wilhelm Schulz	*U 124*	4 April 41
Korvettenkapitän	Günther Seibicke	*U 436*	27 Mar 43
Oberleutnant zur See	Heinz Sieder	*U 984*	8 July 44
Kapitänleutnant	Georg Staats	*U 508*	14 July 43
Korvettenkapitän	Hans-Gerrit von Stockhausen	*U 65*	14 Jan 41
Korvettenkapitän	Siegfried Strelow	*U 435*	27 Oct 42
Oberleutnant zur See	Hermann Stuckmann	*U 621*	11 Aug 44
Korvettenkapitän (Ing)	Gerd Suhren	*U 37*	21 Oct 40
Fregattenkapitän	Reinhard Suhren	*U 564*	3 Nov 40
Kapitänleutnant	Max-Martin Teichert	*U 456*	19 Dec 43
Kapitänleutnant	Rolf Thomsen	*U 1202*	4 Jan 45
Korvettenkapitän	Karl Thurmann	*U 553*	24 Aug 42
Kapitänleutnant	Hans Diedrich von Tiesenhausen	*U 331*	27 Jan 42
Korvettenkapitän	Heinrich Timm	*U 862*	17 Sept 44
Fregattenkapitän	Erich Topp	*U 552*	20 June 41
Kapitänleutnant	Hans Trojer	*U 221*	24 Mar 43
Korvettenkapitän (Ing)	Johann-Friedrich Wessels	*U 198*	9 Mar 43
Oberleutnant zur See	Otto Westphalen	*U 968*	23 Mar 45
Oberleutnant zur See	Karl-Heinz Wiebe	*U 178*	22 May 44
Korvettenkapitän	Werner Winter	*U 103*	5 June 42
Korvettenkapitän	Hans Witt	*U 129*	17 Dec 42
Korvettenkapitän	Helmut Witte	*U 159*	22 Oct 42

Rank	Name	Boat	Date
Kapitänleutnant	Herbert Wohlfarth	U 137	15 May 41
Kapitänleutnant	Erich Würdemann	U 506	14 Mar 43
Fregattenkapitän	Richard Zapp	U 66	23 April 42
Korvettenkapitän	Erich Zurn	U 48	23 April 41

TOP TWENTY U-BOAT ACES

Name	Tonnage sunk
Fregattenkapitän Otto Kretschmer	314,000
Kapitän zur See Wolfgang Lüth	253,000
Fregattenkapitän Erich Topp	240,000
Korvettenkapitän Günther Prien	195,000
Korvettenkapitän Herbert Schultze	185,000
Fregattenkapitän Heinrich Lehmann-Willenbrock	185,000
Kapitän zur See Victor Schütze	180,000
Kapitän zur See Karl Friedrich Merten	180,000
Fregattenkapitän Heinrich Liebe	170,000
Korvettenkapitän Georg Lassen	165,000
Korvettenkapitän Heinrich Bleichrodt	165,000
Korvettenkapitän Werner Henke	155,000
Korvettenkapitän Carl Emmermann	152,000
Fregattenkapitän Reinhard Suhren	148,000
Kapitänleutnant Joachim Schepke	146,000
Kapitänleutnant Engelbert Endrass	142,000
Korvettenkapitän Adolf Piening	141,000
Korvettenkapitän Robert Gysae	140,000
Korvettenkapitän Reinhard Hardegen	138,000
Korvettenkapitän Johann Mohr	135,000

LIST OF ALL E-BOAT RITTERKREUZTRÄGER

Rank	Name	Unit	Date
Korvettenkapitän	Niels Bätge	4. S-Flotille	4 Jan 42
Korvettenkapitän	Heinz Birnbacher	1. S-Flotille	16 June 40
Korvettenkapitän	Hermann Büchting	1. S-Flotille	22 April 43
Korvettenkapitän	Georg Christiansen	1. S-Flotille	8 May 41
Korvettenkapitän	Klaus Feldt	2. S-Flotille	25 April 41
Korvettenkapitän	Kurt Fimmen	1. S-Flotille	14 Aug 40
Kapitänleutnant	Heinz Haag	3. S-Flotille	25 Nov 44
Kapitänleutnant	Kurt Johannsen	5. S-Flotille	14 June 44
Kapitänleutnant	Karl-Erhard Karcher	4. S-Flotille	13 Aug 43
Korvettenkapitän	Friedrich Kemnade	3. S-Flotille	23 July 42

Rank	Name	Unit	Date
Korvettenkapitän	Bernd Klug	1. S-Flotille	12 Mar 41
Kapitänleutnant	Karl-Friedrich Künzel	1. S-Flotille	12 Dec 43
Kapitänleutnant	Jens Matzen	6. S-Flotille	2 May 45
Korvettenkapitän	Götz Frhr. von Mirbach	1. S-Flotille	14 Aug 40
Kapitänleutnant	Albert Müller	3. S-Flotille	13 Dec 43
Kapitänleutnant	Karl Müller	5. S-Flotille	8 July 43
Korvettenkapitän	Hermann Opdenhoff	2. S-Flotille	16 May 40
Korvettenkapitän	Rudolf Petersen	2. S-Flotille	4 Aug 40
Kapitänleutnant	Klaus-Degenhard Schmidt	10. S-Flotille	22 Dec 43
Korvettenkapitän	Werner Töniges	1. S-Flotille	25 Feb 41
Kapitänleutnant	Horst Weber	3. S-Flotille	5 July 43
Kapitänleutnant	Siegfried Wupperman	3. S-Flotille	3 Aug 41
Korvettenkapitän	Felix Zymalkowski	8. S-Flotille	10 April 45

THE MOST HIGHLY DECORATED ACES OF THE U-BOATS, E-BOATS AND AUXILIARY CRUISERS

Rank	Name	Boat	Date
DIAMONDS WINNERS			
Fregattenkapitän	Albrecht Brandi	*U 967*	23 Nov 44
Kapitän zur See	Wolfgang Lüth	*U 138*	9 Aug 43
SWORDS WINNERS			
Fregattenkapitän	Otto Kretschmer	*U 99*	26 Dec 41
Fregattenkapitän	Reinhard Sühren	*U 564*	1 Sept 42
Fregattenkapitän	Erich Topp	*U 552*	17 Aug 42
OAKLEAVES WINNERS			
Korvettenkapitän	Heinrich Bleichrodt	*U 48*	23 Sept 42
Korvettenkapitän	Otto von Bülow	*U 404*	25 April 43
Korvettenkapitän	Georg Christiansen	1. S-Flotille	13 Nov 43
Grossadmiral	Carl Dönitz		7 April 43
Korvettenkapitän	Carl Emmermann	*U 172*	4 July 43
Kapitänleutnant	Engelbert Endrass	*U 567*	10 June 41
Korvettenkapitän	Klaus Feldt	2. S-Flotille	1 Jan 44
Kapitänleutnant	Friedrich Guggenberger	*U 513*	8 April 43
Korvettenkapitän	Robert Gysae	*U 96*	31 May 43
Korvettenkapitän	Reinhard Hardegen	*U 123*	23 April 42
Kapitän zur See	Werner Hartmann	*U 37*	5 Nov 44
Korvettenkapitän	Werner Henke	*U 515*	4 July 43
Korvettenkapitän	Friedrich Kemnade	3. S-Flotille	27 May 43
Korvettenkapitän	Bernd Klug	1. S-Flotille	1 Jan 44
Kapitän zur See	Ernst-Felix Kruder	*Pinguin*	15 Nov 41

Rank	Name	Boat	Date
Kapitänleutnant	Hans-Günther Lange	*U 711*	29 April 45
Korvettenkapitän	Georg Lassen	*U 160*	7 Mar 43
Fregattenkapitän	Heinrich Lehmann-Willenbrock	*U 96*	31 Dec 41
Fregattenkapitän	Heinrich Liebe	*U 38*	10 June 41
Kapitän zur See	Karl-Friedrich Merten	*U 68*	16 Nov 42
Korvettenkapitän	Götz Frhr. von Mirbach	1. S-Flotille	14 June 44
Korvettenkapitän	Johann Mohr	*U 124*	13 Jan 43
Kapitänleutnant	Rolf Mützelburg	*U 203*	15 July 42
Kapitän zur See	Rudolf Petersen	2. S-Flotille	13 June 44
Korvettenkapitän	Günther Prien	*U 47*	20 Oct 40
Vizeadmiral	Bernhard Rogge	*Atlantis*	31 Dec 41
Kapitän zur See	Hellmuth von Ruckteschell	*Michel*	23 Dec 42
Kapitänleutnant	Joachim Schepke	*U 100*	20 Dec 40
Korvettenkapitän	Adalbert Schnee	*U 201*	15 July 42
Kapitän zur See	Klaus Scholtz	*U 108*	10 Sept 42
Kapitän zur See	Victor Schütze	*U 103*	14 July 41
Korvettenkapitän	Herbert Schultze	*U 48*	12 June 41
Kapitänleutnant	Rolf Thomsen	*U 1202*	29 April 45
Korvettenkapitän	Werner Toniges	1. S-Flotille	13 Nov 42
Kapitänleutnant	Siegfried Wuppermann	3. S-Flotille	14 April 43

EINZELKÄMPFER (SINGLE-ACTION) RITTERKREUZTRÄGER

Rank	Name	Date
Oberfernschreibmatrose	Herbert Berrer	5 Aug 44
Kapitän zur See	Friedrich Böhme	26 Aug 44
Schreibermaat	Walter Gerhold	6 July 44
Leutnant zur See	Alfred Vetter	12 Aug 44
Vizeadmiral	Hellmuth Heye	18 Jan 41

AUXILIARY CRUISER RITTERKREUZTRÄGER

Rank	Name	Ship	Date
Kapitän zur See	Theodor Detmers	*Kormoran*	4 Dec 41
Konteradmiral	Robert Eyssen	*Komet*	29 Nov 41
Leutnant zur See	Heinrich Garbers	*Passim*	1 Nov 44
Kapitän zur See	Günther Gumprich	*Thor*	31 Dec 41
Kapitän zur See	Ernst-Felix Kruder	*Pinguin*	22 Dec 40
Vizeadmiral	Bernhard Rogge	*Atlantis*	7 Dec 40
Kapitän zur See	Hellmuth von Ruckteschell	*Michel*	31 Oct 40
Konteradmiral	Kurt Weyher	*Orion*	21 Aug 41

MILITARY UNIT ORGANIZATION

Any book on the German forces of the Second World War will probably
contain a bewildering array of abbreviated unit titles, with roman or Arabic
numerals, honour titles, etc. For the benefit of any reader unfamiliar with
German military terminology, a brief look at the basic make-up of German
military units follows.

The Army
The basic Army unit was the Zug or platoon. Its commander, or Zugführer
was usually a senior NCO or junior officer. After the platoon came the
Kompanie or company, usually commanded by a rank of Hauptmann. A
Kompanie was usually indicated by an Arabic numeral before the
Regimental designation, i.e., 2/Infanterie Regiment 10. This would
represent 2nd Company of Infantry Regiment 10, and would normally be
abbreviated further to 2/Inf Regt 10.

The next unit size was the Bataillon (battalion), commanded perhaps by
a Major. A Bataillon was usually indicated by a roman numeral before the
Regimental Designation, i.e., II/Panzer Grenadier Regiment 111. This
would represent the 2nd Battalion of Armoured Infantry Regiment 111 and
would be further abbreviated to II/Pz Gren Regt 111. The regiment itself
would usually be referred to as an individual entity rather than as a
formation within a division, and would have the regimental number or title
to identify it, i.e. Infanterie Regiment Grossdeutschland, Panzer Regiment
33. As with the regiment, the division was usually known by its number
and or name. The number, however, which normally followed the name of
the regiment, preceded the name of the division, i.e., 21 Panzer Division,
5 SS-Panzer Division Wiking.

Higher formations, such as Korps, Armee or Heeresgruppe level units,
will not normally be encountered when considering the units to which
individual soldiers were allocated, unless the soldier were of very high rank.

The Luftwaffe
The basic flying unit was the Gruppe (RAF equivalent, Wing) totalling
about 30 aircraft. Bomber and fighter units had individual Geschwader
(RAF equivalent, Group) comprising three Gruppen, that is a strength of
about 90 aircraft.

Each Gruppe had three or four Staffeln (squadrons) each of about nine
or ten aircraft which were deployed in Rotte (two aircraft) or Schwarm (four
aircraft).

The Gruppe would be commanded by a Gruppenkommandeur, probably
a Hauptmann or a Major. It would be indicated by a roman numeral before
the Geschwader, i.e., II/Jagdgeschwader 54, that is 2nd Wing of Fighter
Group 54.

The Staffel would be commanded by a Staffelkapitän, usually of junior
officer rank such as Oberleutnant. A Staffel was designated by an Arabic

numeral before the title of the Geschwader, i.e., 1/Jagdgeschwader 51, which indicates 1st Squadron of Fighter Group 51.

The Geschwader itself was identified by its type and number, and occasionally its honour title, i.e., Jagdgeschwader 54, Jagdgeschwader 26 Schlageter. The type of Geschwader was usually abbreviated to initials, i.e., Jagdgeschwader – JG, Kampfgeschader – KG, Lehrgeschwader – LG. Higher units of the Luftwaffe were the Fliegerkorps and the Luftflotte or Air Fleet.

The Navy

Thankfully, the navy is a far more simple matter for the casual reader because the aces of the Kriegsmarine were usually commanders of individual vessels, and so a Captain will be associated with the particular ship in which his victories were won. Original references, too, will list these aces as commander (usually abbreviated Kdr) of a specific vessel, rarely mentioning the flotilla in which the ship served.

THE IRON CROSS, FIRST AND SECOND CLASSES

Although the Knight's Cross of the Iron Cross and its additions in the form of the Oakleaves and Swords and Oakleaves are undoubtedly the awards most associated with the great aces, mention should perhaps be made of the more modest Iron Crosses First and Second Class, it being a prerequisite of the award of the Knight's Cross that the recipient already hold these lower grades. For what reasons then, were these lower grades awarded? There is in fact no clear and concise answer. No hard and fast criteria were laid down; they could be awarded for a whole range of meritorious deeds in the face of the enemy.

For the Luftwaffe, The Iron Cross Second Class might well be awarded to a fighter pilot on achieving his first aerial victory or for taking part in a particularly successful sortie. The First Class could be awarded to a pilot on gaining ace status after his fifth kill, or perhaps to a bomber pilot after having flown a suitable number of missions.

In the Navy both grades of Iron Cross were not infrequently awarded to the entire crew of a vessel after a particularly successful mission. As an example of this, when *U 47* under command of Günther Prien sank the *Royal Oak* at Scapa Flow, Prien was decorated with the Knight's Cross of the Iron Cross and his entire crew received the Iron Cross Second Class.

As for the Army, typical examples are given in the wartime publication *Der Lohn der Tat*, an official publication from 1944 which gives examples of deeds that must be acknowledged by a range of Army awards. For the Second Class, an example is given of a corporal in a Grenadier unit who led his group in an attack on a bunker in which the enemy were only eliminated after hard hand-to-hand combat. For the First Class, the example given is of a sergeant who swam across a river covered by enemy machine-guns to capture and swim back with a small boat. The sergeant then collected his men, and recrossed the river in the boat. In the action which followed, two machine-gun nests were eliminated and five prisoners taken. These were the sort of deeds that might entitle a soldier to the award of the Iron Cross.

In many of the photographs in this book, the pin-backed Iron Cross First Class can be seen worn on the left breast pocket, while the ribbon of the Second Class is worn in the buttonhole, or less commonly, on a ribbon bar above the left breast pocket. The Iron Cross Second Class itself was normally only worn on the actual day the award was made, or with full dress parade uniform.

BIBLIOGRAPHY

This list includes books that are recommended to the reader who wishes to research further into the lives of the aces who were decorated with the Knight's Cross of the Iron Cross. Many of them were primary reference sources for this book.

The awards

Angolia, John R. *For Führer and Fatherland.* vol. 1, Bender Publishing, San Jose, 1979

Klietmann, Dr Kurt G. *Deutsche Auszeichnungen.* Die Ordenssammlung, Berlin, 1971

— *Auszeichnungen des Deutsches Reiches.* Motorbuch Verlag, Stuttgart, 1984

The aces

Alman, Karl. *Ritterkreuzträger des Afrikakorps.* Erich Pabel Verlag, Rastatt, 1975

Angolia, John R. *On the Field of Honour.* vols 1 and 2, Bender Publishing, San Jose, 1979 and 1980

Brütting, Georg. *Das waren die Deutsche Kampffliefer Asse.* Motorbuch Verlag, Stuttgart, 1986

Bender, Roger J., and Law, Richard D. *Organization, Uniforms and History of the Afrikakorps.* Bender Publishing, San Jose, 1973

Bender, Roger J., and Petersen, George A. *Hermann Göring, from Regiment to Fallschirmpanzerkorps.* Bender Publishing, San Jose, 1975

Diroll, Bernd. *Die Hamburger Ritterkreuzträger.* Verlag Klaus Patzwall, Hamburg, 1984

Fraschka, Günther. *Mit Schwertern und Brillanten.* Erich Pabel Verlag, Rastatt, 1970

Hoyt, Edwin P. *U-Boats, A Pictorial History.* Stanley Paul, London, 1987

Jones, Geoffrey. *U-Boat Aces.* William Kimber, London, 1987

Kratschmer, Ernst G. *Die Ritterkreuzträger der Waffen-SS.* Verlag K. W. Schutz, Preussische Oldendorf, 1955.
(A massive tome, expensive but superbly produced. A must for any reader interested in the Knight's Cross winners. Very highly recommended.)

Kessler, Leo. *SS Peiper.* Leo Cooper, London, 1986

Klein, Egon, and Kuhn, Volmar. *Tiger, die geschichte ein legendären Waffe, 1942–1945.* Motorbuch Verlag, Stuttgart, 1981

Kurowski, Franz. (1987) *Die Träger des Ritterkreuzes des Eisernen Kreuzes der U-Boot Waffe.* Podzun Pallas Verlag, 1987.
(A small gem of a volume with photographs and career details of every single U-boat Knight's Cross winner.)

Lefevre, Eric. *Panzers in Normandy Then and Now*. Battle of Britain Prints, London, 1983
— *Battle of the Bulge Then and Now*. Battle of Britain Prints, London, 1984
Lenfeld, Erwin, and Thomas, Franz. *Die Eichenlaubträger, 1940–1945*. Weilburg Verlag, Wiener-Neustadt, 1983
(Another must for any historian. Lavishly produced, covering every one of the 882 winners.)
Luther, Craig. *Blood and Honour*. Bender Publishing, San Jose, 1987
Mallmann Showell, Jak P. *U-Boats under the Swastika*. Ian Allan, London, 1973
— *The German Navy in World War Two*. Arms & Armour Press, London, 1979
Mitcham, Samuel W. *Hitler's Legions*. Leo Cooper, London, 1985
Möller-Witten, Hans. *Mit den Eichenlaub zum Ritterkreuz*. Erich Pabel Verlag, Rastatt, 1962
Muggenthaler, August Karl. *German Raiders of World War Two*. Robert Hale Ltd, London, 1978
Obermaier, Ernst. *Die Ritterkreuzträger der Luftwaffe*. vols 1 and 2, Dieter Hoffmann Verlag, Mainz, 1966 and 1975
Ott, Alfred. *Die Weissen Spiegel*. Podzun Pallas Verlag, Friedberg
Perrett, Bryan. *The Tiger Tanks*. Osprey Vanguard, London, 1981
Range, Clemens. *Ritterkreuzträger der Kriegsmarine*. Motorbuch Verlag, Stuttgart, 1974
Rogge, Bernhard, and Frank, Wolfgang. *The German Raider Atlantis*. Ballantine Books
Schmalenbach, Paul. *German Raiders*. P.S.L. Cambridge, 1977
Schneider, Jost W. *Their Honour was Loyalty*. Bender Publishing, San Jose, 1977
Von Seemen, Gerhard. *Die Ritterkreuzträger*. Podzun Pallas Verlag, Friedberg, 1984
Spaeter, Hellmuth. *Panzerkorps Grossdeutschland*. Podzun Pallas Verlag, Friedberg, 1984
Steinhoff, Johannes. *The Straits of Messina*. Andre Deutsch, London, 1971
Thomas, Franz, and Wegmann, Günther. *Die Ritterkreuzträger der Deutschen Wehrmacht, 1939–1945*. vol. 1 Sturmartillerie; vol 2 Fallschirmjäger. Biblio Verlag, Osnabrück, 1985 and 1986
(The first two volumes in what will become the standard work on the subject. Printed on top quality art paper and expensively bound. Lavishly illustrated, this work will eventually cover every known Ritterkreuzträger, a massive undertaking.)

Periodicals

Das Ritterkreuz, Magazine of the Knight's Cross bearers Association
Der Freiwillige, Magazine for Waffen-SS veterans
Der Landser, Magazine for German ex-servicemen
Info, German militaria collectors' magazine
Militaria, French militaria collectors' magazine

Miscellaneous
The following photo-histories published by Munin-Verlag of Osnabrück were consulted for photographic records of various Waffen-SS Ritterkreuz-träger. These books, though mostly photographic and with only limited text, are nevertheless a mine of information.

Lehmann, Rudolf. *Die Leibstandarte im Bild.* (1 SS-Panzer Division) 1983

Weidinger, Otto. *Division das Reich im Bild.* (2 SS-Panzer Division) 1981

Ullrich, Karl. *Wie ein Feld im Meer.* (3 SS-Panzer Division) 1986

Truppenkameradschaft der 4. SS-Pol. Div. *Die guten Glaubens waren.* (3 SS-Polizei Division) 1977

Proschek, Rolf. *Verweht sind die Spuren.* (5 SS-Panzer Division) 1979

Meyer, Hubert. *Die Kriegsgeschichte der 12 SS Panzer Division.* 1987

Schulze-Kossens, Richard, and Ertel, Karl Heinz. *Europaische Freiwillige im Bild.* (European volunteers) 1986

H.I.A.G. *Wenn alle Brüder schweigen.* (General book on the Waffen-SS)

GLOSSARY

Abwehr	Germany's military counter-intelligence service
Abzeichen	badge, insignia
Abteilung	battalion-sized military unit; detachment
Armee	army
Armeegruppe	army group
Aufklärung	reconnaissance
Aufklärungsabteilung	Reconnaissance battalion or detachment
Armee Oberkommando	Army High Command
Artillerie	artillery
Bataillon	battalion
Batterie	battery
Befehlshaber	commander
Begleit	escort
Brigade	brigade
Brigadeführer	Brigade Commander (Waffen-SS rank)
Beobachter	observer
Deutsche Kreuz	German Cross
Fahnenjunker	officer cadet
Fähnrich	ensign
Fallschirmjäger	paratrooper
Flieger	flyer, pilot
Flotille	flotilla
Flotte	fleet
Freiherr	baron
Freiwillige	volunteer
Feldwebel	sergeant
Geschütz	gun, cannon
Geschwader	Equivalent of an RAF Group. Normally about 90 aircraft
Gruppe	Equivalent of RAF Wing. Normally three Gruppen formed a Geschwader
Gruppenführer	wing leader
Heer	Army
Heeresgruppe	Army Group
Infanterie	infantry
Jäger	rifleman
Jagdflieger	fighter pilot
Jagdgeschwader	fighter squadron (actually nearer in size to a fighter wing)

Junkerschule	military academy
Kavallerie	cavalry
Kampf	battle
Kampfgruppe	battle group
Kampfwagen	combat vehicle
Kampfgeschwader	bomber squadron
Kommando	command
Kommandeur	commander
Kommandierender General	General Officer in Command
Kommodore	Commodore, the rank in command of a Geschwader. Roughly equivalent to a wing commander and usually a major or colonel
Kompanie	company
Korps	corps
Kradschutzen	motor-cycle infantry. Krad = KRaftrAD = motor cycle
Kraftfahr	motor, motorized
Kreuzer	cruiser
Kriegsakademie	Staff College
Kriegsberichter	war correspondent
Kriegsmarine	Navy
Lehr	training
Lehrgeschwader	training squadron
Luftflotte	Air Fleet
Marine	naval
Mitte	centre
Motorisiert	motorized
Minensucher	minesweeper
Nachrichten	signals
Nachtjagdgeschwader	night fighter squadron
Nahkampft	close combat
Oberbefehlshaber	Commander-in-Chief
Oberkommando	High Command
Oberkommando der Wehrmacht	High Command of the Armed Forces
Ordonanz Offizier	orderly officer
Panzer	armour, tank
Panzerabwehr	anti-tank
Panzergrenadier	armoured infantry
Panzerjäger	tank destroyer
Panzer Korps	Armoured Corps
Pioniere	pioneers, engineers
Reichsarbeitsdienst	State Labour Service, in which all able-bodied males were obliged to spent six months
Reichskanzlei	State Chancellery, in Berlin
Reichsmarine	Navy of the Weimar Republic, later

	changed by Hitler to Kriegsmarine
Reichswehr	State armed forces of the Weimar Republic, later changed by Hitler to Wehrmacht
Ritter	knight
Ritterkreuz	Knight's Cross
Ritterkreuzträger	Knight's Cross bearer
Schlachtgeschwader	assault squadron, ground support
Schnellboot	fast patrol boat
See	sea
Schwere	heavy
SS – Schutz Staffel	protection squad
SS-Verfügungstruppe	Order troops, the first military units of the SS
SS-Verfügungsdivision	SS combat unit later to evolve into the Das Reich Division
Stab	staff
Standarte	regimental-sized unit
Sturmgeschütz	assault gun
Sturzkampfflieger	dive-bomber pilot (Sturzkampf normally abbreviated to Stuka)
Totenkopf	death's head
Unterseeboot	U-boat, submarine
Urkunde	certificate
Verband	unit
Wache	watch, guard
Wachabteilung	guard battalion
Wach Offizier	officer of the watch
Waffen-SS	Armed SS. SS military units
Wehrkreis	military district
Wehrmacht	armed forces
Zerstörer	destroyer, also Me 110 twin-engined fighter-bombers were known as destroyers
Zug	platoon
Zugführer	platoon commander
zBV	for special purposes – zur Besondere Verwendung

INDEX

A

Arnold, Hauptmann Friedrich, 27

B

Bachmann, SS-Obersturmführer Erwin, 27, 28
Bahr, Oberfeldwebel Gunther, 97
Bär, Oberstleutnant Heinz, 97, 98
Bargsten, Kapitänleutnant Klaus, 151, 197
Barkhorn, Major Gerd, 99, 100, 191
Barkmann, SS-Oberscharführer Ernst, 29, 30, 31, 32, 33
Batz, Major Wilhelm, 100, 101, 191
Bauer, Korvettenkapitän Ernst, 152, 153, 197
Baumbach, Oberst Werner, 101, 102
Baurmann, Hauptmann Heinz, 34
Bochmann, SS-Oberführer Georg, 35, 36
Börngen, Major Ernst, 103
Bose, Leutnant Georg, 36, 37
Brandner, Major Josef Wilhelm Sepp, 37, 38, 39
Büchting, Korvettenkapitän Hermann, 153, 154, 201

C

Carius, Oberleutnant Otto, 39, 40, 190

D

Detmers, Kapitän zur See Theodor, 154, 155, 203
Deutsch, Oberleutnant Heinz, 40, 41
Dönitz, Grossadmiral Karl, 147, 198
Doring, Leutnant Arnold, 104, 105
Dreike, SS-Hauptsturmführer Franz-Josef, 41, 42
Drewes, Major Martin, 105, 195
Druschel, Oberst Alfred, 106, 107, 197

E

Eder, Major Georg-Peter, 107, 108, 195
Egger, SS-Obersturmführer Paul, 43

Ehrler, Major Heinrich, 108, 109
Eick, Kapitänleutnant Alfred, 156, 198
Emmermann, Korvettenkapitän Karl, 157, 158, 198

F

Falck, Oberst Wolfgang, 110, 111
Flögel, Oberfeldwebel Josef, 111, 112
Franke, Kapitänleutnant Heinz, 158, 159, 198

G

Galland, Generalleutnant Adolf, 92, 112, 113, 114, 115, 116, 193, 196
German Army Divisions:
15 Infanterie Division, 34
208 Infanterie Division, 34
292 Infanterie Division, 37
3 Panzer Division, 50
13 Panzer Division, 52
20 Panzer Division, 34, 39
23 Panzer Division, 55
Panzergrenadier Division Grossdeutschland, 37, 46, 83, 84
German Army Regiments, etc:
Artillerie Regiment 12, 81
Artillerie Regiment 51, 34
Artillerie Regiment 74, 63
Artillerie Regiment 102, 38
Artillerie Regiment 209, 81
Artillerie Lehr Regiment 2, 36, 63
Infanterie Regiment 2, 127
Panzer Regiment 4, 46
Panzer Regiment 5, 75
Panzer Regiment 6, 105
Panzer Regiment 25, 49
Panzer Regiment 35, 77, 78
Panzer Artillerie Regiment 19, 54
Artillerie Abteilung 58, 36
Artillerie Ersatz Abteilung 100, 27
Artillerie Reserve Abteilung 58, 36
Führer Grenadier Brigade, 46
Jagdpanzer Abteilung 512, 40
Panzer Abteilung 66, 49

schwere Panzer Abteilung 502, 39, 48,
49, 52, 53
schwere Panzer Abteilung 503, 50, 51,
52
schwere Panzer Abteilung 505, 53
schwere Panzer Abteilung 507, 56, 85,
86
Panzer Ersatz und Ausbildungs
Abteilung 500, 39
Sturmgeschutz Abteilung 177, 37
Sturmgeschutz Abteilung 200, 70
Sturmgeschutz Abteilung 201, 27, 54
Sturmgeschutz Abteilung 202, 38
Sturmgeschutz Abteilung 237, 27, 81
Sturmgeschutz Abteilung 322, 54
Sturmgeschutz Abteilung 667, 34, 70,
71
Sturmgeschutz Batterie 640, 83
Sturmgeschutz Brigade 191, 64
Sturmgeschutz Brigade 210, 54
Sturmgeschutz Brigade 300, 34
Sturmgeschutz Brigade 322, 34
Sturmgeschutz Brigade 912, 38
Sturmgeschutz Ersatz und Ausbildungs
Abteilung 300, 37
Sturmgeschutz Ersatz und Ausbildungs
Abteilung 500, 27
Sturmgeschutz Ersatz und Ausbildungs
Abteilung 600, 34
Sturmgeschutz Ersatz und Ausbildungs
Abteilung 700, 27, 64, 71
Graf, Oberst Hermann, 115, 116, 191,
196
Grasser, Major Hartmann, 116, 117
Guggenberger, Kapitänleutnant
Friedrich, 159, 198
Gustavsson, SS-Hauptsturmführer Karl-
Heinz, 43, 44, 45

H
Hardegen, Korvettenkapitän Reinhard,
160, 161, 198
Hartmann, Major Erich, 117, 118, 191,
196
Hein, SS-Hauptsturmführer Willi, 45
Heinrich, Leutnant Willi, 46, 47
Helbig, Oberst Joachim, 119, 120
Henke, SS-Hauptsturmführer
Friedrich, 47, 48, 198, 201
Herzig, SS-Sturmbannführer Fritz, 48,
49
Hrabak, Oberst Dieter, 120, 121, 192

I
Ihlefeld, Oberst Herbert, 121, 192, 196

J
Jabs, Oberstleutnant Hans-Joachim,
121, 122
Jähde, Major Willy, 49, 50
Jähnert, Major Erhard, 122, 123
Jope, Oberstleutnant Bernhard, 123

K
Kaganeck, Major Clemens Graf von, 50,
51
Kausch, SS-Obersturmbannführer Paul
Albert, 49, 51, 52
Kemnade, Korvettenkapitän Friedrich,
162, 163, 201
Kerscher, Oberfeldwebel Albert, 52, 53,
54
Köhler, Leutnant Heinrich, 54, 55
Koitschka, Kapitänleutnant Siegfried,
163, 198
Koltermann, Oberleutnant Wolfgang,
56
Kraus, Kapitänleutnant Werner, 164,
165, 198
Kretschmer, Korvettenkapitän Otto,
165, 166, 167, 168, 198, 201
Kujacinski, Major Norbert, 55

L
Lobmeyer, SS-Hauptsturmführer
Jakob, 57, 58
Luftwaffe Units:
Fallschirmjägerabteilung 22, 40
Fallschirmsturmbrigade 12, 40
FallschirmPanzerDivision Hermann
Göring, 34, 75, 76
7 Fallschirm Division, 40, 41
Flakabteilung 491, 40
Flak Ersatz Abteilung 51, 36
Flak Regiment 12, 41
Jagdgeschwader 1 Oesau, 98, 104, 107,
108, 117, 121, 133
Jagdgeschwader 2 Richthofen, 99,
107, 113, 119
Jagdgeschwader 3, 98, 129, 132
Jagdgeschwader 5, 109
Jagdgeschwader 7, 109
Jagdgeschwader 11, 121
Jagdgeschwader 26 Schlageter, 113,
135, 136, 142, 143

Jagdgeschwader 27, 103, 113, 141, 142
Jagdgeschwader 51, 98, 116, 126, 132
Jagdgeschwader 52, 99, 100, 101, 115, 116, 117, 120, 121
Jagdgeschwader 53, 127
Jagdgeschwader 54, 120, 121, 130, 131
Jagdgeschwader 77, 98, 121, 135
Jagdgeschwader 103, 121
Jagdgeschwader 210, 117
Jagdgeschwader 300, 104, 137
Jagdverbande 44, 98, 99, 115, 130, 143
Kampfgeschwader 2, 134
Kampfgeschwader 30, 101
Kampfgeschwader 40, 123, 124
Kampfgeschwader 53 Legion Condor, 104, 145
Kampfgeschwader 55, 104
Kampfgeschwader 66, 134
Kampfgeschwader 77, 134
Kampfgeschwader 100, 123
Lehrgeschwader 1, 144
Nachtjagdgeschwader 1, 106, 122, 126, 138
Nachtjagdgeschwader 3, 105, 122
Nachtjagdgeschwader 4, 138
Nachtjagdgeschwader 5, 126
Nachtschlachtgruppe 5, 111, 112
Schlachtgeschwader 1, 107, 139, 140, 141
Schlachtgeschwader 3, 123
Schlachtgeschwader 10, 146
Schlachtgeschwader 102, 146
Schlachtgruppe 77, 146
Schlachtkampfgruppe 210, 97
Zerstörergeschwader 1, 110
Zerstörergeschwader 2, 107, 116
Zerstörergeschwader 76, 105, 122
Lützow, Oberst Gunther, 129, 130, 193, 196

M
Marbach, Kapitänleutnant Karl-Heinz, 168, 169, 199
Marseille, Hauptmann Hans-Joachim, 124, 125, 126, 191, 196
Mehl, Korvettenkapitän Waldemar, 169, 170, 199
Meierdress, SS-Sturmbannführer Erwin, 58
Metzler, Korvettenkapitän Jost, 172, 199
Merten, Kapitän zur See Karl-Friedrich, 170, 171, 199, 201
Meurer, Hauptmann Manfred, 126, 127
Meyer, SS-Oberführer Kurt, 60, 61
Mölders, Oberst Werner, 127, 128, 129, 192, 196
Müller, Oberstleutnant Alfred, 63, 64
Mühlenkamp, SS-Standartenführer Johannes-Rudolf, 61, 62, 63

N
Nicolussi-Leck, SS-Hauptsturmführer Karl, 64, 65, 66
Nowotny, Major Walter, 130, 133, 192, 196

O
Oesau, Oberst Walter, 132, 133, 192, 196

P
Peiper, SS-Standartenführer Joachim, 66, 67, 68, 69, 189
Peltz, Generalmajor Dietrich, 133, 134, 135
Pichler, Leutnant Johann, 135
Piening, Korvettenkapitän Adolf, 172, 173, 199, 201
Priller, Oberst Josef, 135, 136, 193, 197
Primozic, Leutnant Hugo, 70, 71

R
Raeder, Grossadmiral Erich, 149
Rauh, Major Herbert, 138
Rall, Major Gunther, 136, 137, 191, 197
Ribbentrop, SS-Hauptsturmführer Rudolf von, 71, 72
Richter, SS-Hauptsturmführer Wilfried, 73, 74
Rogge, Vizeadmiral Bernhard, 174, 175, 176, 177, 203
Rudel, Oberst Hans-Ulrich, 138, 139, 140

S
Sailer, SS-Obersturmführer Johann, 74
Sandrock, Major Hans, 75, 76
Schnee, Korvettenkapitän Adalbert, 177, 178, 179, 200
Schrijnen, SS-Unterscharführer Remi, 76, 77
Schroeteler, Kapitänleutnant Heinrich, 179, 180, 200

Schultz, Major Fritz-Rudolf, 77, 78, 190
Seibold, SS-Hauptscharführer Emil, 78, 79
Senghas, SS-Hauptsturmführer Paul, 80, 81
Ships:
  Albert Leo Schlageter, 174
  Anton Schmidt, 187
  Atlantis, 174, 175, 176, 177
  Aviso Grille, 172
  Emden, 162
  Goldenfels, 174
  Gorch Fock, 153, 156, 160, 174, 181
  Karlsrühe, 153, 160, 181
  Köln, 154, 187
  Königsberg, 170
  Kormoran, 154, 155
  Leipzig, 177
  Nurnberg, 181
  Orion, 174, 186
  Schlesien, 156
  Schleswig-Holstein, 170
  Stiermark, 154
  3 Schnellbootsflotille, 162
  5 Torpedobootsflotille, 154
  Widder, 174
Siegel, SS-Sturmbannführer Hans, 79, 80
Spranz, Hauptmann Bodo, 81,82
Stahlschmidt, Oberleutnant Hans-Arnold, 141, 142
Steinhoff, Oberst Johannes, 142, 143, 144, 191, 197
Storp, Generalmajor Walter, 144, 145
Suhren, Fregattenkapitän Reinhard, 180, 181, 200

T
Tiesenhausen, Kapitänleutnant Hans Dietrich von, 181, 182
Tonne, Hauptmann Wolfgang, 145
Topp, Fregettenkapitän Erich, 183, 200, 201
Tychsen, SS-Obersturmbannführer Christian, 33, 82, 83, 199

U
U-Boats:
  U 6, 177
  U 23, 165, 177
  U 35, 165
  U 46, 183
  U 47, 164
  U 48, 172, 180, 181
  U 57, 183
  U 60, 177
  U 62, 169
  U 68, 170, 171
  U 72, 169
  U 81, 159
  U 83, 164
  U 93, 182
  U 99, 151, 165, 166
  U 101, 168, 169
  U 107, 187
  U 121, 185
  U 123, 161, 162
  U 124, 160
  U 126, 152
  U 147, 160
  U 155, 173, 174
  U 159, 187
  U 172, 157
  U 176, 156
  U 199, 164
  U 201, 177, 178, 179
  U 262, 158
  U 331, 182
  U 371, 169, 170
  U 438, 151
  U 471, 156
  U 510, 156
  U 513, 160
  U 521, 151
  U 552, 151, 178, 183, 184
  U 563, 151
  U 564, 180, 181
  U 566, 185
  U 616, 163
  U 667, 179
  U 1023, 179
  U 2502, 159
  U 2511, 159, 179, 181
  U 2513, 185
  U 3008, 159

W
Waffen-SS Units:
  Divisions:
  1 SS-Panzer Division Leibstandarte SS Adolf Hitler, 42, 47, 51, 57, 60, 66, 67, 68, 72, 79, 86, 87
  2 SS-Panzer Division Das Reich, 29, 31, 32, 33, 44, 78, 82, 84

3 SS-Panzer Division Totenkopf, 41, 42, 51, 59, 73
5 SS-Panzer Division Wiking, 48, 57, 62, 63, 65, 66, 76, 80
9 SS-Panzer Division Hohenstaufen, 74
10 SS-Panzer Division Frundsberg, 27
11 SS-Freiwilligen Panzer Grenadier Division Nordland, 39, 78
12 SS-Panzer Division Hitlerjugend, 61, 79, 80, 89
17 SS Panzer Grenadier Division Götz von Berlichingen, 36
18 SS-Freiwilligen Panzer Grenadier Division Horst Wessel, 35
Regiments, etc:
SS-Panzer Regiment 2, 33, 78, 82, 84
SS-Panzer Regiment 3, 35, 74
SS-Panzer Regiment 5, 45, 80
SS-Panzer Regiment 9, 35
SS-Panzer Regiment 10, 27, 28
SS-Panzer Regiment 11, 49
schwere SS-Panzer Abteilung 102, 43
schwere SS-Panzer Abteilung 501, 56, 87, 88
schwere SS-Panzer Abteilung 502, 43

SS-Panzer Abteilung 11 Hermann von Salza, 49
SS-Kradschützen Regiment Thule, 35
SS-Standarte Germania, 29, 44
SS-Freiwilligen Legion Flandern, 44
SS-Sturmbrigade Langemark, 44, 76
Kampfgruppe Peiper, 67, 68, 69
SS-Junkerschule Braunschweig, 48, 58, 62, 66, 71, 82
SS-Junkerschule Tölz, 27, 42, 44, 45, 57, 65, 74

W
Wegner, Leutnant Wilhelm, 83
Weiss, SS-Obersturmbannführer Hans, 84
Westphalen, Oberleutnant zur See Otto, 185, 200
Weyher, Konteradmiral Kurt, 186, 203
Wirsching, Hauptmann Max, 85, 86
Witte, Korvettenkapitän Helmut, 187, 188, 200
Wittmann, SS-Hauptsturmführer Michael, 86, 87, 88, 89, 90, 181
Wosnitza, Oberfeldwebel Alois, 145, 146

and Binding By:
Clays Ltd.
ungay
Suffolk
R 35 IED
England